Deep Culture

Mixed Sources
Product group from well-managed
forests and other controlled sources
www.fsc.org Cert no. TT-COC-2082
© 1996 Forest Stewardship Council

LANGUAGES FOR INTERCULTURAL COMMUNICATION AND EDUCATION
Editors: Michael Byram, *University of Durham, UK*
Alison Phipps, *University of Glasgow, UK*

The overall aim of this series is to publish books which will ultimately inform learning and teaching, but whose primary focus is on the analysis of intercultural relationships, whether in textual form or in people's experience. There will also be books which deal directly with pedagogy, with the relationships between language learning and cultural learning, between processes inside the classroom and beyond. They will all have in common a concern with the relationship between language and culture, and the development of intercultural communicative competence.

Other Books in the Series
Developing Intercultural Competence in Practice
  Michael Byram, Adam Nichols and David Stevens (eds)
Intercultural Experience and Education
  Geof Alred, Michael Byram and Mike Fleming (eds)
Critical Citizens for an Intercultural World
  Manuela Guilherme
How Different Are We? Spoken Discourse in Intercultural Communication
  Helen Fitzgerald
Audible Difference: ESL and Social Identity in Schools
  Jennifer Miller
Context and Culture in Language Teaching and Learning
  Michael Byram and Peter Grundy (eds)
An Intercultural Approach to English Language Teaching
  John Corbett
Critical Pedagogy: Political Approaches to Language and Intercultural Communication
  Alison Phipps and Manuela Guilherme (eds)
Vernacular Palaver: Imaginations of the Local and Non-native Languages in West Africa
  Moradewun Adejunmobi
Foreign Language Teachers and Intercultural Competence
  Lies Sercu with Ewa Bandura, Paloma Castro, Leah Davcheva, Chryssa Laskaridou, Ulla Lundgren, María del Carmen Méndez García and Phyllis Ryan
Language and Culture: Global Flows and Local Complexity
  Karen Risager
Living and Studying Abroad: Research and Practice
  Michael Byram and Anwei Feng (eds)
Education for Intercultural Citizenship: Concepts and Comparisons
  Geof Alred, Mike Byram and Mike Fleming (eds)
Language and Culture Pedagogy: From a National to a Transnational Paradigm
  Karen Risager
Online Intercultural Exchange: An Introduction for Foreign Language Teachers
  Robert O'Dowd (ed.)

For more details of these or any other of our publications, please contact:
Multilingual Matters, Frankfurt Lodge, Clevedon Hall,
Victoria Road, Clevedon, BS21 7HH, England
http://www.multilingual-matters.com

**LANGUAGES FOR INTERCULTURAL
COMMUNICATION AND EDUCATION 16**
Series Editors: Michael Byram and Alison Phipps

Deep Culture
The Hidden Challenges
of Global Living

Joseph Shaules

MULTILINGUAL MATTERS LTD
Clevedon • Buffalo • Toronto

Library of Congress Cataloging in Publication Data
Shaules, Joseph.
Deep Culture: The Hidden Challenges of Global Living / Joseph Shaules.
Languages for Intercultural Communication and Education: 16
Includes bibliographical references and index.
1. Intercultural communication. 2. Multicultural education.
3. Language and languages--Study and teaching. I. Title.
P94.6.S48 2007
302.2–dc22   2007020122

British Library Cataloguing in Publication Data
A catalogue entry for this book is available from the British Library.

ISBN-13: 978-1-84769-017-3 (hbk)
ISBN-13: 978-1-84769-016-6 (pbk)

Multilingual Matters Ltd
UK: Frankfurt Lodge, Clevedon Hall, Victoria Road, Clevedon BS21 7HH.
USA: UTP, 2250 Military Road, Tonawanda, NY 14150, USA.
Canada: UTP, 5201 Dufferin Street, North York, Ontario M3H 5T8, Canada.

The policy of Multilingual Matters/Channel View Publications is to use papers that are natural, renewable and recyclable products, made from wood grown in sustainable forests. In the manufacturing process of our books, and to further support our policy, preference is given to printers that have FSC and PEFC Chain of Custody certification. The FSC and/or PEFC logos will appear on those books where full certification has been granted to the printer concerned.

Typeset by Bookcraft Ltd.
Printed and bound in Great Britain by the Cromwell Press Ltd.

Contents

Foreword

'People and things are increasingly out of place', James Clifford suggested in his book *The Predicament of Culture* (1988). In the twenty years since he wrote that, the tempo of movement has accelerated further. It has never been as easy as it is now to cross borders physically. More people then ever before are living 'away from home'. But at the same time, we are discovering that the most heavily policed frontiers are not physical but linguistic and cultural. These borders are embedded in the everyday life of ordinary people and we ourselves do more to police them than any security force could hope to achieve.

In this context, Joseph Shaules's book is a timely intervention in the field of intercultural communication and the forms of learning that underpin it. It takes issue with existing approaches that construe intercultural learning as a largely linear process and argues that things are considerably more complex. The extent to which a visitor resists, accepts or adapts to a host culture may vary considerably over time, but in ways that are neither homogeneous nor predictable. A great deal rests on the 'habitus' of individuals: the dispositions, attitudes and values they bring to an encounter. But intercultural relations are rooted in dialogue and interaction, where individuals have scope to choose the ways in which they will engage with their cultural environment. Long-term sojourners can thus shape their engagement, and familiarity may breed contempt as well as affection.

To a significant extent the responses to intercultural encounter are personal and subjective, easier to guess at than to analyse, and frequently discussed on the basis of anecdotes rather than evidence. Joseph Shaules has achieved valuable access to evidence, through detailed interviews with a sample of informants, and has teased out the patterns of intercultural development they reveal. In this way he has been able to delve beneath the surface of their behaviour and the way they themselves view it. His concept of 'deep culture' is a challenging one, designed to understand the processes going on in sensitive personal areas, without adopting an inappropriately normative perspective. As he demonstrates, this understanding is an essential requirement for developing effective strategies of intercultural learning.

The approach developed here has clear theoretical groundings and is supported by detailed examination of the evidence. I have been happy and privileged to play a part in its gestation. Its value will be assessed by its ability to inform the process of learning and to provide people with the knowledge and skills to move around the world in creative and satisfying ways. It may thereby assist us in attaining a positive 'cultural footprint' so that the places in which we stay will be enriched by our sojourn there.

Michael Kelly
Southampton, March 2007

Acknowledgements

My interest in deep culture originated from reading the works of Edward
Hall during studies at the School for International Training (SIT), in
Brattleboro, Vermont. This interest was supported by Lou Spaventa with
additional impetus provided by training at the Intercultural Communication Institute (ICI) in Portland, Oregon. The work of Milton Bennett and
Janet Bennett, whom I met there, figure prominently in this work. Their
openness and supportive attitude is greatly appreciated. During the
writing of this book, the support of colleagues at Rikkyo University has
been indispensable. Particular thanks is owed to Torikai Kumiko and
Hiraga Masako. At the University of Southampton, Michael Kelly and
Patrick Stevenson have been wonderful advisors and mentors during
doctoral studies there. Thanks also to Alison Phipps for her encourage-
ment to turn that work into this book. The Japan Intercultural Institute has
been indulgent in allowing me to test out the ideas contained here in
intercultural seminars. Thanks in particular to Nobuo Nishikawa, Takeshi
Enomoto, Ellen Kawaguchi, Kanami Uchida and Valerie Hansford.
Throughout 20 years of intercultural wanderings many people have
provided inspiration and support. They include: Alma Church, David
Shaules, James Shaules, Elizabeth Hamilton, Michiyo Oshiro, Steve
Ziolkowski, Haruko Ishii and especially Estelle Bisch. Friends and family
in the US, Mexico, Japan and France have enriched both my sojourns and
my homecomings. Thanks to all.

Introduction

At an intercultural communication conference not long ago, I heard a speaker comment that globalization was rendering the concept of cultural difference invalid. Some weeks later, during a reunion with a friend who had just completed an 18-month trip around the world, I asked about this assertion. My friend commented that to find cultural difference you have to 'get off the internet and get on a bus'. He went on to argue that often the intercultural contact we have in our 'global village' doesn't amount to us having 'intercultural experiences'. While globalization may bring diversity into our living room, we usually aren't required to *adapt* to it in any significant way. Even meeting people from other countries can be a relatively shallow experience if we don't need to change much about ourselves in order to get along. Living or traveling abroad, however, implies that we are obliged to go through a process of learning to function better in our new environment.

The distinction my friend made – that intercultural contact is not the same as intercultural adaptation – is important for understanding the goals of this book. It will look at the process of *cultural learning* that sojourners go through as they learn to function in a new cultural environment. Currently, an ever wider range of people are facing this challenge; whether as an expatriate employee, a student studying abroad, a volunteer working for a non-profit organization, a round-the-world traveler, or even as a tourist in a resort hotel. This book will argue that despite the wide variety of intercultural experiences, those who enter into a new cultural environment go through a learning process that is fundamentally similar, sharing a common need to respond to the adaptive demands found in their new environment. In facing these demands sojourners learn not only about their new surroundings but they may learn deeper, at times even transformative, lessons as well. This book will introduce a theoretical model to make sense of this process. It is hoped this will serve as a basis for intercultural training and education.

The title of this book, *Deep Culture*, refers to the unconscious frameworks of meaning, values, norms and hidden assumptions that we use to interpret our experiences. Cultural differences at this deep level are an often unnoticed obstacle to intercultural learning which trip up sojourners by letting them fall into ethnocentric judgments about their new surroundings. One of the 'dirty little secrets' of intercultural education is that experiences abroad don't always raise the awareness or tolerance of sojourners. They can also reinforce stereotypes, make sojourners critical or dismissive of the people they meet and cause them to denigrate differences. Worst of all, this usually happens without sojourners realizing it. In this book, for example, we will meet Australian students who, after having spent a year learning the ins-and-outs of a French university, conclude that as a rule 'the French are inefficient'. We meet a flight instructor whose experience with Asian students has convinced him that Asians have 'no survival instinct'. One French student, when asked if her attitudes towards Americans have changed after living in the United States for a year replies simply, 'Yes, for the worse'. Other sojourners, of course, have positive, even life-changing experiences. Some sojourners seem to be very positive about some parts of their experiences and negative about others. Fully understanding these varying reactions requires an in-depth look at the intercultural learning experience.

The goals of this book are ambitious: (1) to present a new model of intercultural learning that is both straightforward and theoretically sound; and (2) to focus attention on the importance of deep cultural difference. This book is divided into two parts. Part 1 (Chapters 1 to 6) examines the cultural learning experience, while Part 2 introduces a formal model of intercultural learning. Part 1 first takes a detailed look at the concept of *deep culture*, including ways in which differences in deep culture create obstacles to cultural learning. It also anticipates some objections to the concept of culture itself. Currently, we have linguists who speak of a universal language instinct (discounting linguistic relativism), anthropologists who argue that culture is an anachronistic concept and communication specialists who argue that the way we speak is not primarily a product of our cultural background. Much of this debate is tied to changes brought about by globalization. I will argue that many interculturalists have lost sight of some fundamental insights about culture and culture difference. Using this work's conceptualization of deep culture as a starting point, Part 1 then also examines the process of cultural learning, negative learning outcomes and the goals of cultural learning.

The *Deep Culture Model* in Part 2 of this book draws on the theoretical knowledge from a variety of academic fields. In its broad outlines it is simple. Cultural learning is seen as developmental – it involves (hope-fully) an ever greater ability to construe the perceptual world found in a new environment. The development of this ability is driven by the need to respond to the gap between the internal competencies of the sojourner and the external adaptive demands of the environment. Yet not all sojourners accept the validity of the adaptive demands they face. They also may resist them. Sojourners' reactions to adaptive demands are not conceptualized in terms of behavior, but rather in terms of changes to the cognitive categories that sojourners use to conceptualize cultural difference. These reactions – *resistance, acceptance* and *adaptation* – are not absolute or exclusive. Sojourners may resist one element of their experience and adapt to another. This distinction between *surface* and *deep* cultural experiences is seen as central to understanding the complex and sometimes contradictory reactions that sojourners have to a new environment.

Throughout this work quotations from sojourners are used to illustrate the points discussed. This approach emphasizes the phenomenology of cultural learning and keeps theory grounded in the lived experience of sojourners. The quotations found in this book come from a research project involving interviews with approximately two dozen expatriates. The goal of this research was to compare the accounts of sojourners' cultural learning with existing theoretical models of cultural learning. Sojourners were asked about the challenges they faced in getting used to life in a new place, their foreign language ability, the types of relationships they had with their cultural hosts and what languages those relationships were carried out in. These sojourners are not necessarily a representative sample of sojourners around the globe. All of them chose to go abroad, generally under fairly advantageous circumstances. In this sense they represent a kind of 'best case' sample. Yet, even among this privileged group, deep cultural learning was often a difficult process. The understanding of this process gained from this research, together with contributions from existing cultural learning theory, have been integrated in the Deep Culture Model of cultural learning found in Chapters 7 to 12. For a full account of the research that led to this model, see Shaules (2004a).

As we will see, the way that sojourners talk about cultural difference can give us insight into their cultural learning process. When Jack, an American expatriate in Tokyo, talks about 'typical Japanese overpoliteness', he is passing judgment on the patterns of deference he has experienced. This judgment is not based on an assumption that Japanese patterns of deference are normal (for Japanese) but rather that they are excessive in some absolute way. On the other hand, Mayumi, a Japanese woman living in Korea with her Korean husband, finds interacting with her in-laws stressful. She feels humiliated, for example, by the fact that her mother-in-law bleached the inside of her teapot while she was away. Yet despite these demands, she accepts that her in-laws are trying to be helpful and simply acting in accordance with Korean expectations. She manages to avoid the negative judgments that Jack makes. She _accepts_ and _adapts_ where Jack _resists_.

While it is clear that some sojourners react less constructively to adaptive challenges than others, we must not moralize about intercultural learning. Resisting change is a natural reaction to adaptive pressure. It is naïve simply to call for greater tolerance and assume that intercultural contact will, in and of itself, bring about greater _awareness_ or some kind of _global identity_. We must recognize that it is also natural for intercultural experiences to engender conflict (at least sometimes), misunderstanding and denigration. Sojourners (and educators) need a neutral vocabulary of cultural learning as well as theoretical frameworks that allow us to talk about the full range of reactions to new environments. This work proposes such a vocabulary as well as a way to diagram the intercultural learning process using statements sojourners make about cultural differences. For an overview of the key terms of the Deep Culture Model, see the Glossary. In Chapter 13 there is a discussion of some of the educational implications and possible applications of this model.

The overall approach of this work has been heavily influenced by the intuitive understanding of cultural learning I have gained while growing up in the United States, learning Spanish and living in Mexico (3 years), learning Japanese during 14 years in Japan, and learning French and living in France (2 years). It has also been informed by 20 years of language teaching experience as well as experience in intercultural training and education. As an expatriate who has integrated fairly deeply into host communities where I have lived, I have long been interested in the question of why people seem to respond so differently to the challenges of living abroad. As a language teacher, I have been interested in the cultural barriers to effective communication in a foreign language. As a trainer, I have been involved with helping people prepare for their stays abroad and have puzzled over how to give prospective sojourners some help in coping with the challenges that await them.

It was fascinating to talk to the sojourners whose voices appear in this book. It was also a challenge to connect what they said to cultural learning theory. The learning model presented in this book was motivated in part by a desire to bring some clarity to the fragmented professional literature related to culture, cultural learning and the effects of globalization. Sojourners' stories are used to illustrate the contention that the deeper elements of intercultural learning can be understood in relatively straightforward terms if we have the right conceptual frameworks to do so. They also reinforced my personal belief that deep cultural learning is an increasingly important issue in an age of globalization and the frequent crossing of cultural boundaries. While the total amount of cultural differences in the world may be decreasing, the number of deep intercultural experiences is increasing dramatically. Hopefully, this book will be of some use to the educators and sojourners that have to manage this largely hidden learning process.

Part 1
The Intercultural Experience

Chapter 1

Intercultural Contact in the Global Village

Japan is predictable. Lots of times that's a good thing. I know my train's going to come on time. I know I'm going to get good service.
Jack, talking about life in Tokyo after fourteen years in Japan.

Sojourns as a Learning Experience

Spending time in a foreign country is a learning experience. On a short trip abroad travelers see previously unfamiliar places and increase their knowledge of the world. They may try *gnocchi* for the first time, learn to buy gasoline in Turkish or simply familiarize themselves with the landmarks of Paris or Shanghai. Those who spend a longer time abroad – immigrants, study-abroad students, expatriates, etc. – must go through a longer and deeper process of learning about and adapting to their new environment. They often must struggle to learn a new language, get used to a new lifestyle and form relationships with people they may not fully understand. Each in their own way, both short-term visitors and long-term sojourners go through a learning process as they interact with environments that they don't fully understand.

These learning experiences change the people that go through them. We think of people who have traveled extensively as being *international*. Those who have lived abroad and learned a foreign language are seen as having gained intercultural awareness or an appreciation of cultural difference; they may have faced culture shock; they may have become more tolerant or changed their personal values. Some people seem even to 'go native', taking on the lifestyle and values of people from another country. These experiences may even have provoked an identity crisis. Long sojourns can teach transformative lessons far beyond gaining the ability to 'get by' in a foreign land necessary for short-term visits.

Adapting to life in a new cultural environment – in this book, *cultural learning* – can be a very powerful experience. At the same time, its outcomes are difficult to predict and explain. When language teachers send students off on a study-abroad program, they know that some will have their lives altered in fundamental ways. Others, however, may spend their time with their compatriots and return having learned seemingly few deep lessons. Some will become fascinated by their temporary new homes while others may have negative stereotypes reinforced. Some students may even find the experience so stressful that they return home early. Explaining how these different outcomes come about is not easy. Life abroad is an all-encompassing experience, and personalities and living situations are so varied that it can be difficult to conceptualize the changes that sojourners go through.

Educators and trainers who prepare sojourners for stays abroad know they can try to do so by giving concrete information about the geography, history or literature of a particular country. Yet, the intangible challenges of living abroad – gaining insights into values, learning to communicate in a new way, discovering one's own prejudices, etc. – are much harder to teach prospective sojourners. Deciding what one's educational goals should be and what elements of the intercultural experience to focus on is a constant question. For their part, sojourners who have never been abroad often have little idea of the challenges they will face and may wildly under- or overestimate how easy or difficult it will be. Asking sojourners what they are likely to learn while they are abroad often draws puzzled looks. Asking sojourners how their values or worldview might change is an unfair question: the process is so deep and living in another country is so unlike other experiences that it is difficult even to have a point of comparison.

Goals of This Book

This book focuses on the hidden challenges of living abroad. Its goal is to present an intercultural learning model which gives both educators and sojourners a way to think and talk about the hidden *adaptive challenges* of a long-term stay in a new cultural environment. Entering any new environment creates a learning challenge, but longer-term sojourners are often challenged to adapt to their new environment in deep ways. Adapting more 'deeply' to a new environment refers to a need to rethink the out-of-awareness beliefs, values and assumptions that we normally use to make sense of the world and get along with others. Changes in behavior may be accompanied by concurrent changes in how we view the world. And because our worldview is greatly influenced by our own cultural conditioning, it often takes an experience with those who have different cultural backgrounds to make us aware of our own cultural perspective.

As we will see, in spite of all that specialists have learned about the nature of intercultural experiences, there is little agreement on how to describe the process of intercultural learning. Part of this results from the fact that intercultural learning is studied from a wide range of different perspectives. Yet even among educators and intercultural communication specialists there is little consensus on questions as simple as: What constitutes a successful intercultural experience? What is intercultural *awareness*? What is the role of culture in determining behavior? Is it possible to go 'beyond' cultural difference? Is cultural difference even a valid concept in our globalized world?

This book will attempt to find some answers to these questions. In doing so, it will attempt to avoid vague idealized intercultural goals such as 'increased awareness' or 'global consciousness'. It will also attempt not to moralize about what people *should* learn as a result of intercultural experiences. Instead, it will look at both positive and negative outcomes, and try to understand how they come about. It will not deal with issues of social justice or equality. Prejudice will be dealt with, but only in the context of coming into contact with cultural difference. This work assumes that while some intercultural learning outcomes may be more desirable than others – acceptance of cultural difference is preferable to denigration – all are normal human reactions to the intercultural learning process. This work also assumes that ethnocentrism is a product of human evolutionary biology and thus the starting point of intercultural learning. The ways in which inculcated prejudice affects human relations is beyond the scope of this book.

An important difficulty in understanding the process of intercultural learning is that every intercultural situation is different and individuals differ widely in their responses to apparently similar situations. It is difficult to compare the challenges faced by an extroverted tourist, a frustrated economic immigrant, an idealistic Peace Corps volunteer and a fun-loving student on a homestay program. Yet the assumption of this book will be that all intercultural learning experiences share certain elements which make the intercultural learning process, if not predictable, at least comprehensible. Part 1 of this book will focus on three areas in particular: (1) the nature of culture and cultural difference; (2) the demands that encountering cultural difference imposes on sojourners; and (3) the *depth* of intercultural learning experiences. Part 2 of this book will bring these three areas together into a model of intercultural learning meant to help sojourners and educators talk in a more explicit way about a process which normally takes place at an intuitive level.

Deep Culture

The recurring theme in this book will be the concept of *deep culture*. In the context of this book, *deep culture* refers to the unconscious meanings, values, norms and hidden assumptions that allow us to interpret our experiences as we interact with other people. These shared meanings form a framework which acts as a starting point for our sense of what it means to be human, what constitutes normal behavior, how to make moral or ethical choices and what we perceive as reasonable. (Hampden-Turner & Trompenaars, 2000; Trompenaars & Hampden-Turner, 1998) Deep culture generally functions out of awareness at the intuitive level and we usually remain unaware of it until confronted with a need to interact with people who have different cultural assumptions. It is our 'cultural programming' or, as Barnlund (1989) puts it, our 'collective unconscious'. Geert Hofstede (1997) describes it as the 'software of the mind'. To take the computer analogy further, if our body and biological predilections are our hardware, then deep culture is the operating system – the learned framework of perception, interpretation and judgment – that allows us to run the interpretive programs with which we engage in the tasks of daily living.

Living in or visiting other countries often brings us into contact with people who have different deep-culture settings. This does not necessarily refer to witnessing behavior one might find unusual (e.g. washing in cow urine, reportedly practiced by the Masai in East Africa). Deep culture does not refer to specific behaviors but rather to the values and assumptions that underlie those actions. Some examples of deep culture are: differing cultural assumptions about the role of men and women; differing orientations towards time and feelings of identity (e.g. collective versus individual); differing senses of morality and ethical behavior (e.g. feelings of 'face' or individual morality); and many others. This book will argue that cultural difference at this deep level constitutes the most fundamental challenge of intercultural learning. It is the foundation upon which ethnocentrism rests and it constitutes the raw material for our cultural biases.

In many intercultural contexts, deep culture is not noticed or understood in any profound sense. An English visitor to Thailand may experience a profound sense of cultural difference when seeing monks with begging bowls. The visitor hasn't – strictly speaking – had a Thai experience but an English experience in Thailand. The *deep* elements of Thai culture are not those that are the most sacred or symbolically important, they are those that are most fundamental and subtle. What seems 'spiritual' to our visitor may seem simply an everyday routine to many Thais. Thai communities place an importance on ancestry or family relations that our English visitor will find hard to grasp. The levels of formality in the Thai language may seem impossibly complex and hinge on social distinctions that our visitor is unaccustomed to making. The meaning of simple concepts – family, responsibility, independence, morality, shame, fun, adulthood, etc. – may seem very different when viewed from a Thai perspective.

As our visitor participates more fully in Thai communities, however, the perception of Thais may change. This change occurs when the visitor shares more of the hosts' worldview. The visitor's understanding may be transformed from that of an outsider, observing and interpreting an explicit cultural phenomenon, to that of an insider sharing the meaning and interpretation of the community that produced the phenomenon. This change is primarily intuitive, not intellectual. It requires a willingness to suspend one's outsider's judgment and attempt to see the world from a new point of view. In doing so, the internal logic of that community becomes clearer and one may learn to operate within these new cultural frameworks. *It is this intuitively felt internal logic, the unspoken assumptions behind a community's behavior, which constitutes deep culture.* The process of acquiring the ability to step into these new frameworks of meaning is *deep cultural learning.*

The deeper 'hidden' side of the intercultural experience has been recognized at least since 1959, when Edward Hall (1959) published his seminal book *The Silent Language.* Since then, cultural frameworks and worldview have widely been recognized to function primarily out of conscious awareness; in the same way that fish don't notice water, we don't notice our own hidden cultural programming. Unfortunately, the implications of this fundamental insight are seldom focused on. This book will argue that not having a clear conceptualization of the hidden structure of deep culture leads to confusion about fundamental issues in intercultural relations such as: whether *culture* is a useful concept given increasing globalization; whether being socialized into a particular cultural community can predict particular behavior; and how to understand the difference between the role of personality and culture in influencing behavior.

This book will also argue that it requires more than a brief trip abroad or simply meeting someone from a foreign country for *deep cultural learning* to happen. To support this argument we will examine the experiences of expatriates who were interviewed as part of a research project on intercultural learning. We will explore the deep culture lessons that these sojourners learn (or don't) and try to understand the stages in their learning process. As we will see, sojourners have a variety of reactions and learn widely different lessons as a result of experiencing life in a new cultural community. Some adapt readily and report very positive experiences while others seem to resist change, complain or openly criticize their cultural hosts. Linda, for example, a British woman living in France, describes her new life as a 'voyage of discovery', while Adele, an American living in Japan, describes bitterly her four years abroad by saying: 'I think one thing I've learned [in Japan] is that I really like the United States, and I'm glad that I was born there.' In addition, some people have deeper intercultural learning experiences than others. Jack (quoted at the start of the chapter) has lived a contented life in Tokyo for 14 years yet speaks only rudimentary Japanese, has few Japanese friends and is barely integrated into Japanese life. We will try to make sense of these different reactions.

Deep culture and the global village

It is important to understand the experiences of people like Jack, Adele and Linda because globalization is revolutionizing intercultural relationships. As early as 1964 Marshall McLuhan (1964: 4) argued that the world was turning into a 'global village' in which communication technology was 'extend[ing] our central nervous system in a global embrace, abolishing both space and time'. McLuhan (1968:11) also predicted that people everywhere would soon 'adjust to the vast global environment as if it were his little home town'. And while some argue that global interconnectedness heralds the advent of a new 'transcultural community' (Agar, 2002), deep culture differences still pose a challenge to most people who spend an extended period abroad. Even within a village there are prejudice, conflict, discrimination and inequality. Increased contact does not always lead to harmony. It can also lead to a vicious cycle of misunderstanding and aggression as we can see, for example, between Catholics and Protestants in Northern Ireland, Palestinians and Israelis, The Singhalese and Tamils in Sri Lanka, and relations between India and Pakistan or Ethiopia and Eritrea.

The 'global village' metaphor can also be carried too far. Though contact in our new global village is extensive it often remains shallow. Communities in cyberspace not only bring disparate people together, they allow for an escape from many of the difficulties of deeper more involved human relations. And although people around the world increasingly share brand names, consumer goods and popular culture, objects often mean different things to different people. A hamburger may be a status food to one person and a symbol of economic imperialism to another. News coverage is tailored to suit what a local or national audience expects and entertainment media images often do not accurately portray life in distant places. While mass media brings cultural difference into our homes, it may be a very shallow experience that doesn't fundamentally change our way of looking at the world. Put into more constructivist terms, these shallow intercultural experiences are put into pre-existing categories of meaning and don't fundamentally threaten the underlying framework of one's values and hidden cultural assumptions.

In addition, as individuals gain increasing power over the media content they consume and the communities that they belong to, they can choose to interact only with people who reinforce their particular view of the world. With increasing numbers of insulated in-groups defining themselves by who they are against, differences and intolerance can be exacerbated. Perhaps because of this, an increased access to technology, higher levels of income and more education around the world have not led to a lessening of intercultural conflict, nor agreement on universal standards of human beliefs or behaviors. Indeed, the opposite may be true as Brooks (2006) argues:

> We now know that global economic and technological forces do not gradually erode local cultures and values. Instead, cultures and values shape economic development. Moreover, as people are empowered by greater wealth and education, cultural differences become more pronounced, not less, as different groups chase different visions of the good life, and react in aggressive ways to perceived slights to their cultural dignity.

Violent religious extremism, ethnic separatism and alienated immigrant populations show us that this is not only happening in cyberspace. A tendency towards 'regionalization' is even found in linguistic analysis in the United States. Recent research shows that despite national broadcast and entertainment media, regional accents, instead of blending into a single standard American English, are actually increasing (Labov *et al.*, 2005). This reminds us that globalized media doesn't automatically create globalized communities.

This is not to say, of course, that face-to-face contact with people from different cultural, social, religious and ethnic backgrounds is not increasing. Nearly 700 million people a year visit a foreign country (Scott, 2003) and the number of people with the means to travel abroad – an activity once reserved for only the smallest elite – is expanding at a breathtaking pace. The number of people living abroad for longer times is increasing rapidly although it is difficult to quantify the phenomenon. The study of the effects of tourism on individual tourists – what someone learns from coming into contact with new people and places – is only just beginning. Jack and Phipps (2005: 157) argue that tourism can be a transformational experience that has the potential to 'teach radical lessons about the possibility of living a different, everyday life when we are not tourists'. But while foreign travel may bring travelers to the realization that great diversity exists, it may provide only a limited view of life in a different place. Resort hotels can shield tourists from the need to adapt to the norms of their host country. Ease of travel can also lead to a trivialization of a host community; when a country or region is reduced to a list of 'must see' temples and monuments or 'must visit' tribes encountered on a pre-packaged trek. And what of tourists who have negative experiences? If we feel that a country we visit is dirty; its people dishonest; its food too heavy, spicy or expensive: does this lead to greater intercultural understanding and positive personal transformation?

It seems clear that simply being physically present in a foreign land does not automatically bestow increased intercultural understanding. It also seems intuitively obvious that being a Peace Corps volunteer, or immigrating to a foreign country, is a more challenging and engaging experience than taking a short vacation abroad. And in spite of globalization it is still a challenge to move to a new country, learn a foreign language, work abroad, or immigrate. Unlike the past, however, it is a challenge being faced by millions. Even if globalization is reducing the cultural difference between groups of people in an absolute sense, the number of people facing the challenge of intercultural living is growing. For the first time in history, deep intercultural learning is happening on a mass scale, yet our understanding of the personal learning challenges that this entails has not kept pace with the change in our global environment.

Avoiding deep intercultural learning

Globalization not only increases the number of people crossing national and cultural boundaries, it also changes *how* people interact with people from other cultural communities. With all of the emphasis on multiculturalism and increased intercultural contact, we sometimes overlook how globalization has increased our ability to avoid deeper intercultural experiences when we are abroad. More than ever before, we can be in the proximity of people who are different from us, yet avoid deeper interaction. We can see this with Jack, an English teacher who has lived in Japan for fourteen years, and was quoted at the beginning of this chapter. He is happy with his life as an expatriate and enjoys his relationship with his students at his High School. His girlfriend is Japanese, he lives comfortably and he functions very well in Tokyo. Yet Jack speaks only basic conversational Japanese and when he is asked about friendships he has with Japanese, he reports:

... actually I don't have that many Japanese friends; actually my male friends are all foreigners. Actually my only close Japanese friends have been my girlfriends. I don't have one close Japanese male friend.

If you ask Jack whether he has adapted himself to Japan, we can sense the barriers he feels:

You could learn the language fluently, do everything to be accepted, but they never really would ... according to what I heard from other foreigners. So that was enough for me to not try.

So Jack seems to be blaming the Japanese for not being open to foreigners, though it seems that he has not tried that hard to overcome whatever barriers may exist.

Naturally, speaking Japanese is an important part of getting to know Japanese culture more deeply. Jack has had trouble making much progress:

I've only learned what I needed to learn to survive and get by ... what I need in my job, being an English teacher. I don't have a chance to use Japanese. I've made some attempts at times, joining language schools. I guess there are other things I've been interested in. I can experience the culture doing other things. I can experience the culture with people through English.

One wonders whether the Japanese would agree that it is possible to deeply understand Japanese culture without learning Japanese. So why hasn't Jack learned more?

I really don't have the opportunities. I would have to create opportunities. For example I could go to the store – even though I don't need tuna fish – I could ask for the tuna fish. I could call a department store on the phone and ask for something.

And this affects the kinds of relationship he has with the people around him:

And the other English teachers that don't speak English very well avoid me. Other colleagues outside of the English department use a mix of Japanese and English, but I have much less contact with them, very little. I could go days without using Japanese, I'm sure I have.

Given that Jack lives in Tokyo some might find it difficult to understand his assertion that he has little opportunity to use Japanese. If you have spent time with expatriates, however, you soon understand that Jack's reaction to his environment is not that unusual. Because his work centers on English – he has easy access to English media, an English-speaking community (consisting both of Japanese and non-Japanese), international food, etc. – he's not really under that much pressure to adapt. And he doesn't. Not all expatriates react like Jack, of course. But Jack is not unusual, and as we will see, some sojourners have an even more discouraging reaction to their intercultural experiences: an *increase* in prejudice, negativity and criticism of the host cultural community.

Our globalized world has thus increased the number of people having all sorts of intercultural contact; from email exchanges and virtual communities to ecotourism and globalized business, to study abroad and immigration. These experiences exist along a continuum of more superficial to more involving. Yet the effects of these differing degrees of intercultural contact are not yet clearly understood. Superficial contact and technological convergence across borders can mask the deeper more subtle cultural differences that often create intercultural misunderstanding. And more than ever before, sojourners *choose* the degree to which they will engage with a new environment. If differences in deep culture result in choices of isolation rather than engagement, our global community will see increasing intercultural conflict.

Perspectives on Intercultural Learning

Professional literature related to the process of adapting to new cultural and social environments is extensive but fragmented. Because it touches upon so many different disciplines, including anthropology, sociology, psychology and education, among others, it is, as Kim (2001: 11) puts it, 'far from intellectually cohesive'. In the United States, a country with a long history of immigration, *acculturation* has been studied by anthropologists and sociologists throughout the 20th century. There has been great interest in looking at changes in immigrant communities as they became 'Americanized' or more integrated into mainstream American culture (Amersfoort, 1984; Marrett & Leggon, 1982; Redfield *et al.*, 1936; Spiro, 1955). This 'macro' perspective looks at acculturation as a group phenomenon in which individuals belonging to social categories go through a process of *assimilation* or exist in a state of *marginality* (Ansari, 1988; Gordon, 1973; Schuetz, 1963; Simmel, 1950). There has been increasing interest in these issues in other countries as well, including Australia,

Canada, England, Germany, Israel and Sweden (see Abbink, 1984; Berry *et al.*, 1987; Coleman, 1987; Noels *et al.*, 1996; Wilpert, 1984).

The macro processes studied by anthropologists and sociologists have been referred to using various terms including *acculturation, assimilation* and *integration*. Acculturation – the process of internalizing the cultural patterns of a new cultural environment – can be contrasted with enculturation, the socialization process that children go through as they grow up, absorbing the shared cultural frameworks of their home community. Assimilation emphasizes the internalization of the cultural patterns of the host community, while integration emphasizes an acceptance and participation in the host environment.

In this work, however, we are interested in cultural adaptation at the micro level, with an emphasis on the internal process of change within an individual as he or she interacts in a new environment. This focus takes us beyond anthropology and sociology into education, psychology and intercultural communication. Terminology used in these fields includes: *coping, adjustment, culture shock, adaptation* and *cross-cultural adaptation*. Terms such as coping, adjustment and culture shock are often used when referring to the psychological stresses of fitting into a new environment (Kim, 2001) while adaptation refers more generally to the process of changing to fit a new environment. The term *cross-cultural adaptation* is defined by Kim (2001: 31) as 'the dynamic process by which individuals, upon relocating to new, unfamiliar, or changed cultural environments, establish (or reestablish) and maintain relatively stable, reciprocal, and functional relationships with those environments'.

This work will generally use the term *intercultural learning* or *cultural learning* to describe the lived experience of dealing with an unfamiliar cultural environment. This term is intended to include not only the process of immigrants and long-term residents, but also of tourists and short-term visitors. The starting assumption is that both short and long stays in a new cultural environment are learning experiences and involve facing adaptive demands. The depth and intensity of those demands may vary widely but it is assumed that the dynamic at work is fundamentally the same. Crossing borders opens a gap between one's existing internal competencies and the competencies necessary to function in a new environment. This gap is more than simply a lack of information. New cultural environments differ in *systematic* ways and once one has learned how things work, whether this refers to how to use chopsticks, ride a subway, speak a new language or express humor and friendliness, one is better able to get things done and interact with people. In this work, this systematic difference will be referred to as *cultural difference*. Dealing with this difference creates stress and a need for adaptation and adjustment. Intercultural learning will therefore be defined as: *the process of responding to the adaptive demands that result from interacting with a new cultural environment.*

The term *intercultural learning* is not new. It has been used, particularly in Europe, to refer to efforts by educators to improve communication between new immigrants and indigenous populations (Hu, 1999; Kramsch, 2005). *Intercultural learning,* as used in this work, is closer in meaning to Kim's usage of the term *cross-cultural adaptation.* Yet the word *learning* was specifically chosen to widen the scope of the definition. Whereas the term *cross-cultural adaptation* implies that some sort of 'fitting in' has taken place, this work assumes that not fitting in is also a common result of the intercultural learning process. Increased prejudice towards a host community among expatriates would not normally be referred to as cross-cultural adaptation, yet negative or ethnocentric reactions to intercultural experiences are not unusual. Some sojourners may live abroad for years yet never change much in response to the cultural differences found in the host society. Others may 'go local' and develop a new sense of identity or change their values. It is assumed, however, that all of these outcomes are part of the same fundamental process. It is also assumed that as globalization makes intercultural contact more common and more varied, an increasingly wide range of reactions to intercultural experiences can be expected.

The word *adaptation* typically implies the process of learning to function in or feel comfortable in a new environment; a question of 'fitting in' with the external environment and the 'satisfaction' of one's internal state. Yet someone may be emotionally adapted to their life abroad – i.e. they are happy in their situation – without having learned much about how to get along with local residents. Conversely, someone may have learned a lot about local customs or lifestyle, yet still find their stay very frustrating. This work will focus on the broader lessons that sojourners learn from their intercultural experiences. It is assumed that even those who don't adapt to their new environment learn something and those who have negative experiences also go through a learning process, although perhaps, with negative outcomes.

Regardless of the terminology used, the processes associated with intercultural learning have been studied extensively by a wide range of specialists, each with goals related to their discipline. The variety of viewpoints in the professional literature is both a blessing and a curse. While there are many sources to draw on, the fragmented and specialized nature of what is written makes it difficult to achieve an integrated, unified view. But each area of inquiry mentioned has something to offer to our overall understanding. This book will draw on the contributions which different areas of specialization have to offer. These ideas will be integrated into a theoretical whole, which will attempt to be well founded on established insights and theory, yet represent a new theoretical synthesis. This synthesis draws on the insights of many different fields.

The fields of anthropology, intercultural communication and cross-cultural psychology contribute an understanding of the competing uses of the word 'culture'. The work of intercultural communication specialists such as Hall (1959; 1976), Triandis (1972), Tomalin & Stempleski (1993), Trompenaars & Hampden-Turner (1998) and Hofstede (1997) can help us understand the *deep structure* of cultural values, beliefs and hidden assumptions. The field of language education offers an understanding of the relationship between communication and intercultural learning. In the UK and Europe the work of scholars such as Byram (1987; 1997; Byram & Feng, 2004; Byram *et al.*, 2001) and Muller (2003) sheds light on the different elements that make up the competencies necessary to communicate and function in a new linguistic and cultural environment. In the United States there has been a focus on intercultural education in the field of English language teaching (Damen, 1987; Moran, 2001). This work can be combined with the perspective of intercultural training. This type of Scholarship examines questions such as how to conceptualize and carry out intercultural training and education (Dinges, 1983; Dinges & Baldwin, 1996; Goldstein & Smith, 1999; Landis & Bhagat, 1996; Paige, 1993). There is an extensive body of work which examines what is meant by intercultural sensitivity or intercultural awareness, what the goals of intercultural learning should be and how best to describe the stages of intercultural learning (Adler, 1975; J. Bennett, 1998; Oberg, 1960; Stone & Ward, 1990; Ward *et al.*, 2001). There is also an increase of literature on how intercultural experiences can encourage personal growth and development (Cornes, 2004; Jack & Phipps, 2005; Nagata, 2005).

The field of cross-cultural psychology offers research on the mental and emotional states of those facing intercultural learning challenges. This has often been related to attempts to predict the kinds of personal qualities associated with success and failure in a new cultural environment (Babiker *et al.*, 1980; Dinges & Lieberman, 1989; Kamal & Maruyama, 1990; Stone & Ward, 1990) and the stress-coping strategies associated with intercultural success (Matsumoto *et al.*, 2001). At a more fundamental level, the field of general psychology offers us an understanding of the unconscious with the starting assumption that parts of ourselves which we are not fully aware of affect us in many ways. This parallels our discoveries about the deep structure of cultural values and beliefs examined by specialists who study cultural differences (Hampden-Turner & Trompenaars, 2000; Hofstede, 1983, 1986, 1997; Kim *et al.*, 1994; Kluckhohn & Strodbeck, 1961; Lewin, 1936; Ting-Toomey, 1994; Ting-Toomey & Oetzel, 2001; Trompenaars & Hampden-Turner, 1998, 2004).

This book is not, however, about how different academic disciplines have looked at the question of intercultural learning. Instead, we will put the process of intercultural learning at the center of our inquiry. This perspective builds on Kim's (2001) view that, in order to come to an integrated perspective of the intercultural learning experience, we must view cross-cultural adaptation as a universal phenomenon. This implies that intercultural learning is not simply an incidental process related to language learning or working abroad but rather a fundamental learning process that humans, as social animals and participants in cultural communities, go through any time they must come to grips with the need to function in a new, systematically different social environment. Interacting with a new cultural environment creates a gap between the existing internal knowledge and competencies of the individual and the systems, expectations and demands of the external environment.

This view of intercultural learning emphasizes its ongoing developmental nature. This perspective originates in open systems theory, which views living things as sharing certain life processes, such as 'the metabolism of matter energy and the metabolism of information' (Ruben, 1972: 120). Or, as Kim (2001: 35) describes it, 'each person is seen not as a rather static package of more or less stable internal structure, but as a dynamic and self-reflexive system that observes itself and renews itself as it continuously interacts with the environment. Humans are seen as having an 'innate self-organizing drive and a capacity to adapt to environmental challenges'. In phenomenological terms this self-organizing drive involves an innate desire to make sense of our experiences in terms of our existing perceptual categories. In a new intercultural environment, however, our existing schema may not be adequate to effectively interpret or interact in our new environment. Here, our innate capacity to adapt – to restructure our inner world as a result of interaction with our new environment – comes into play. This view of intercultural learning places cultural difference at the center of the intercultural experience. Cultural difference is defined as *the gap between a sojourner's existing internal cultural competencies and those required in his or her new host environment.* This work assumes that, although all humans share certain universal traits and biological drives, the challenge of dealing with difference in a new environment is what drives intercultural learning. Certain facial expressions, for example, are recognizable to most or all cultural groups and do not cause intercultural misunderstanding or place any adaptive pressure on a sojourner. The fact that the same facial expression – a smile, for example – is used and interpreted in widely different ways by different cultural groups does create an intercultural learning challenge (Matsumoto & Juang, 2004).

As will be argued throughout this book, the greatest difficulties in intercultural learning come primarily from cultural differences that are out of awareness. Many sojourners have intercultural experiences that they don't recognize as such. They make ethnocentric judgments about their cultural hosts without realizing that the phenomena they are reacting to are cultural and systematic rather than personal and idiosyncratic. Put in phenomenological terms sojourners experience a failure of empathy, an inability to understand the perceptual criteria of their cultural hosts. The source of this failure is, at least at first, ignorance; a gap between the internal worldview of the sojourner and the expectations and shared meanings of the host community. The process of responding to this gap is intercultural learning. In the next chapter we will look at competing conceptualizations of culture. Following that will be an examination of what is meant by deep culture followed by an examination of how intercultural learning can fail. An examination of these issues will lay the groundwork for the model of intercultural learning presented in Part 2 of this book.

Chapter 2
Objections to Culture

The things that make living here easier represent Japan losing its
culture. I wonder how long it will be before you have to go to the ends
of the earth to see Japanese architecture.
Adele

Interviewer: What are your feelings about Japanese culture?
Jack: How do you define 'culture'?
Interviewer: The way that people live ... how they communicate ...
their values.

The Struggle to Define 'Culture'

So far, this work has referred to 'cultural difference' without looking specifically at how we are using the word 'culture'. In common usage, the word culture is often used to refer to the visible products that represent the creative accomplishments of a group of people; things like art, literature, food, monuments and so on. In the quote above, Adele seems to have these things in mind when she talks of Japan losing its culture. For her, Japanese culture is epitomized by Japanese architecture. It is perhaps understandable that Adele thinks this way as she is a specialist in Japanese literature. She equates Japan's culture with Japan's artistic output and modernism as the loss of what is special about Japan. Jack, on the other hand, wants an explicit definition. The definition given by the interviewer was until recently mostly the domain of specialists but is increasingly passing into common use. This view of culture is wider and includes the everyday behavior, customs, values and beliefs of people from different places. A recent series of advertisements for an international bank uses this broader perspective when it shows images of differing cultural customs while touting the importance of its 'local knowledge' for doing business abroad. The assumption behind this view of culture includes a greater emphasis on the idea that visible differences in how people do things reflect deeper more hidden differences in values, beliefs or world views.

As with any word used to describe such a broad phenomenon, the word *culture* is used by many people in many ways. Currently, the word *culture* figures prominently in debates regarding the effects of globalization, diversity, issues of social justice, increasingly multicultural societies, the cultural identity of ethnic minorities, and so on. In this work, the focus is less on these macro-level social issues and more on the experience of individual sojourners living in unfamiliar surroundings. That particular focus calls for a usage of the term *culture* suitable to examining that process. In order to bring some clarity to the issue this chapter will give an overview of different conceptualizations of culture and how they have been used over time. It will also look at the argument, made by some, that the concept of culture is no longer valid in our globalized and multicultural world.

Competing conceptualizations

Among academics, the understanding of the nature of culture has changed over time and the details of its definition constitute an unresolved debate. The Encyclopedia of Social and Cultural Anthropology (Barnard & Spencer, 1996), for example, does not even offer a definition, choosing, rather, to trace the history of competing conceptualizations. Etymologically, culture is linked to words such as *cultivate* and *agriculture* and started to be used in the 17th century to refer to the potential for human development when referring to someone as being 'cultured'. Starting in the 19th century, culture was used in two different ways: (1) to describe a set of desired qualities, some people are more cultured than others; and (2) to describe, in the anthropological sense, the world being divided into any number of cultures, each with intrinsic value (Williams, 1958).

The development of this more relativistic sense was important because until the early to mid 20th century, a dominant view of human difference was racial determinism; the notion that physiological differences in race were important factors in determining behavior. Genetic superiority was often seen as a reason for industrial development and modernism. In the first half of the 20th century however, anthropologists and sociologists such as Boas (1928), Lévi-Strauss (1958), Mead (1961), Benedict (1934), Durkheim (1938) and Weber (1968) argued strongly that one's social and cultural environment – not racial difference – was the dominant force in shaping our behavior and that different *cultures* held self-contained and alternative valid worldviews.

These researchers held contrasting views of how precisely to define culture. One influential early definition was created by Taylor (1871):

> Culture or civilization, taken in its wide ethnographic sense, is that complex whole which includes knowledge, belief, art, moral, law, custom, and any other capabilities and habits acquired by man as a member of society. (p. 1)

Taylor's definition emphasizes the shared knowledge, values and physical products of a group of people. When we visit another place, we see
that buildings and food are different, and that the thinking and values that
brought about those cultural products contrast with those we are used to.
In addition, this definition reminds us that culture is not a static object, but
something that is modified and re-created in an ongoing process.
Throughout the 20th century, social scientists argued extensively about
further refinements of the definition of culture. The debate often reflected
the context and purpose of the definition. For example, Benedict's (1943:
9–10) definition of culture as 'behavior which in man is not given at birth,
which is not determined by his germ cells as is the behavior of wasps or the
social ants, but must be learned anew from grown people by each generation', was an attack on genetic determinism.

For many of these early researchers the study of cultural systems was a
method to gain insights into the ways in which our own socialization
limits our self-understanding. As Margaret Mead (1995: 1) put it: 'I have
spent most of my life studying the lives of other peoples, faraway peoples,
so that Americans might better understand themselves.' Mead and others
analyzed different social systems in order to 'illuminate the social practices of our own times, and ... show us, if we are ready to listen to its teachings, what to do and what to avoid' (Boas, 1928). Accordingly, these
researchers became interested not only in social organization and gene-
alogy but in everyday behavior and communication styles. Benedict (1934:
9) remarks that in the past 'custom did not challenge the attention of social
theorists because it was the very stuff of their own thinking: it was the lens
without which they could not see at all'. These social scientists were joined
by linguists such as Sapir (1921) and Whorf (J.B. Carroll, 1956) who
emphasized that our perception of the world is determined in large part by
the language we speak and the socialization of our cultural environment.
They argued that the influence of culture and socialization is often invis-
ible from the inside, that culture is to us like water is to a fish, and so much
a part of our world that it is difficult to separate from our experience and
examine objectively.

This greater understanding of cultural relativism in the early 20th
century corresponded with the development in the field of psychology of
the concept of the unconscious. A fundamental insight of Freud (Brill,
1995) and Jung (Jaffe, 1979) was that experience shapes behavior in unseen
ways. Thus, while psychoanalysts were exploring at the individual level
how our experiences shape our personality and behavior in ways of which
we are only vaguely aware, anthropologists were discovering the same
thing at the macro levels of cultural communities. Barnlund (Valdes, 1986)

describes the ideas of 'individual unconscious' first developed by Freud (Brill, 1995) and 'cultural unconscious' (used by Barnlund to refer to shared cultural frameworks) as some of the greatest insights of this modern age. (Barnlund, 1989)

Naturally, the world has changed since anthropologists were studying relatively isolated peoples. One obvious effect of globalization has been increasingly interconnected and diverse cultural communities. It may no longer be possible – if, indeed, it ever was – to accurately speak of *Russian culture* or *Italian culture*. If there is a general consensus around this term, it may be the understanding that *culture* is not a singular deterministic entity which controls behavior or which one 'belongs' to, but rather a network of products, meanings and expectations which communities share. Each individual participates in multiple cultural communities in a variety of roles so we can more easily refer to *cultural experience* or *cultural frameworks* than *culture* itself. One can as easily speak of the *culture* of a football team as that of a nation.

The complex and shifting nature of *culture*, however, should not obscure the powerful influence of one's cultural socialization and the potential challenge of adapting to a new cultural environment. As we have seen even with this small example with Jack, despite globalization and increasingly multicultural communities, it is still a challenge to learn a new language, live and work in another cultural environment. In many ways, the discovery of the power of implicit cultural frameworks by social scientists early in the last century parallels the experiences of today's sojourners as they discover that going abroad implies not only getting used to a new physical environment, but also making sense and adapting to different worldviews and confronting an array of new cultural communities.

Edward Hall – from culture to intercultural

For the anthropologists mentioned above, the study of culture was primarily a pursuit of specialists who viewed culture as a self-contained system and who attempted to describe how that system worked. After World War II, however, there was increased interest in understanding what happens when people from differing cultural frameworks come into contact with each other. Edward Hall was the first person to use the term *intercultural communication* while studying culture as it relates to cross-cultural miscommunication and misunderstanding. Hall (1959) elaborated a view of culture as an unconscious framework of shared meaning which makes communication possible but makes intercultural conflict inevitable. He argued that people were generally unaware of their cultural conditioning and that hidden difference in how we think and communicate creates barriers to intercultural understanding.

Hall focused in particular on finding ways to describe objectively these hidden differences. He attempted to identify concepts that could be used as neutral points of comparison – a kind of universal grammar to describe cultural difference. His work rests explicitly on the premise that intercultural communication is difficult because we are unaware of our own hidden patterns of thinking and communicating. He was particularly interested in differing cultural orientations regarding the use of time and space and felt that by understanding our own cultural patterns we would be freed from cultural constraints. Hall developed concepts such as a distinction between high and low context communication and cultures (Hall, 1959, 1976). High-context communication was described as that in which communicators rely relatively more on the context of a message and less on the words themselves. Thus, 'one word says it all'. In low-context communication, meaning relies more on the actual content of the message and less on when, how and by whom it is expressed. This type of communication is the 'say what you mean' way of expressing meaning.

Hall's concept of high and low context communication was useful because it acted as a criterion by which communication styles or cultural groups could be compared. According to this view, for example, Japanese communication was said to tend towards 'high context' as typified by the Japanese expression 'hear one and understand ten' (*ichi wo kite, juu wo shiru*). Anglo-American communication patterns tend more towards lower context and therefore value a more direct and explicit communication style (Hall & Hall, 1987). By using this category of cultural comparison, cultural conflict between, say, Japanese and Americans becomes easier to understand.

Hall's ideas were also important because his work created the framework for subsequent researchers' attempts to describe cultural difference. Hall, like the earlier generation of anthropologists, believed that an important goal of studying culture was cultural self-understanding. He saw this as a way to solve intercultural conflict and develop human potential. He states:

> Theoretically, there should be no problem when people of different cultures meet. Things begin, most frequently, not only with friendship and goodwill on both sides, but there is an intellectual understanding that each party has a different set of beliefs, customs, mores, values, or what-have-you. The trouble begins when people have to start working together, even on a superficial basis. Frequently, even after

years of close association, neither can make the other's system work! The difficulties I and others have observed persist so long and are so resistant to change that they can be explained only in psychological terms: people are in and remain in the grip of the cultural type of identification ... Man must now embark on the difficult journey beyond culture, because the greatest separation feat of all is when one manages to gradually free oneself from the grip of unconscious culture. (Hall, 1976: 239–240)

For Hall (1976: 17), bringing the hidden patterns of one's own cultural orientations to light was of primary importance, but also very difficult, because 'it is frequently the most obvious and taken for granted and therefore least studied aspects of culture that influence behavior in the deepest and most subtle ways'. Hall's contribution was to point out in concrete ways, as Freud had done half a century before, that much of what humans say and do is regulated at levels of the self of which we are not fully aware.

Edward Hall's ideas have been enormously influential yet there seems to have been relatively little explicit focus of late on the hidden side of the intercultural experience. Perhaps this is a bias of the seeming cultural convergence of our globalized world. It is true that many researchers have developed categories of cultural comparison following, in effect, Hall's lead. In addition, there has been a lot written about issues related to hidden culture, such as awareness, consciousness and cultural identity (Adler, 1977; Chalmers, 1996; Friedman, 1994; Gaston, 1984; Hall & Du Gay, 1996; Hanvey, 1979; Ingulsrud et al., 2002; Kemp, 1995; Muller, 2003; Noels et al., 1996; Schuetz, 1963; Shaules, 2003; Shaules et al., 2004; Singer, 1968; Smith, 1999; Sparrow, 2000; Tomalin & Stempleski, 1993; Tomlinson, 2000), yet it seems that Hall's desire to make more explicit the hidden elements of intercultural experiences has not been fully realized.

Objections to 'Culture'

Two recent trends have made, for some people at least, the use of the word culture – when used in the context of, say, 'Polish culture' – rather suspect. One is political correctness, which sometimes equates making generalizations about groups of people with the use of negative stereotypes. The other is globalization itself. Given that populations are so fluid, that multiculturalism is becoming so widespread, some doubt that it is even possible to talk of culture in a meaningful way. Within the field of cultural studies there has been vigorous debate about the nature of cultural identity in the postmodern world, with a particular emphasis on how issues such as gender, ethnicity, nationality, politics, media and values interact in the context of globalization to produce highly fragmented patterns of self-identification (Friedman, 1994; McGuigan, 1999; Sherbert *et al.*, 2006; Singer, 1968). Some argue that the traditional boundaries of cultural identity have become so fragmented in modern societies that the concept of culture and cultural identity itself is called into question (Hall & Du Gay, 1996).

In a similar way, some communication specialists argue that communication is so highly contextual that it is unreasonable to claim that culture plays a large deterministic role. As Kramsch (2005: 15) puts it: 'To assume that "German culture" speaks through the discourse of a speaker of standard German is an inappropriate assumption in our days of hybrid, changing, and conflicting cultures. ... [C]ulture has become, for many speakers, a de-territorialized, imagined community.' Scollon and Scollon (2001: 138) state that 'the word culture often brings up more problems than it solves' and Agar (2002) argues that the whole concept of culture is no longer valid:

> The 'culture' part of the term 'transcultural' is now a major problem. For most anyone today, the 'cultures' that affect him/her at any given moment are multiple, local to global, partial and variable in their impact. Culture used to be a way to describe, generalize and explain what a person was doing. It is not so easy – maybe even impossible – to do that any more. (p. 15)

Agar prefers the concept 'community of practice' – a term from the field of business communication referring to the informal networks which develop in collaborative relationships (Sharp, 1997: 15) – and argues that it is a 'more powerful tool than the old idea of "culture"'. He calls for us to give up the aspiration to talk about *culture* in the sense of predicting behavior and making generalizations and narrow the focus to a particular situation:

> A situation is dynamic – in fact it is a nonlinear dynamic system. The situation has people in it. Like any nonlinear dynamic system, the situation is an interaction between an environment and a model of that environment, the two co-evolving over time. Let's call that moving environment the flow, and the model will be called a framework, or frames for short. Much of the time the navigation is straightforward. Sometimes the flow moves in unexpected directions and you adjust the frames. Sometimes you get a bright idea and change the frames

and the interaction with the flow goes more smoothly. The transcultural moment comes when a disruption occurs, something the frames can't handle. A transcultural self can understand and explain such disruptions and resolve them with positive outcomes. (p. 15)

Taken at face value, this line of argument would seem to imply that any attempt to explain the learning process of those living abroad in terms of cultural groups or cultural difference is bound to flounder on the jagged shores of the individualized, globalized identities of sojourners. In this view, the diversity of the individual goes beyond the social cohesiveness traditionally attributed to cultural communities, thus *culture* becomes an anachronistic conceptual framework.

Social identity versus communities of shared meaning

There are, however, some important distinctions that need to be made. The first is the differing purposes to which the term *culture* is being applied. We need to be careful to distinguish between cultures as: (1) a form of personal, ethnic or social identity and (2) a community of shared meanings. Cultural studies and postmodernism are often interested in the elements that contribute to one's sense of social identity – how race, gender, ethnicity, power relations, etc. affect one's sense of self and view of the world. The children of immigrants, for example, may find themselves caught between the expectations of family and a desire to participate in the society that they grew up in. They may face prejudice as an ethnic minority. To blithely refer to the bilingual and bicultural children of Hong Kong immigrants to Canada simply as 'Canadian' would not do justice to the richness of their cultural identities and intercultural experiences. With an increase in multiculturalism and globalism, the importance of creating inclusive societies has created great interest in the questions of cultural and social identity and may have pushed the definition of culture in this direction.

Yet, social identity is not the same as the ability to understand the frameworks of meaning that another cultural community shares. An African-American, for example, may feel a strong personal connection with Africa as part of his social identity. That does not mean, however, that when he arrives in Senegal for the first time that he will be able to interpret Senegalese behavior better than any other tourist. He still may be uncomfortable eating with his fingers and he won't automatically understand Wolof, one of the principle languages of Senegal. As for any American, it will take time for him to understand Senegalese values, social relations, food, communications styles, etc. His cultural identity may change his *attitude* towards Senegalese and make it easier to learn these things, but the frameworks of shared meaning that allows Senegalese to communicate with each other is separate from the African-American's sense of social identity. Likewise, an Indian immigrant who grows up in England attending English schools may feel very alienated from mainstream English values, but he still has been exposed to an English worldview and can most likely better interpret English behavior than someone who did not grow up in England.

Confusing these two usages of the term *culture* can lead to overestimating cultural similarity. If one focuses on culture as a form of social or personal identity, one might say that two teenagers from different countries – let's say, Iran and Peru – who see themselves as rebels and share a love of similar video games, hip hop stars and football players, share more cultural identity than either of those teenagers with their own grandparents. Yet the Iranian teenager would largely be incompetent to function in the social environment that his Peruvian friend takes for granted and vice versa. Even if the Iranian and Peruvian teenagers can form a relationship with each other based on their shared interests, the Peruvian teenager would have to first learn Farsi to communicate with his friend's grandmother, shop in his friend's neighborhood stores, interact with his friend's friends, and so on. To function as a teenager in Iran involves linguistic and social competencies that go far beyond abstractions about personal tastes or interests that we may use to define ourselves. In the same way, growing up speaking a particular language – Italian, for example – does not mean that someone will necessarily *feel* a strong Italian identity or adhere to a particular set of personal values. But language is a reflection of the worldview of its speakers and being socialized into a linguistic community gives one an intuitive sense for the worldview of others in that community. It also provides a shared framework that allows for interaction and allows for the expression of an individual identity relative to the expectations and meanings of that community.

Bennett addresses the issue of the shared meaning of social communities by describing culture as existing at different levels of abstraction:

National groups such as Japanese, Mexican, and US American and pan-national ethnic groups such as Arab and Zulu are cultures at a high level of abstraction – the qualities that adhere to most (but not all) members of the culture are very general, and the group includes lots of diversity. At this level of abstraction we can only point to general differences in patterns of thinking and behaving between cultures. For instance, we might observe that US American culture is more characterized by individualism than is Japanese culture, which is more collectivist.

Analysis at a high level of abstraction provides a view of the 'unifying force' of culture. The very existence of interaction, even through media, generates a commonality that spans individuals and ethnicities. For instance, despite their significant individual and ethnic differences, Mexicans spend more time interacting with other Mexicans than they do with Japanese. They certainly spend more time reading Mexican newspapers and watching Mexican television than they do consuming Japanese media. This fact generates Mexican 'national character' – something that distinguishes Mexicans from Japanese (and from other Latin Americans as well.) (M.J. Bennett, 1998: 4)

Bennett reminds us that broad cultural labels are meaningful as long as we remember that they only imply the sharing of particular cultural frameworks. They don't imply that any individual will necessarily identify themselves in a particular way.

Cultural as a causal agent

The view of culture as shared frameworks of meaning must also be distinguished from the assumption that culture is a causal agent – something which makes people act in a certain way. Kramsch (2005), for example, argues that we shouldn't assume that German culture speaks through the discourse of a speaker of German, yet this is an indictment of the view that culture causes particular behaviors, not that German speakers share frameworks of meaning. Individual speech acts are not predetermined by the language one speaks. Despite this, language use and discourse is not arbitrary and Germans understand the complex expectations of how behavior will be interpreted by their fellow Germans better than non-Germans.

Likewise, when Agar (2002: 15) argues that the 'cultures that affect [one] at any given moment are multiple, local to global, partial and variable in their impact', he is arguing against the causal 'impact' of culture. But his characterization of culture as something that 'affects' people differs greatly from the perspective of Hall and others who characterize culture as the lens through which we see things, rather than something that controls us. His statement that culture may not be able to 'describe, generalize and explain what a person is doing' seems to be a rejection of the idea that membership in a cultural community is deterministic and absolute. Yet, a salient feature of intercultural experiences is a lack of the frameworks of meaning – including in particular language – for *interpreting* behavior and events in our new environment. Culture conceptualized as influencing behavior and culture seen as a guide to interpreting behavior are two different things.

The view of culture as a deterministic force is deeply embedded in the discourse of intercultural studies. Hofstede (1997: 4), who has done influential studies on cultural variation, explains cultural difference by saying that behavior is 'partially predetermined by [one's] mental programs'. Hofstede goes on to claim that the 'patterns of thinking, feeling, and potential acting which were learned' throughout one's lifetime must be 'unlearned' before being able to learn something different. This seems to characterize culture as an internal essence that drives actions, much as personality is seen as a stable quality that makes certain behavior more likely. Nisbett (2003: 123) has argued that this approach to explaining interaction is a particularly Western conceptualization of humans, founded in a tendency to make a 'fundamental attribution error' that overemphasizes causality in its view of human behavior. In the field of psychology it has been strongly argued that measurement of internal psychological qualities is a poor predictor of specific behavior (Kraus, 1995; LaPiere, 1934; Wicker, 1969). If so, it should not be a surprise that knowing someone's cultural background does not allow us to predict behavior with much accuracy.

Different conceptualizations of culture are appropriate for the purposes to which they are put. For sojourners, an important contribution of Edward Hall, (1959; 1976; 1984) has been to recast our understanding of the relationship between culture and behavior. He argued that when interacting with people from other cultural communities we are, in effect, interacting with other worldviews and that surface behavior is tied to deep and hidden networks of meaning, values and expectations that our hosts share with each other, yet which we do not yet fully understand. As we will see, this approach to understanding intercultural interaction has not been lost. Within the field of intercultural relations it is reflected, for example, in M.J. Bennett's (1993) phenomenological view of intercultural sensitivity and Trompenaars and Hampden-Turner's (1998) view of the hidden assumptions that underlie cultural value dilemmas. These authors share with Hall the view that culture acts as a perceptual framework, which is used to make sense of the world and in turn acts as an arbiter of choices about particular behavior. And while this view is not *correct* in an absolute sense, it does seem to fit well with the experiences reported by those who face intercultural learning challenges.

Culture as Experienced by Sojourners

In this book we are interested primarily in culture as it is experienced by those living in new cultural communities. Hall's view of culture as a system of shared meaning and expectations fits well with the way that expatriates describe their intercultural learning experiences. Overwhelmingly, when they talk of their experience abroad, they talk about their experiences in terms of cultural difference or perhaps 'patterns of difference'. Jack, for example, when talking about his relationships with Japanese says:

> The Japanese I know – the students – treat me with respect ... my students, they respect a professional. They heap adoration on me. How much of it is legit and how much of it is typical Japanese over-politeness, I don't know.

Regardless of whether we agree with his conclusions, when Jack talks about 'typical Japanese over-politeness', he is running into systematic patterns of difference between the values or communication styles he finds in Japan, and what he is more used to as an American. Regardless of our definition of culture it is this systematic difference that constitutes the intercultural learning challenge for those crossing cultural boundaries. And when these systematic differences function out of awareness, they can trip up sojourners who are unable to get at the root cause of their discomfort or communication difficulty. In Jack's case, he seems unsure as to whether he can trust the *adoration* of his students because it goes beyond what he would experience with American students.

Of course, what Jack experiences as *adoration* is probably only partly a result of warm feelings that *individual* students have for him. In addition, it is most likely also a result of the deference that Japanese students express *in general* towards their teachers. This specific behavior is a functional part of a Japanese worldview that defines the role of teachers as deserving of more deference than what Jack would consider *normal*. At least to some degree, Jack's students are not heaping *adoration*, they are simply treating him normally as they would treat all teachers. The fact that Jack describes this treatment as *over-politeness* shows that he is still judging his students by American standards and hasn't fully stepped into a Japanese worldview in which relatively greater deference towards teachers is to be expected.

It is beyond the scope of this book to discuss in depth the differences between the more hierarchical, collectivist, Confucian-based values system which underlie the behavior of Jack's students and the more individualist, egalitarian thinking behind Jack's view of what constitutes normal relationships between students and teachers. Much research into cross-cultural difference attempts to provide descriptions of these kinds of meta-level differences. Of more importance here is the fact that regardless of how we define the word culture, crossing cultural and social boundaries put us in contact with people who are different than we are in systematic ways. Just as a language is a communication system which allows for meaningful interaction, the shared meanings, values, norms and hidden assumptions of cultural groups represent a systematic, albeit diffuse, framework of meanings and expectations which enable human interaction.

The importance of *deep culture* may sometimes be overlooked due to technological convergence. It is easy to forget that the existence and importance of culture is a relatively recent insight. The first researchers who explored these issues emphasized a need for us to use cross-cultural experiences to come to a greater understanding of ourselves. They also spoke of the difficulties of going beyond our cultural programming. These issues are more relevant than ever as they represent precisely the challenges being faced by millions of sojourners today. Rather than redefining or rejecting culture as a useful concept, it may be necessary to go back to the roots of the discovery of culture. Doing this may show us that a principle insight of the first intercultural specialists – becoming aware of the hidden patterns of our own behavior has important lessons to teach us – is being forgotten among specialists just at the time when millions of people are in the position to take advantage of it. The next chapter will look in more detail at what is meant by *deep culture* and start to look at the kinds of challenges that difference in deep culture creates for sojourners.

Chapter 3

Understanding the Deep Structure of Culture

> *Eun Suk: For Japanese [sitting separately from colleagues at lunch]*
> *may be totally normal, but from my Korean point of view, it's*
> *something I simply can't fathom. [Here in Japan] If I'm at a*
> *restaurant and a teacher from my same department is there, I'm not*
> *sure if I should join them or not.*
> *Interviewer: So you're not sure what a Japanese would do in this*
> *situation?*
> *Eun Suk: Yes, it's very hard to read the situation.*
> *Interviewer: After 12 years in Japan it's still hard to read? Sounds*
> *difficult.*
> *Eun Suk: [laughing] Yes, it is.*

Cultural 'Rules' and Diffuse Cultural Difference

Eun Suk is Korean and has been living in Japan for 12 years. She is a fluent Japanese speaker, completed doctoral studies in Japan and has worked as a tenured faculty of a prestigious university in Tokyo for five years. Her level of interaction with Japanese is high – she teaches courses, advises graduate students and works on university committees – yet she is still not sure whether or not to join her colleagues at lunch. She is not socially incompetent or insensitive; she simply has trouble understanding the expectations and intentions of her Japanese colleagues.

The challenges faced by long-term sojourners like Eun Suk go beyond the typical behavioral maxims often heard when discussing life abroad, such as, 'In France, you should always greet shopkeepers when you enter a store' or a list of taboos, such as, 'In Japan, you should never pass food from one set of chopsticks to another'. Admonitions like this give the impression that it is possible to reduce cultural learning to a set of rules. Yet no one can tell Eun Suk the 'rules' of when to sit with her colleagues because cultural expectations are not a set of 'do's and don'ts'. She knows that she *can* sit with her colleagues in this situation, but she's not sure what it will mean to them. Will she be seen as pushy? Friendly? It will most likely depend on the particular situation: Are they on campus or off? Is the colleague alone? Are they older or younger, male or female? How much contact have they had in the past? No one could devise a set of rules to cover all of these eventualities.

Eun Suk's dilemma illustrates some of the difficulties faced by long-term sojourners. They face cultural difference which is subtle and diffuse. This makes it difficult to describe or predict – even for intercultural specialists. But that doesn't mean that cultural difference doesn't exist or that it is arbitrary. As Eun Suk understands instinctively, the interpretations people give to actions or the values and worldview that people use to explain their behavior, are neither arbitrary nor simply a matter of personal choice. For Eun Suk, sitting separately from colleagues at lunch is *unfathomable* because of real, yet hidden differences between Korean and Japanese cultural norms, values and implicit beliefs. Normally, these deep cultural differences are felt intuitively but there have also been attempts to describe them in systematic ways. This chapter will give an overview of these efforts and try to show how hidden cultural difference can create adaptive challenges for sojourners.

Culture as stable frameworks of interpretation

In Chapter 1 it was argued that culture is not so much a controlling agent as a way to make sense of the world. In Eun Suk's case, this implies that she won't easily be able to determine the rules that govern people's behavior. That doesn't mean, however, that stable standards are not applied to the interpretation of behavior. We can draw a linguistic parallel by asking the question: 'In England, what do the English say when meeting someone for the first time?' Of course it is difficult to make rules to predict the use of language in this way. One could list some things that you *can* say, but that doesn't allow us to predict what people will say. It doesn't even allow us to predict the language usage in a similar situation or by a particular type of person since use of language is highly contextual and tied to the personality and idiolect of each individual. If we suppose that people say 'How do you do?' when they meet someone, we may find that people often say nothing at all or that young people say something different. There is almost always a contextual variable which can disprove an assertion that a particular utterance belongs in a particular situation.

Yet the assertion of contextual variation doesn't mean that use of language is arbitrary. If someone chooses to say 'How do you do? It's a pleasure to meet you', English speakers know that this choice represents a more formal register than saying 'Hey there. What's up?' While we cannot predict the behavior, the system that is used to interpret the behavior is relatively stable. Individuality is expressed in how we use the system, i.e. the choice of what to say given the unspoken interpretive frameworks that are taken for granted in a situation like this. For her part, Eun Suk finds herself in the same situation as a learner of French not sure whether he should use the formal 'vous' or the informal 'tu' in a particular situation. He knows that he can use either, but isn't sure which one best represents his communicative intention.

Another argument against the importance of culture as a factor in successful interaction is that people who don't speak a common language or share a similar background are often able to communicate well or form satisfying relationships. Yet the cases in which this happens reinforce rather than weaken the argument that frameworks of meaning are necessary for communication and human relationships. Two engineers from different cultural backgrounds who successfully work together despite language barriers share the framework of engineering to base their relationship on. When football players from different countries gather for a game, it is a mutual understanding of the rules of football that allow them to play. The further away those players are away from the context of playing football, the more difficult their communication becomes. And even when players share the same rules, cultural difference can create conflict. A basketball player who grows up playing a razzle-dazzle style of game in the US may be seen as selfish and pretentious playing in China where cooperation by team members is given great importance. Engineers from China and Germany may have different culturally-based ideas about the best way to solve problems or the best way to organize a project. One may find Feng Shui normal while the other superstitious.

And in the soccer analogy, even when there are different rules, as long as those rule differences don't cause two players to interpret a play differently, things proceed smoothly. In the same way, an ignorance of the rules doesn't necessarily prohibit play, it simply creates a potential for misunderstanding. Someone can play football without understanding the rules for what constitutes an offsides infraction. If players are of good will and there are no important consequences to the ignorance, the game goes on. But the danger of conflict will continue, and sooner or later, either the player will come to understand the rule and play accordingly, or will create conflict by not meeting the expectations of other players at a key moment.

The deep structure of cultural difference

It has been argued that culture can be conceptualized as frameworks of shared meaning that allow for interaction and relationship building. What those frameworks are, however, has not been discussed. To better understand the learning challenge faced by Eun Suk, it is necessary to come to a clearer understanding of what constitutes deep cultural frameworks, and how differences in those frameworks can create adaptive challenges in a new environment. Within the professional literature, a starting point for examining this question is the distinction between *subjective* and *objective* culture. Objective elements of culture are said to be the products and artifacts of culture such as clothing, food and architecture. The subjective elements are said to be the aspects that we cannot see or touch, such as values, beliefs, attitudes and norms (Triandis, 1972). This distinction has lead to taxonomies that attempt to identify the different elements of culture that function out of awareness. One common image used for this purpose is that of the cultural 'iceberg' in which unconscious elements of culture remain out of sight. A typical example (Terreni & McCallum) is shown in Diagram 3.1.

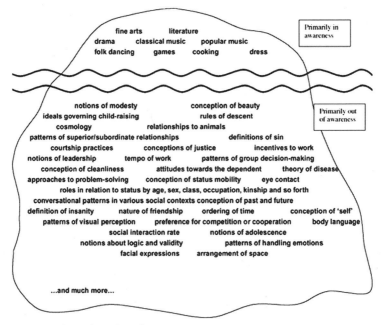

Diagram 3.1 The cultural 'iceberg'

Taxonomies such as this are useful because they remind us of the many elements of deep culture that we often take for granted. It is instructive to look at each of the items in the diagram above and consider that all of them represent significant areas of cultural commonality within particular groups, yet that a list like this could also be extended nearly indefinitely. Given the number of hidden elements of culture, it is understandable that deep cultural learning can be difficult.

Yet taxonomies such as this are frustrating as well, because they don't provide us with a way to systematically compare cultural frameworks. While it may be true that, as is shown in this diagram, the *ordering of time* and *patterns of handling emotions* are elements of hidden culture, this diagram doesn't explain what different approaches there are for ordering time or handling emotions. It also doesn't make clear how some of these categories may be related to each other. For example, are *patterns of group decision making* related in some way to *preference for cooperation or competition*? Put differently, can this vast list be divided into superordinate categories that might constitute a fundamental structure to deep culture? And finally, this type of taxonomy doesn't clarify whether certain elements of culture may be more out of awareness than others.

In spite of a lack of consensus on which elements constitute an overall structure of deep culture, there has been a lot of research on the particular elements found within the hidden part of the cultural iceberg. As mentioned previously, Hall (1959; Hall, 1976) was the first to attempt this kind of systematic comparison in examining differing systems for 'ordering of time'. Many others have followed Hall's lead in examining specific elements of deep cultural difference. One challenge with any attempt to create an overall description of deep culture comes from the vast number of elements that can be included. One way to deal with this problem is to organize these components into categories which allows for systematic comparison of different cultural groups. Fortunately, there have been important advances in research designed with this goal in mind.

Research into Deep Cultural Difference

The earliest research into cultural difference is rooted in cultural anthropology. Traditionally, an important goal of cultural anthropological research has been a descriptive understanding of cultural groups (Barnard, 2000). Often, using ethnographic methodologies, anthropologists would attempt to come to an emic – or an insider's perspective of a cultural group – by questioning cultural informants as to their view of their social world. This methodology is well suited to developing descriptions of social systems, rituals, cosmologies, taboos and explicit belief structures. The work of Edward Hall (1959; 1976), himself an anthropologist, reminds us, however, that what people are capable of explaining about their own culture is often limited to the more explicit, objective elements. The hidden elements of culture are more difficult to describe and measure, Still, there is research from several different fields that can contribute to our understanding in this area.

Linguistic relativity

One approach to understanding the hidden influence of culture has been through the study of the effects of language on cognition – particularly in connection with the Sapir–Whorf hypothesis. This hypothesis, also known as *linguistic relativity*, proposes that the language that one speaks affects cognitive processes. Because different languages categorize objects, relationships and meanings differently, one's view of the world is said to reflect perceptual categories learned in the process of acquiring one's native language. As Sapir (1958[1929])states:

> Human beings do not live in the objective world alone, or alone in the world of social activity as ordinarily understood, but are very much at the mercy of the particular language which has become the medium of expression for their society. It is quite an illusion to imagine that one adjusts to reality essentially without the use of language and that language is merely an incidental means of solving specific problems of communication or reflection. The fact of the matter is that the 'real world' is to a large extent unconsciously built upon the language habits of the group. No two languages are ever sufficiently similar to be considered as representing the same social reality. The worlds in which different societies live are distinct worlds, not merely the same world with different labels attached... We see and hear and otherwise experience very largely as we do because the language habits of our community predispose certain choices of interpretation. (p. 69)

A great deal of research has been carried out to test the Sapir–Whorf hypothesis in a variety of ways. Some research which supported this hypothesis, for example, showed that Navajo speakers categorize objects differently from English speakers, presumably as a result in a rich vocabulary for handling objects of different shapes in Navajo (Carroll & Casagrande, 1958). Other studies looked at the ability to classify colors (Kay & Kempton, 1984); the propensity of Chinese speakers to give hypothetical interpretations to a hypothetical story (Bloom, 1981); or the effects of language on visual memory (Santa & Baker, 1975). While research of this sort has provided evidence that language affects cognition to some degree, there has been a great deal of disagreement on how and to what degree it does so. Research which challenges the conclusions of the kinds of research mentioned above include Au (1983) and Davies *et al.* (1998). Pinker (1995) argues for what he calls a language 'instinct', refuting the idea that we are obliged to perceive in a particular way due to the influence of language.

For intercultural learners, the claims and counterclaims of this debate obscure some important limitations of the questions being asked. The quote by Sapir above and the issue of relevance for those crossing cultural boundaries, relate not so much to the ability to classify or categorize particular elements of the physical environment such as colors or shapes, but rather the fact that language is a symbolic system which represents our *social reality*. It is important to distinguish between the word 'perception' as used to describe the neural act of processing sensorial stimuli, and 'perception' as used to describe one's worldview or opinion about an issue. Regardless of whether speaking one language or another affects our ability to easily *perceive* (identify) differing shades of color or classify particular shapes, one's *perception* (interpretation) of what is right, good and reasonable in a given situation is clearly related to one's social worldview. The ability to perceive a wedding dress as white doesn't confer on an observer the knowledge that white is considered a sign of purity, or that sex before marriage has generally been considered a sin in a traditional Christian worldview.

Deep culture and cognitive processes

For research into differences in cognition to be of more use for intercultural learners, it would be necessary to show not only that some particular cognitive process varies depending on cultural background, but also how that difference relates to the worldview and social reality of those socialized to think in that way. This could help sojourners make more sense of their intercultural experiences and allow them to suspend judgment when faced with a different way of seeing things. Nisbett (2003) has carried out a series of experiments comparing the thought processes of East Asians (Chinese, Koreans and Japanese) and Westerners (Western Europeans and Americans) in which he argues that approaches to cognition vary between these two cultural groups in fundamental and important ways – ways which relate clearly to the intellectual traditions of Western and Asian cultures and also to current values and social practices.

Nisbett (2003) wanted to test the supposition – found in comparative cultural studies – that Westerners tend toward more discrete, analog thinking while East Asians have more holistic, context oriented cognitive processes. He specifically wanted to test the ideas that:

> European thought rests on the assumption that the behavior of objects – physical, animal, and human – can be understood in terms of straight-forward rules. Westerners have a strong interest in categorization, which helps them to know what rules to apply to the objects in question, and formal logic plays a role in problem solving. East Asians, in contrast, attend to objects in their broad context. The world seems more complex to Asians than to Westerners, and understanding events always requires consideration of a host of factors that operate in relation to one another in no simple, deterministic way. Formal logic plays little role in problem solving. In fact, the person who is too concerned with logic may be considered immature. (p. xvi)

According to Nisbett, these differences are important in ways beyond laboratory tests because:

> the social structures and sense of self that are characteristic of East-erners and Westerners seem to fit hand in glove with their respective belief systems and cognitive processes. The collective or interdepen-dent nature of Asian society is consistent with Asians' broad, contex-tual view of the world and their belief that events are highly complex and determined by many factors. The individualistic or independent nature of Western society seems consistent with the Western focus on particular objects in isolation from their context and with Westerner's belief that they can know the rules governing objects and therefore can control the objects' behavior. (p. xvii)

Nisbett's experiments dealt with a wide range of questions related to a variety of fields, including: (1) science and mathematics; (2) attention and perception; (3) causal inference; (4) organization of knowledge; and (5) reasoning. He proposes that differences in these areas are related to social conditions and systems of thought which developed thousands of years ago and which have maintained a consistency since then. He uses the thinking and social practices of ancient China as a point of comparison with the social systems and approach to thought associated with ancient Greece. According to this view, the tenets of Confucianism and Taoism reflect not only a philosophical cosmology, but were both a reflection of society at the time and a powerful shaper of the way people come to perceive their existence. Likewise, in ancient Greece the tradition of subject–object thinking, linear reasoning and search for essential qualities within nature have shaped thinking patterns and social views up until the present.

To support these assertions, Nisbett carried out and reviewed clinical experiments comparing cognitive tasks by people from different countries. Nisbett found that: (1) East Asians are better able to see relationships among events than Westerners; (2) it is harder for East Asians to distinguish an object from its surroundings; (3) Westerners are more likely to overlook the influence of context on how both objects and people behave; (4) Easterners have a tendency to have a 'hindsight bias', which makes them believe that they 'knew it all along'; and (5) East Asians tend to group things by relationships, while Westerners tend to use categories.

One of the experiments Nisbett uses to support his assertions relates to what Nisbett refers to as 'holism' versus 'analysis'. He found differences in, for example, the tendency to view things as an object or a substance. When seeing a pyramid-shaped object made of cork, Americans are more likely to group that object with other pyramid-shaped objects (seeing it as an object), while East Asians are more likely to group it with other things made of cork (seeing it as a substance). Nisbett sees a connection between these experimental results and the philosophical traditions and social practices of China which emphasizes process and context, and the more atomistic tradition of subject–object reasoning developed by the Greeks.

Another example of Nisbett's experiments related to the relative importance of context in the thinking of Westerners and East Asians. In one experiment subjects were shown a 20 second scene of an aquatic environment with a variety of fish, plants and moving objects. Among these was a 'focal fish', which stood out from the background because it was larger, moved more, etc. When asked to recall this scene, Japanese subjects made 60 percent more references to the background elements such as bubbles, rocks, and so on. The first sentence of the Japanese participants was likely to be an explanation of the environment ('It looks like a pond') whereas Americans were three times as likely to first refer to the focal fish ('There was a big fish on the left'). Nisbett argues that research done by Morris and Peng (1994) shows that the focus on context was not limited to physical objects. In content analysis of Chinese and American newspaper crime reports, they found that Chinese are more likely to attribute behavior to the context of an event ('did not get along with his advisor', 'rivalry with the slain student'), while Americans are more likely to internal qualities of the actor ('very bad temper', 'sinister edge to his character').

The research that Nisbett draws on to make his case for cultural difference between East Asians and Westerners comes primarily from laboratory research. He argues, however, that these differences are reflected in social practices and worldviews. He gives examples in:

(1)   Medicine – Western medicine is more object oriented and interventionist while traditional Chinese medicine is more holistic, focused on processes and the balance of different elements.

(2)   Law and conflict resolution – The West has a much higher number of lawyers and emphasis on rule-based conflict resolution (adversarial justice and lawsuits) rather than the emphasis on mediation in conflict resolution and flexibility and interpretation in contracts in Eastern Asia.

(3)   Debate – decision making in Asia is much more likely to be based on consensus, rather than an adversarial dialectic (debate) commonly used as a way to look for truth in the West.

(4)   Science – In the 1990s, the number of Nobel prizes were awarded to 44 Americans and only one to a Japanese, despite the fact that funding for Science in Japan is half that of the United States. This can be seen as an emphasis on Confucian respect for elders which funnels research funds to mediocre older scientists and also a lesser emphasis on peer review, open debate and criticism in Japan.

(5)   Rhetoric – Western rhetoric involves linear thinking that focuses on background, problems, hypothesis, testing, evidence, arguments about evidence, refutation of counterarguments, conclusions and recommendations. This linear reasoning is not universal and is much less common in Asian communication patterns.

(6)   Contracts – In Asia, contracts are seen more as a framework within which a relationship is maintained, rather than a set of rules that is used to arbitrate behavior and resolve conflict.

(7)   Human rights – Westerners tend to see the individual as the primary social unit that has a relationship with the state that entails certain rights and obligations. Asians, on the other hand, see society as holistic organism rather than a collection of individuals. The Chinese view is based on a part/whole conception rather than one/many conception.

(8)   Religion – Religion in the West tends to center on a right/wrong mentality, whereas there is a both/and tendency in Asia. It's possible to be Confucian, Buddhist and have a Christian wedding in Japan. Monotheism and God as an absolute good is contrasted with the cycles and reoccurrences in Buddhism and Taoism.

Nisbett (2003: 201) does not argue that there is a direct cause and effect relationship between cognitive processes that are tested in the laboratory and the social phenomena listed above. Rather, his claim is that 'cognitive differences are inseparable from the social and motivational ones'. 'People hold the beliefs they do because of the way they think and they think the way they do because of the nature of the societies they live in.' This conclusion has important implications for those who are crossing cultural boundaries, and as such, find themselves in the position of needing to adapt to environments that differ in such deep and fundamental ways.

One implication of Nisbett's ideas is that if one knows where to look, it is possible to discern deep-seated cultural differences in the day-to-day cognitive behavior of people from different cultures. Another implication is that the influence of culture goes much deeper than globalization might seem to imply. The measurable cognitive differences that Nisbett found seem to have been stable for several thousand years. The basis of these differences is more than explicit beliefs about particular teachings, i.e. it goes beyond whether one *believes* in God or some particular cosmology or set of social strictures. Attitudes, values and beliefs may be different as a consequence of having fundamental, yet hidden differences in approaches to making sense of the world. As Nisbett (2003) puts it:

> If people really do differ profoundly in their systems of thought – their worldviews and cognitive processes – then differences in people's attitudes and beliefs, and even their values and preferences, might not be a matter merely of different inputs and teachings, but rather an inevitable consequence of using different tools to understand the world. And if that's true, then efforts to improve international understanding may be less likely to pay off then one might hope. (pp. xvii–xviii)

His statement that international understanding may be more difficult than we might hope is reflected in the difficulties than Eun Suk has fitting in with her Japanese colleagues. What may seem like a simple behavior on the surface – sitting down or not – exists within a worldview that is not easily accessible to outsiders.

Dimensions and domains

In attempting to explain the deeper levels of culture's influence on human behavior, and as a way to break down deep culture into elements that can be measured and compared, cross-cultural psychologists make a distinction between cultural *domains* and cultural *dimensions*. Matsumoto and Juang (2004: 46) define domains as 'specific sociopsychological characteristics that are considered to be meaningful outcomes, products, or constituents of culture, including attitudes , values, beliefs, opinions, norms, customs, and rituals'. These domains are considered to represent separate psychological processes. Dimensions, on the other hand, are seen as 'general tendencies that affect behavior and reflect meaningful aspects of cultural variability'. The assumption behind this view of subjective culture is that dimensions of culture can be manifested in many different domains. A tendency for a group of people to emphasize the needs of the group over the needs of the individual, for example, could manifest itself in values, beliefs, customs, rituals, and so on of different cultural groups. The relative emphasis on the group or the individual is a dimension of cultural difference. That implies that there exist patterns of collective differences at deep levels which permeate the social practices of groups of people and play a role in shaping the behavior and artifacts of people in that cultural group.

Cultural domains exist at a high level of abstraction in the sense that they cannot be observed directly. Rather, it is necessary to infer their existence from observable behavior and categories of meaning shared by cultural groups. When a French visitor to Japan first sees one Japanese bow to another, she is seeing a single instance of behavior which can be observed, but the meaning of which depends on interpretation. By observing Japanese in a wide range of circumstances, this visitor may be able to distinguish patterns of bowing – who bows to whom, in what way, and in what situations. These norms that dictate expectations about bowing – deeper bows imply a higher degree of deference – are one domain in which deeper cultural qualities are manifested. Likewise, Japanese values related to bowing – the importance of showing respect – are another separate domain which manifests itself in these patterns of behavior.

While the distinction between domains and dimensions is relatively clear, there is little agreement on what constitutes essential dimensions of cultural difference. The area of research that is perhaps of most use to sojourners who face the day-to-day challenges of living in a new cultural environment is related to dimensions of cultural difference relative to value orientations. While cultural values are expressed in many forms, such as heroes, laws, myths and moral strictures, the study of value orientations allows us to have points of comparisons between different cultural groups – precisely what sojourners need as they navigate through new cultural environments.

Approaches to Understanding Value Orientations

One approach to understanding value orientations focuses on identifying key concepts to help us make sense of cultural behavior, yet without trying to make quantitative comparisons between different cultural groups. An example of this is the concept of *face* or *facework* (Goffman, 1967; Hu, 1944; Ting-Toomey, 1994). Asian cultural values, for example, can be examined from the point of facework as a way of understanding interaction within a variety of Asian cultural communities. Also, some researchers focus on individual cultural groups and attempt to explain salient features of a given community from the point of view of the insider. Examples include studies of Latin American cultural patterns using the concept of *dignidad* (Triandis *et al.*, 1984) and analysis of the Japanese concept of *amae* (Doi, 1995).

Work of this sort attempts to find key concepts which represent fundamental and deep organizing principles around which a constellation of other cultural values and assumptions revolves. For example, in Japanese, *amae*, sometimes translated as *dependence*, is conceptualized in its purest form as the dependence for nurture felt by an infant for its mother. More broadly, however, *amae* describes a form of hierarchical dependence and caregiving said to constitute a fundamental element of human relations within the Japanese worldview. A child who runs up to his mother for affection is said to *ameru* (used as a verb), while an employee who expects undeservedly lenient treatment from a superior is also said to *ameru*. If someone's attitude is described as *amae* it can indicate an unrealistic optimism based on an immature inability to judge the reality of a situation. The uses of the term and its connections to other important value words in Japanese is argued to make it an indispensable concept for understanding the Japanese worldview, particularly in terms of Japanese feelings about hierarchy, responsibility, learning, and so on. For a non-Japanese, trying to understand these basic concepts represent an attempt to gain access to a Japanese linguistic and social world.

A more comparative approach to understanding different value orientations is the attempt to define universal categories of cross-cultural comparison (Hall, 1959; Hofstede, 1983, 1997; Kim *et al.*, 1994; Kluckhohn & Strodbeck, 1961; Ting-Toomey, 1994; Triandis, 1995; Trompenaars & Hampden-Turner, 1998). As of yet, there is not an absolute *cultural grammar* – a single set of categories for cross-cultural comparison which is accepted as all-inclusive – but research in this area has produced a series of concepts, such as *'individualism/collectivism, power distance* (the degree to which a cultural community makes status explicit) and *affective/neutral* (the degree to which emotion is expressed openly) which act as a widely accepted set of conceptual tools. These studies may represent the closest we have come yet to a functional description of deep culture in the context of intercultural learning.

Two influential schemas for describing value orientations have been created by Geert Hofstede (1980; 1983; 1997; Hofstede & Spangenberg, 1984) on the one hand, and Trompenaars and Hampden-Turner (2000; 1998; 2004) on the other. Both of these schemas attempt to describe universal categories of cultural comparison and both share important conceptual elements, such as individualism and collectivism. There are, however, significant differences between them as well. Not only are the categories within these two schemas different, the theory used to explain value orientations is different and the research methodology to test for these differences is different.

Hofstede's value orientations

Hofstede is a social psychologist who examines the emotional and psychological characteristics of people from different cultural groups. Hofstede (1980; 1983; 1997) asked about preferences and attitudes in the workplace among IBM employees in 40 countries. Based on the patterns of the answers given, he has extrapolated what he argues are underlying cultural dimensions. He asked employees, for example, to choose the qualities that would represent the ideal job. By performing factor analysis he discovered that respondents' answers for certain items correlated with certain others. For example, the people who tended to value (1) *earnings* also tended to value (2) *recognition*, (3) *advancement* and (4) *challenge*. On the other hand, those who valued (1) *good relationships* also tended to value (2) *cooperation*, (3) *desirable living areas*, and (4) *employment security*.

Extrapolating from what Hofstede found to be the unifying quality behind the patterns of answers and borrowing concepts from social psychology, Hofstede then labeled the clusters of answers. In the example given above, he described the unifying concept behind the shared desire for (1) *earnings*, (2) *recognition*, (3) *advancement*, and (4) *challenge* as 'masculinity', while he describes the desire for (1) *good relationships*, (2) *cooperation*, (3) *desirable living area*, and (4) *employment security* as 'femininity'. Ultimately, Hofstede proposed five distinct cultural value orientations: (1) power distance; (2) individualism/collectivism; (3) masculinity/femininity; (4) uncertainty avoidance and 'Confucian dynamism'. Hofstede's value orientations are outlined in Table 3.1.

We cannot say that cultural difference *causes* people to answer a certain way on his workplace value questionnaire since it is simply a higher percentage of answers that is *associated* with national origin. In Hofstede's sample, one's nationality increases the likelihood that someone will choose a particular answer. The degree to which culture influences the

Table 3.1 Value orientations of Geert Hofstede

Dimension	Definition	Measured traits associated with orientation
Power distance	How cultures handle inequality – the emotional distance between those of differing status	(1) Employee fear of expressing disagreement (2) Superiors have autocratic or paternalistic style (3) Preference for autocratic or paternalistic style
Collectivism and individualism	Individualism: ties between individuals are loose, each looks after oneself Collectivism: ties are integrated into strong, cohesive ingroups	Individualist (1) personal time (2) freedom (3) challenge Collectivism (1) training (2) physical conditions (3) use of skills
Masculinity and femininity	Masculinity = assertive, competitive, tough Femininity = nurturance, focus on relationships and living environment	Masculinity (1) earnings (2) recognition (3) advancement (4) challenge Femininity (1) good relationships (2) cooperation (3) desirable living area (4) employment security
Uncertainty avoidance	The extent to which one feels threatened by uncertainty or the unknown	(1) level of job stress (2) rule orientation (3) desire for job stability

Table 3.1 Value orientations of Geert Hofstede *continued*

Dimension	Definition	Measured traits associated with orientation
Confucian dynamism	Long term (dynamic) or short term (static) orientation as related to virtue	Long-term orientation (1) persistence (2) hierarchy (3) thrift (4) sense of shame Short-term orientation (1) personal steadiness (2) protecting "face" (3) respect for tradition (4) reciprocation of favors

answers given is statistically significant, but not enough to allow one to predict with a high degree of individual probability how people will answer (and presumably, behave) based simply on national origin.

Hofstede's starting assumption seems to be that culture is best understood as a form of emotional and psychological programming which inclines us to certain emotional and psychological reactions. Once this initial programming is imprinted, our affective lives are attached to these particular patterns, and for this to change we would have to relearn different affective and psychological reactions. In this view, those socialized into a more collectivist society identify with in-groups and are seen as emotionally attached to the well-being of other group members. This attachment is associated to values that emphasize cooperation and harmony. Those who live in more individualistic communities feel more separated from other members of their community and this is manifested in values such as independence.

The 'cultural onion' model of Trompenaars and Hampden-Turner

Fons Trompenaars and Charles Hampden-Turner (2000; 1998; 2004) have developed a theoretical framework which attempts to explain cultural difference in terms of fundamental challenges that humans face when organizing social communities. Based on these ideas, they have constructed a series of questions designed to gather data related to these constructs across different national cultural groups. While Hofstede talks about cultural difference in terms of a sort of psycho-emotional programming, Trompenaars and Hampden-Turner attempt to identify the varying internal logics used by different cultural groups to explain their value choices.

The idea that people are not aware of their own socialization and value orientations is a prominent element of Trompenaars and Hampden-Turner's (2000; 1998; 2004) conceptualization of culture. They see culture fundamentally as the way in which groups of people solve problems and reconcile dilemmas. Their assumption is that the most fundamental problem that cultural organization looks for is an answer to survival. Thus, as African cultures dealt with the problems of droughts, the Dutch to rising waters, and the Inuits to bitter cold, they developed solutions which, once solved, became automatic and institutionalized. Problems have a variety of equally viable solutions, but once one solution is chosen over another it becomes reified and self-perpetuating. Solutions became standards which were passed on and which acquire symbolic significance. The fact that there are other possible solutions may disappear from everyday awareness and become part of a system of absolute assumptions about how things are done.

Trompenaars and Hampden-Turner (1998) propose that value orientations represent a cultural group's solution to fundamental human dilemmas related to living together and interacting with the environment. The misunderstandings between people who cross cultural boundaries are seen as being a result of differing *logics* underlying the solutions to these dilemmas. The value orientations of Trompenaars and Hampden-Turner can be found in Table 3.2.

These varying orientations are considered dilemmas because they are related to an attempt to deal with a problem that has opposing solutions. For example, it is argued that one of the most fundamental challenges of social organization is the potential conflict between the needs and desires of the individual and those of the social group that the individual belongs to. For example, in any group that must live or work together, cases will arise where an individual's needs may be different from what the group

Table 3.2 Value orientations of Trompenaars and Hampden-Turner

Value dimension	Dilemma Type	Dilemma
universal vs. particular	Relationships between people	Should behavior be regulated with universal rules, or an emphasis on particular context?
individualism vs. communitarianism	Relationships between people	Which contributes more to the common good? Emphasizing the development of the individual even at the expense of the group, or emphasizing the well-being of the group even at the expense of the individual?
affective vs neutral	Relationships between people	Should emotion be expressed freely, or controlled?
specific vs. diffuse	Relationships between people	To what degree should we separate our lives into different realms or compartments?
status from achievement vs. performance	Relationships between people	Should status be awarded based on standards of achievement defined by the individual, or standards that are formally recognized by society?
time orientations	Relationship between people and time	Does time follow a discrete, linear progression, or is it cyclical and adaptable to the needs of particular events.
internal or external control	Relationship between people and nature	Are humans fundamentally in control of nature and their own destiny, or is fate beyond human control?

sees as appropriate. Cultural groups find alternative yet valid solutions to these dilemmas. Some cultural groups may develop social practices that emphasize the responsibility of each person to care for and support members of their community. Individuals will be able to develop themselves within the framework of the support of those around them. The assumption behind this approach is that each individual human forms an integral and necessary part of the broader community. Individuals should recognize the important connection they have to others and the responsibility to make a contribution to the community. This orientation is referred to as *communitarianism* by Trompenaars and Hampden-Turner.

The opposing solution to this dilemma is an emphasis on the development of the individual. The starting assumption is that the common good is best achieved when individuals develop themselves independently of the group. This allows them to go beyond the expectations and limitations of following others, so that they will ultimately have a greater capacity to contribute to the community. This does not mean that individuals should only think about themselves, which would be selfish, but that they contribute to the group by first developing the qualities which are particular to them as individuals. The assumption is that each individual is a separate entity that needs independence to develop fully. Each individual must not only be independent, but also individually responsible for his or herself and his or her actions. This implies that individuals will sometimes need to go against the wishes of the group, but this is seen as a natural (and perhaps even desirable) result of each person fully expressing his or her individuality. The locus of producing well-being for the community is focused on the individual, thus the term *individualism*.

An essential element to understanding culture as the resolution of dilemmas is that differing solutions are functional. It is possible to build a successful community on assumptions that focus more on either the group or the individual. Neither approach can be said to be better than the other. At the same time, these solutions form a kind of mirrored opposite of each other. Since each system is functional in its own right, those who are used to the assumptions of one system may find the assumptions or practices of another system threatening or incomprehensible. For example, if a group of friends is trying to decide where to eat, a more individualist approach to making this decision might involve each person openly giving opinions and debating the final outcome. The underlying reasoning is that each person should be given the chance to contribute their ideas and state their opinions as an individual. Each person, then, is responsible for speaking up and giving a clear opinion and this egalitarianism is seen as the basis for constructive relationships.

A more communitarian approach to the same situation, however, might be to assume that it is of primary importance to be sensitive to the desires and needs of other members of the group. This willingness to adapt to the needs of those around you then allows for close nurturing relationships in which everyone's needs are taken into consideration. It may also mean that individuals look to leaders of the group to take an active role in making the decision and that leaders would be expected to take into consideration the needs and desires of everyone, not just the leader's personal preference. Being in a role of influence within the group confers a responsibility to exercise that influence in the best interests of everyone.

Trompenaars and Hampden-Turner do not describe these orientations as absolute. Even the most individualistic people recognize and take into account the needs of others and collectivist thinking does not mean that people never focus on individual needs. Both options – focusing either on the wants of the individual or on the needs of the group – are used by any group of people at different times. Trompenaars and Hampden-Turner's point, however, is that groups of people have a tendency to approach a similar situation in different ways. Not only are particular behaviors different, but behaviors are based on fundamentally opposing assumptions on how to build constructive relationships and provide for the well-being of everyone. Not only are the resulting behaviors different, but the logic which underlies the behavior has differing starting points.

Norms, values and hidden assumptions

According to Trompenaars and Hampden-Turner (1998), it is important for those in cross-cultural situations to understand the unspoken assumptions that underlie the cultural dilemmas they describe. An unspoken assumption for someone raised in a more individualist cultural community might be that those who are not independent and separate from others are not fully developed human beings. This assumption contributes to social practices – such as having children sleep separately from their mother – intended to bring about the desired outcome. Another assumption might be that each individual needs to express what is original or different about him or herself. If an individual's opportunity for self-expression is stifled, frustration and conflict will result. Individualist logic would emphasize the importance of everyone having a chance to speak up (or vote), reasoning that anything less would be unfair (since each individual loses their essential need for autonomy) and would create resentment.

The unspoken assumption for more communitarian values, on the other hand, is that humans develop themselves best in relation to others, and

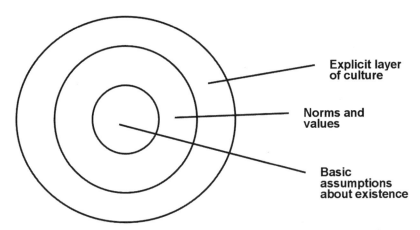

Diagram 3.2 Cultural onion (Trompenaars & Hampden-Turner, 1998)

that mutual interdependence is necessary and desirable for personal development. Positive relationships are described in terms of nurturing and support, which then allows individual development to take place. Thus, for a mother to leave a crying infant alone in a separate room at bedtime for the sake of developing 'independence' (a practice not uncommon in the US and Western Europe) might seem cruel or even abusive to someone more used to communitarian values and assumptions about what is important.

Trompenaars and Hampden-Turner visualize the hidden elements of culture using the image of an onion (Diagram 3.2), with deeper, more out-of-awareness elements of culture at the center. On the outside of the onion lie explicit products of culture, defined by Trompenaars and Hampden-Turner as 'the observable reality of the language, food, buildings, houses, monuments, agriculture, shrines, markets, fashions and art' (p. 21). The visible products of culture are symbols of deeper meaning. If, in an example used by Trompenaars and Hampden-Turner, you see a group of Japanese bowing, you witness explicit culture in the act of bending. The symbolic meaning of that behavior, however, is at a deeper, less explicit layer of cultural interpretation. If you ask Japanese 'Why do you bow?' you arrive at the next layer of the cultural onion called *norms* and *values*.

According to Trompenaars and Hampden-Turner, *norms* are the 'mutual sense a group has of what is "right" and "wrong"' (pp. 21–22), whether they are formalized, as in laws, or informal as in customs about how to shake hands or eat food. *Values*, on the other hand, reflect a cultural group's definition of good and bad and serve as criteria to choose between alternatives. Whereas norms define how one *should* behave, values define how one *wants* to behave. If you ask a Japanese why they bow, they might say that they do so because everyone does it (norm) or because it is important as a show of respect (value).

Trompenaars and Hampden-Turner describe the core of their cultural onion as basic assumptions about existence. It is rare for people to question the underlying or *deep assumptions* behind their norms and values. If you ask a Japanese why they bow, they might say that they want to show respect – a value – but if you ask why it is important to show respect, you may be given a puzzled look. Asking about basic assumptions raise questions that are never asked and this can provoke irritation. If you ask an American why they call their boss by the first name, they may reply that everyone in the company does so (norm) or because it is good for people to be treated equally (value). If you ask why being treated equally is good, the person may express surprise because the answer seems so self-evident. If you go on to question the legitimacy of equality by arguing that equality is not ever possible since there must be hierarchy for people to work effectively, your line of reasoning may seem like an attack.

The *deep assumptions* that underlie norms and values are highly abstract, but they can be extrapolated from looking at meaningful patterns in behavior and meaning systems. For Japanese, language, social structure and communication patterns hint at an implicit assumption that hierarchy is a natural and normal element of human existence. In language, hierarchical relationships are made explicit. The word for 'you' changes depending on the relationship with the speaker. Status can be considered a grammatical feature and even basic words such as 'to eat' (*taberu, meshiagaru, kuu*) change depending on the relative status of the interlocutors. The norms related to bowing reflect this hidden assumption, yet are so taken for granted that they aren't even a topic of discussion among Japanese themselves.

The values and communication patterns typically associated with mainstream American culture, on the other hand, emphasize explicit social equality. Being on a 'first-name basis' is considered a mark of a good relationship. In practices that would be inconceivable in many cultural contexts, even teachers or step-parents are sometimes called by their first names and treated as friendly equals, rather than seniors. An American who refuses to call friends by their first name risks seeming bizarre or perhaps causing offense, just as a Japanese would who did not show deference to seniors or spoke too formally to juniors. Thus, we find that American cultural patterns hint at an assumption of social equality and emphasize horizontality in their relationships. They may do so – as when an employee calls a boss by the first name – in the face of explicit differences in social status or power. Japanese, on the other hand, have a starting point of assumed social hierarchy emphasizing verticality in relationships. It should be pointed out that emphasizing horizontality in social relations does not guarantee economic or political equality nor does emphasis on verticality preclude it. It is evident in terms of income distribution and the gap between rich and poor, that the United States is less equal than Japan (Scully, 2000).

One problem with discussing these issues is that even the language used carries with it implicit associations that shade one's perception of the cultural 'other'. For example, in English the word 'hierarchy' is probably considered emotionally neutral at best, and more often negative, given the emphasis on egalitarianism and individualism found in most English-speaking cultural communities. In East Asian cultural communities, largely as a result of Chinese Confucian influence, hierarchies are seen as representing fundamentally (even if only as an ideal) nurturing relationships. The responsibility of a superior to look out for the well-being of those entrusted to his or her care is felt very strongly. Words that attempt to communicate this sort of relationship in English, such as 'paternalism', tend to have negative connotations precisely because of differences in deep cultural assumptions.

One point for caution is that Trompenaars and Hampden-Turner's diagrams and their focus on national-level culture can create the impression of deep culture as a fixed quality that can be quantified and predicted. But the deep cultural phenomena described by Trompenaars and Hampden-Turner are not a set of rules that people follow but hidden interpretive frameworks. It is difficult, however, to describe cultural difference in a way that both recognizes the diversity and dynamism of particular behaviors, and the deep patterns of similarity that unify people in cultural communities at differing levels of abstraction. Regardless of its limitations, however, the cultural onion model of Trompenaars and Hampden-Turner is a tool which can be used to examine the dilemma faced by Eun Suk with her colleagues. The decision she faces (should I sit down with my colleague or not) is related to the most explicit layer of cultural phenomena, the physical act of sitting down. Answering the question requires an understanding of Japanese norms – what would a Japanese do in this situation – and the values that go along with these norms. The norms and values, in turn, are built on assumptions which function at even deeper levels of the self. It is the challenge of dealing with these hidden differences in norms and values and assumptions that constitute Eun Suk's deep cultural learning challenge.

Human Universals and the Biological Bases of Culture

This work has argued that enculturation produces frameworks of meaning that form the basis of distinct cultural worldviews. It has also argued that there are deep-seated cultural differences in cognitive processes and psychological reactions to phenomena. Some may feel that this view of cultural difference suffers from an overemphasis on difference while ignoring commonality across cultures. Yet, there is no contradiction between the existence of deep-seated differences in the deep structure of a cultural worldview and the existence of cultural universals or the existence of shared biological bases of human behavior. Within the field of evolutionary biology, patterns of behavior such as courtship or cooperation are seen as adaptations that evolve in concert with biological evolution (Futuyma). Humans share a biological basis which acts as the framework for human social systems and includes cultural communities. The formation of cultural communities can reasonably be defined as a biological imperative in that it is our primary survival mechanism and that there are elements common to all cultural communities.

The study of cultural universals can provide us with clues about the deep structure of culture. Brown (1991) has reviewed ethnographic descriptions of culture to produce an exhaustive list which he argues is a blueprint for what he calls 'Universal People'. He believes that reports of exotic behavior by people in different groups can obscure the fundamental similarity found across all cultural communities. His detailed list of proposed human universals includes (among others):

Gossip. Lying. Misleading. Verbal humor. Poetic and rhetorical speech forms. Metaphor. Words for days, months, seasons, years, past, present, future, body parts, inner states, behavioral propensities, flora, fauna, weather, tools, space, motion, speed, location, spatial dimensions, physical properties, giving, lending, affecting things and people, numbers, proper names, possessions. Kinship categories. Binary distinctions, including male and females, black and white, natural and cultural, good and bad. Measures. Logical relations including 'not', 'and', 'same', 'equivalent', general versus particular, part versus whole.

Nonlinguistic vocal communication. Interpreting intention from behavior. Recognized facial expressions of happiness, sadness, anger, fear, surprise, disgust and contempt. Use of smiles as a friendly greeting. Crying. Masking, modifying and mimicking facial expressions. Displays of affection.

Sense of self versus other, responsibility, intention, private inner life, normal versus abnormal mental states. Empathy. Sexual attraction. Powerful sexual jealousy. Childhood fears. Fear of snakes. Face recognition. Adornment of bodies and arrangement of hair. Hygiene. Dance. Music. Play. Manufacture and dependence upon tools. Drugs, both medicinal and recreational. Shelter. Decoration of artifacts.

Living in groups which claim a territory and have a sense of being a distinct people. Institutionalized marriage, socialization of children by senior kin, avoidance of incest between mothers and sons. Great interest in the topic of sex.

Status and prestige, both assigned (by kinship, age sex) and achieved. Some degree of economic inequality. Division of labor by sex and age. More child care by women. More aggression and violence by men. Acknowledgement of differences between male and female natures. Domination by men in the public political sphere. Exchange of labor, goods, and services. Reciprocity, including retaliation. Gifts. Social reasoning. Coalitions. Governmental organization. Leaders. Laws, rights and obligations, including laws against violence, rape, and murder. Punishment. Conflict which is deplored. Rape. Seeking of redress for wrongs. Mediation. In-group/out-group conflicts. Property. Sense of right and wrong. Envy.

Etiquette. Hospitality. Feasting. Diurnality. Standards of sexual modesty. Fondness for sweets. Food taboos. Magic. Theories of fortune and misfortune. Medicine. Rituals, including rites of passage. Mourning the dead.

It may be encouraging for sojourners to be told that no matter what cultural community they visit in the world, they will all share the qualities listed above.

To see what this list may mean to sojourners coming to grips with deep cultural difference, it is important to make some distinctions among the different items. The first and perhaps most discouraging distinction is that the items on this list constitute the *what* of cultural communities not the *how*. While it is true that all communities have a shared sense of etiquette (the *what* that is shared), this doesn't tell a sojourner what particular behavior is considered proper etiquette by a particular community (the *how*, i.e. the way it is expressed or defined by a particular group). While it may be considered polite to burp (not belch) at the end of a meal in China, it is generally considered indiscreet in Denmark. Both cultural communities have expectations about etiquette but the particulars of those expectations depend on the community. On the other hand, knowing that every cultural groups has its own set of expectations for polite behavior (there's no place where 'anything goes') may sensitize sojourners to the need to figure out the particular etiquette of a host community.

The categories themselves can be organized in terms of how they are related to the particular qualities of human existence. For example, a number of these qualities are shared properties of language. Since all human communities use language, the shared human capacity for linguistic cognition and expression creates points in common across all cultural communities. This does not mean, unfortunately, that differences in language don't create barriers to understanding or that most people can ever learn to use a foreign language to the same degree of proficiency as their native language. Our universal capacity to be imprinted with the language of our childhood social environment becomes both a universal feature of human life and a potential source of difficulty for out-group understanding. The same can be said for the deep cultural differences of values, beliefs, cognition, etc.

There are also a number of categories of commonality related to our evolutionary roots as social primates. These include: nonlinguistic vocal communication, interpreting intention from behavior, recognition of facial expressions, living in groups, status and hierarchy, male/female distinctions, sexual jealousy, reciprocity, leaders, and so on. However, unlike other primates such as apes or chimpanzees, humans form communities based on highly elaborated systems of symbolic meaning, i.e. language and a conceptual worldview. While both humans and chimpanzees have hierarchy as an element of their social organization, only humans have government; while primates have competition for mates and mating behavior, only humans have marriage ceremonies. Direct reciprocity exists in the animal kingdom while conceptually elaborated contracts (written and unwritten) exist in human communities. These symbolic systems of meaning include the way that humans explain their own existence to themselves and so include cosmologies, values and beliefs.

The human capacity to develop distinctive, adapted communities based on a single biological blueprint has allowed us to survive in (some would say overrun) nearly all ecological niches on the planet. And while behavioral categories related to biological imperatives – life in groups, hierarchy, and so on – are predetermined, the *how* of assigning particular symbolic meaning to particular behavior within those categories is extremely flexible. And though a traveler may be impressed by the human capacity for internalizing a wide range of behaviors – it is as normal for some people to drink vodka martinis as it is for others to drink cow's blood – the most powerful adaptive ability of human communities does not exist at the level of individual behavior, but in the capacity for systematic deep culture enculturation and adaptation. Whole communities unconsciously develop, maintain and perpetuate particular approaches to solving the challenges of community survival.

We can begin to appreciate the importance of Trompenaars and Hampden-Turner's (2000; 1998) characterization of fundamental human value dilemmas when we relate them to the universal categories above. As we have seen, as a result of our evolutionary biology humans live in groups yet also have a sense of individual self. This fundamental contradiction leads to the dilemma of the group versus the individual. Different cultural groups resolve this dilemma through worldviews, norms, beliefs and values related to *individualism* and *communitarianism*. Likewise, living in groups and claiming territory creates in-group/out-group conflict. This is dealt with a group's collective sense of public versus private spheres, another dilemma described by Trompenaars and Hampden-Turner. One final example is that all human communities have status and prestige which is sometimes assigned (based on who you are: your age, affiliation, title) and sometimes achieved (what you can do, your accomplishments). These competing types of status are at the root of achieved versus ascribed status dilemmas described by Trompenaars and Hampden-Turner.

Tracing some of these cultural values back to their biological origins remind us that humans are not fundamentally designed to be aware of their systematic cultural adaptations. And since the deep structure of our cultural conditioning is related to our biological roots as primates, threats to the symbolic structures of worldviews function at highly intuitive levels. Research into the structure and functioning of the brain teaches us that it is the limbic system – the portion of our brain shared with all mammals – that regulates things such as basic emotions, our sense of territoriality and social hierarchy (Morse, 2006). The portion of our brain – the cortex, and in particular the prefrontal cortex – that allows us to analyze and reason is a relatively recent evolutionary addition. While the *how* of our cultural systems is consciously explained and justified with reasoning that takes place in our prefrontal cortex, the 'what' of our mammalian brains determines our instinctive reactions to perceived threats to our deep cultural systems. And because our symbolic world of meaning is connected so closely with these deeper biological imperatives, our bodies react to threats to our beliefs and values with genuine fight or flight responses. When cultural difference does not 'make sense' or it threatens to undermine our view of reality, it can create cognitive dissonance ('my view is reasonable but those people are being unreasonable') that is dealt with by denigration of the difference encountered (a form of conceptual disarming of the threat) and/or defensive retrenching of one's existing worldview. In this view, ethnocentricity as a form of explaining intercultural experiences is a result of our evolutionary biology. It is an instinctive biological response to a symbolic threat – one that is experienced through the conceptual lens of a culturally inculcated worldview.

Cultural programming and individual choice

While our responses to intercultural experiences may be influenced by instinct and our evolutionary biology, the affective and psychological reactions of any given individual are interpreted and given meaning based on the personality and choices of that particular individual. That is to say, the fact that humans have cultural programming doesn't mean that everyone reacts equally to intercultural experiences. Humans are not static. They learn, adapt and evolve their symbolic relationship with their environment based on ongoing interactions. Thus, they have a capacity to become aware of deep cultural settings and can recalibrate their view of the world.

We can be encouraged by the individual human capacity to change and learn. It seems that nearly everyone who has intercultural experiences learns something new about the world, if not about themselves. Unfortunately, it is not easy to understand and adjust the deepest parts of ourselves – those related to deep culture. In the next chapter we will see how sojourners react to elements in new cultural environments which they have trouble accepting. We have seen in this chapter that Eun Suk finds Japanese behavior 'inexplicable' but she seems to have avoided drawing critical and ethnocentric conclusions about Japanese in general. Unfortunately, many sojourners who face deep cultural difference never fully realize that their personal reactions are influenced in important ways by their deep cultural programming. This lack of recognition leads, at least part of the time, to increased prejudice and negative learning outcomes.

Chapter 4

Deep Cultural Difference and Increased Prejudice

> *Interviewer: Did your opinion about Americans or American culture change when you were there?*
> *Joanna: Yes. For the worse.*

Change for the Worse

Joanna (above) is a French woman who spent a year teaching French at an American high school. Before arriving, she had positive feelings about the United States in general and about Americans in particular. Yet after a year of interacting with Americans she declares that her opinion of them has changed for the worse. She is not saying that she met Americans that she did not like (she made some American friends and seems to have enjoyed their company). Rather, she has developed negative feelings about Americans as a category of people who share certain qualities of 'Americanness'. She is reacting to cultural difference by condemning Americans in general. This discouraging reaction, an increase in negative judgments based on intercultural experiences, is not rare. Yet little attention seems to be paid to it in the professional literature. While we readily use words such as *prejudice* or *ethnocentrism* to describe negative attitudes about cultural groups, these words are often pejorative. Talking with sojourners and travelers, however, shows us that resisting some of the cultural difference that we find seems to be a normal part of intercultural learning.

Educators tend to focus on desired outcomes and the ideals of tolerance increasingly espoused in today's multicultural communities make it difficult to talk about negative reactions to cultural others in neutral terms. But it is necessary to distinguish between learned prejudice and negative reactions to intercultural experiences. Someone who grows up in an environment where a particular group is systematically denigrated can easily develop prejudicial attitudes towards members of that group. Yet, sojourners who do not start with negative stereotypes about another cultural group also sometimes denigrate their cultural hosts. The cause, however, may not be prejudice learned previously but rather a natural product of ethnocentrism. But examining the experience of sojourners

65

teaches us that ethnocentrism is not easy to overcome. Our cultural programming runs deep and ethnocentrism can be very subtle so it is often not recognized as such.

In order to understand how to overcome ethnocentrism it is necessary not to vilify negative reactions to cultural difference, even if they involve denigration and prejudice. Among sojourners, prejudice functions primarily out of conscious awareness and often result from judging behavior based on criteria that the sojourner assumes is neutral and absolute, but which is actually based in hidden cultural assumptions. Shedding light on this phenomenon – and using neutral terminology to do so – can help sojourners become aware of this process and may help them suspend judgment. In this book we will use the term *resistance* to describe a negative reaction to cultural difference which includes denigration. This chapter will examine the negative reactions that sojourners frequently have to their intercultural experiences, often as a result of deep cultural difference.

Deep culture and increased prejudice

Deeper cultural differences create problems when sojourners react negatively to phenomena without recognizing a systematic pattern of cultural difference. For example, Joanna says:

> I didn't appreciate parts of American culture. For me it was a great experience, but just if I look back. I couldn't have stayed in this country. I was definitely not part of it. For one year it was great, but ... it was not groovy enough for me.

But what does 'groovy' mean? Deep patterns of culture are so abstract that sojourners can often give only vague descriptions of what bothers them. When asked, Joanna says she 'was surprised by the lack of international culture'. She sees American attitudes towards the attacks on September 11th as betraying fundamental problems with American culture in general. She states:

> After a while I was a bit fed up with the American reaction, like 'we are at war'. They reacted like they were the victims and they never thought about why it happened or what their responsibilities were. They never thought about it. They didn't think that people might have been your victims some time. I think they overreacted – if that's

possible – the flags everywhere. They never tried to think about it. They were right one more time, and the others were wrong, as usual.

Notice the degree to which Joanna is describing an overall 'American reaction'. She is not making reference to particular opinions, but something deeper. To say that people 'didn't try to think about it' implies a fundamental unreasonableness. She also complains of Americans' political discourse and feels that Americans in general are not interested in knowing the 'truth' about the world outside the United States.

With the people I liked I tried to explain how the reality is, but with others if I realized they didn't have any interest in understanding the truth ... if they thought we all had berets and baguettes – I tried to give some explanation to people who were curious. Some people were very sure of what they were saying and they weren't interested in learning anything other than their own truth. They aren't going to change their mind so there's no reason to talk to them anyway.

So by Joanna's reasoning, Americans' provincial attitudes blind them to the fundamental 'truths' that she finds self-evident. Joanna, of course, fails to notice that her ideas about what constitute 'truth' do not constitute an absolute standard by which all others can be reasonably measured. There is a tragically divisive irony in Joanna's sense that Americans went too far in feeling victimized by a terrorist attack. If she told Americans this, it is easy to imagine that they would have felt defensive, a reaction which would then reinforce her opinions about Americans' unreasonableness. In the worst kinds of ethnic and cultural conflict both sides feel victimized by the other and feel justified in their own criticism or aggression. We can see the beginnings of this dynamic here.

Cultural difference which causes conflict and misunderstanding is not necessarily related to explicitly moral or sociopolitical issues. It is more often the deep culture that underlies differences in daily behavior that contributes to ethnocentric reactions among sojourners. This tendency has been studied by de Nooy and Hanna (2003). They showed how differences in information-gathering strategies reinforced negative stereotypes among Australian students studying in a French university. The study showed:

Australian students at odds with a high context cultural environment as they attempt to operate according to the low context communication principles of their home universities. Three interrelated cross-cultural issues [were] in play here: (1) approaches to the circulation of information; (2) relative importance of task versus relationship during interaction; (3) extent to which information and rules vary according to situation. (p. 69)

The Australian students in this study were accustomed to typically low-context assumptions about information circulation and had the expectation that helpful information should be openly and easily available to all (e.g. on a website) in a way that anyone can understand. A higher context approach to information circulation assumes that 'insiders' (in this case, the students) know where to go and who to ask for the particular information that they need. This difference was also related to the relative importance of personal relationships in gathering information (asking other students, developing relationship with administrative staff), which corresponds with 'particularist' and 'universalist' ways of solving problems:

> The information available in low context communication is likely to be valid for all situations (universalist), whereas information offered in high context communication may well vary according to the particular situation and the relationship (or lack of it) between interlocutors (particularist). (p. 70)

Australian students confronted with these differences made a variety of interpretations as to the reasons for their difficulties gathering information, including lack of ability in French and lack of predeparture support from their home university. By and large, however, the most common interpretation of their difficulties was 'French failures of efficiency'. Typical comments were that 'French administrative employees are "extremely unhelpful, unfriendly and unknowledgeable"', or the advice to '[a]lways remember that [French administration] is arbitrary, illogical and inconsistent'. Much more rarely, students understood that there was systematic difference – i.e. that one could 'work the system' in a different way in order to get what one wants. As for the number of students who recognized not only that there was systematic difference, but that the root of that difference was cultural, discouragingly:

> there were no students who were, so to speak, completely enlightened. Interviewees who propose astute strategies, along with their justification, are still also likely to tell you – or, more importantly, their successors – that 'the French' are hopelessly disorganized. (pp. 76–77)

At issue for these cultural learners is not specifically whether French or Australian universities are better at distributing information, but rather the recognition that the strategies that work in one environment don't necessarily work in another. The ability to adapt one's information strategies to the underlying system was the cultural learning task of these students. The Australian students would certainly have felt less frustration if they adopted the strategies for information gathering typically used by French students. Importantly, the students in this study reported great satisfaction with their experience abroad. Clearly, they learned a lot about France and most of them developed successful strategies for dealing with their new environment. That did not mean, however, that they were able to identify the deeper cultural differences that they were facing, or that they overcame stereotypes and became culturally tolerant.

Cultural Learning as 'Pattern Recognition'

Implicit cultural frameworks manifest themselves in a wide range of situations. Thus for Australian students to unravel French high-context information-gathering strategies, they would have to identify patterns or systems that are manifested in different settings. It is not enough for a student to notice that they have received different information from a friend who talked to a different administrator. They must also notice how this fits into wider patterns of information diffusion. Any one instance is only a single piece of the puzzle that can provide more of an insider's view of what to expect and how to get things done. In a more concrete example, if a traveler visits India, he may meet someone who greets him with a *namaste* (a gesture in which the hands are held with the palms together in front of the chest). This single instance, however, will not be enough to know whether the *namaste* is also used when someone departs or if it can be used to say 'thank you'. This requires contact in a range of different settings that will allow the contextualization of *namaste*. And even after the sojourner has formed an idea of when to use a *namaste*, that will not explain how this gesture fits into the broader worldview of the Indians that use it. Even asking Indians about *namaste* may not be of much help since they themselves use it without thinking.

Encountering deep cultural difference involves a series of encounters from which patterns may emerge. It is the ability to generalize accurately from the isolated manifestations of deep culture that marks successful deep intercultural learning. Unfortunately, this seems quite difficult. It requires a suspension of judgment about experiences that may be inconvenient or unpleasant. It also requires an ongoing engagement since deep cultural patterns are not immediately apparent. It is almost inevitable, if one has an ongoing engagement with cultural difference, that there will be deeper patterns of values, assumptions or worldviews which will make one uncomfortable, seem unreasonable, unfair, and so on. Yet while sojourners often recognize that they are supposed to tolerate or respect difference, they may not identify the things that bother them as cultural in nature. Detached statements about culture as an abstraction are rare because deep cultural difference is often not perceived as being a phenomenon that needs to be examined in order to be understood.

We can see this with Philippe, a French researcher, who studied in Germany. When asked about life in Germany he talks about trash. This is his way to say that he finds Germans overly obsessive about rules and regulations. He recounts receiving a telephone call from the police who had been notified by his landlord that he had failed to properly divide his garbage into the correct classifications used for pickup:

Philippe: It's very hypocritical but anyway this is the way they live. And I took my garbage pack out the wrong day, and in this garbage sack I had lots of nonplastic stuff like food and so on, and completely illegally and in this garbage sack, I was stupid because I took an abstract that I was writing for a journal and there was my name on it, of course, as being an author of the abstract and I took it out and the person in charge of my building saw the *gelbe sack*, opened the *gelbe sack*, took out this piece of paper, realized it was me – and she also knew it was me because there were all these cigarette packs – and so she called the cops.

Researcher: She called the cops?

Philippe: Immediately. And how I knew this was the cops (was) because the cops called my laboratory saying 'Okay, we know it's you'. This is how the conversation actually started.

'Philippe Dupont?'
'Yeah.'
'We know it's you.'
'What do you mean?' I mean I was so far away from imagining that it was my *gelbe sack* that was the problem that, you know, when the police call you and they say 'We know it's you!' it's like, 'What did I do?' and.

(They said) 'We know it's you! You took your garbage, and we know that it's you and there's absolutely no way you can deny this'. And so on, and 'We want to meet you and you will have to pay for this'.

And I was like 'What the fuck are you talking about? Yeah, I took out my *gelbe sack* today, and wasn't I supposed to?'

'No, no, no we want to meet you.'

So I had to go to a police station and there they explained to me for one hour the principles of German legislation on garbage and so on. And so they told me I had to pay 300 marks, or a 150 euros for this. 150 dollars for this!

And I asked 'But ... I mean, how do you know this?' And they said 'What did you expect? You take your garbage out and you don't expect the woman in charge of the building to know that?' So it's a common thing that every German does this.

His story is about deep cultural difference – in effect a horror story to high-light Philippe's feelings that Germans in general are overly concerned with rules and regulations – yet Philippe does not formalize his experience in abstract cultural terms. His statement that 'every German does this' is an indictment of German thinking in general, based on cultural standards that Philippe is only aware of intuitively.

Resisting the Demands of Cultural Learning

Philippe's story can help us understand how differences in deep culture can lead sojourners to make negative judgments about their host commu-nity. In dealing with his new cultural environment, Philippe faces cultural difference which he must respond to. In an important sense, encountering cultural difference involves facing a *demand for change* from one's environ-ment. In Philippe's case, on the explicit level, that demand is simply a tech-nical matter of being required to separate garbage in a particular way. Rules about garbage, however, are related to deeper frameworks of cultural expectations and values. Philippe's telling of the story indicates that he felt a deeper demand being made of him – to adapt to a value system that places too much emphasis (according to Philippe) on following rules to the letter. How he reacts to experiences like this, and the way that his views about his cultural hosts evolve over time, are the essence of Philippe's deep cultural learning. In this case, he finds this deeper demand unreasonable and makes value judgments about Germans in general. Even if he ends up separating his garbage according to the rules, at the deeper level of values and assumptions, he is resisting the change that is being demanded of him.

It is sometimes argued that there is so much cultural diversity within any given cultural framework that generalizations such as 'German culture' are meaningless. In a situation like the above, it might be argued that some Germans would also find the caretaker's actions extreme, and in that sense, there is no difference between Philippe's reaction and the potential reaction of some Germans. This argument says, in effect, that this conflict is one of individual values or preferences rather than culture. But this argument assumes that one's membership in a cultural community is a product of one's personal opinions or sense of individual identity. In terms of intercultural learning this misses the point, as someone who had been raised in German society would have a much more complete understanding not only of the rules of collecting garbage, but the thinking and worldview which generate those rules. Disliking the rules (Philippe and some Germans) and not fully understanding the expectations and thinking related to the rules (Philippe) are two different things.

Does this mean, then, that Philippe must change his values in order to live comfortably in Germany? Not necessarily. The fundamental issue for Philippe is not so much his personal sense of values, but his inability to see as valid the cultural values that underlie German garbage collection. It is possible for Philippe not to like an emphasis on rules (which reflects his personal values) and also to recognize that for many Germans the emphasis on rules is a normal and understandable way to organize human activity. The problem that Philippe faces is not so much one of personal values but of not fully recognizing that the source of his discomfort results, more probably, from the fact that he was raised in a country that had different cultural values and assumptions.

Philippe's story highlights the difficulties of coming to grips with more implicit levels of cultural difference. As with the Australian students described by de Nooy and Hanna (2003), his reaction to the more implicit layers of his intercultural experience is *natural*. In this case, his reactions match the cross-cultural studies that describe German cultural value dimensions as being more universalistic (trusting of rules rather than adapting to particular circumstances) and lower context (the message is given importance rather than the context that the message was given in – in other words, following rules 'to the letter' is important) than French cultural value dimensions (Trompenaars & Hampden-Turner, 1998). Some might even call Philippe's reaction *typical* for someone from France. But for Philippe, cultural difference is not viewed in objective or abstract terms. Like the Australian students trying to make sense of university life in France, he simply reacts personally to the negotiation of his daily life in his new environment. The lessons that he does or does not draw constitute the degree to which he has been able to enter into and accept as valid the implicit cultural frameworks of Germans.

Among the sojourners interviewed for the research project on which this book is based (Shaules, 2004a), very few sojourners spoke about deep cultural difference in neutral relativistic terms. This paralleled the findings about Australian students in France. While nearly all sojourners gain an increased understanding of the explicit layer of cultural difference – in this case Philippe learned how to divide his trash – not all of them gain an understanding of the systematic nature of the underlying layers of culture. In this example, Philippe interprets his experience as an example of the Germans' unreasonable obsession with rules. He does not approach German values and norms regarding trash collection as an equally viable alternative. And it is this conceptual or emotive leap – the ability to see a situation as reasonable based on the point of view of cultural others – that constitutes an understanding of deep culture in a new environment.

What is striking when discussing cultural difference with sojourners is the degree to which cultural difference evokes affective reactions. When confronted with different values or lifestyles, sojourners have either positive or negative affective reactions, yet almost no one, it would seem, has no reaction at all. This reminds us that humans are constantly interacting with our environment whether we are aware of it or not. When our environment is different than what we are used to, we automatically seek to explain, justify or criticize unusual phenomena in order to maintain our sense that we operate in a meaningful world. In that sense, simply being physically present in a new environment constitutes a demand for change. Our perceptual world demands that we make sense of what we experience and modify our worldview accordingly. When affective reactions are negative, it is a short step to increased prejudice.

Deep cultural difference and absolute judgments

A consistent feature of the negative judgments that sojourners make is a belief that they are simply reporting facts. The interpretation of the facts is taken for granted. Philippe doesn't make the statement that Germans are unreasonable, but there is an implicit criticism in his evaluation of his experience. What he reports are the 'facts' of the story – how he was called by the police – while the interpretation of the story is intuited, i.e. Germans are unreasonably concerned with rules. This parallels the experience of the Australian students in France who reported that French bureaucracy was 'inefficient'. They were simply reporting the facts as they saw them and probably wouldn't have seen these statements as either ethnocentric or prejudicial against French people in general.

Judgments like those made by Philippe and the Australian students are *absolute* in the sense that they use criteria for judgment not seen as based on cultural assumptions. Thus, for the Australian students, 'efficiency' is an objective category that is beyond cultural variation. It doesn't occur to them that efficiency is in the eye of the beholder and that a French student in an Australian university might find information on a website or a general information packet 'inefficient' because he has trouble finding the specific information which fits his particular case. The hidden assumptions behind what constitute 'efficiency' or, in Philippe's case, 'reasonableness' produce the deep cultural barriers to intercultural understanding.

It is in trying to understand this kind of reaction that Trompenaars and Hampden-Turner's (1998) conceptualization of culture as dilemmas are extremely useful. In Trompenaars and Hampden-Turner's view, different cultural groups have their own internal logic based on unspoken values and hidden assumptions. In the case of the Australian students, the criteria for what constitutes 'efficiency' depends on hidden assumptions about the nature of efficiency. With universalist logic as described by Trompenaars and Hampden-Turner, an attempt is made to create systems which apply equally to everyone. Efficiency is expected to be built into the rules of the system itself. Systems that cover all possible circumstances yet which are not cumbersome are seen as efficient. There is no expectation that individual cases should require exceptions to be made, since efficient systems cover the total range of individual cases that can be expected. The hidden assumption of universalist logic is that categorizing phenomena into generalizable categories allows us to explain or regulate the world around us.

Particularist logic, however, emphasizes the unique qualities of any given phenomenon. It assumes that any systematic description will fall short of giving a true picture of the phenomenon in question. In the case of information systems at universities, there may be an assumption that each student has particular needs that can only be addressed by treating each individual case as special. Systems and rules are seen as frameworks created to address particular needs; rules need to be interpreted and systems need to have flexibility so that someone with different needs can be accommodated. In practice, this is often accomplished by personalizing the process. In the case of a university, there may be an information desk or administrative counter where students can ask a broad range of questions and get official answers to particular questions. On a more informal level, students might ask classmates how things work, or develop relationships with administrators so that their particular needs can be met, even if it falls outside of what would formally be permitted by the system. A system which is flexible enough to handle many cases, and in which one has access to the information which suits one's particular case, is seen as efficient.

These two logics have opposite starting points – one emphasizes the predictability of the system and the other the flexibility of the system. Because these assumptions are so abstract and out of awareness, however, sojourners may not recognize that there may exist another kind of 'efficiency'. While the Australian students found the lack of clarity in the French administration frustrating, French students in an Australian university may also be frustrated when they approach an administrator to ask a question simply to be told 'you can find the answer on the university website'. This would constitute inefficiency, since the student who has gone to the trouble to visit the administrator now must go back home and look things up on the internet. The efficiency of the Australian system rests in one's ability to find a lot of information in a predictable way through explicit systems. The disadvantage is when individual attention is needed, a particular case falls through the cracks or an exception to the rule is needed, the system may be extremely inflexible or impersonal. The efficiency of the French system is that when a person understands how things work and knows those in a position of authority, then a wide range of needs can be met. The disadvantage is that finding out how things work can take a long time and rules may be applied in an arbitrary way.

Although the differing logics of cultural value dimensions can lead to negative judgments, this does not necessarily mean that sojourners' judgments prejudice them against everyone in a cultural group. The Australian students in de Nooy and Hanna's (2003) study generally reported very positive attitudes towards French people. And Philippe also reports having a very positive overall experience in Germany. He even reports that living in Germany helped him get over some of his own prejudicial attitudes. As a French Jew, Philippe had some very negative associations with Germany:

So in the beginning ... my friends and most of my family thought, 'Okay, you're doing this not only because of the research but also you want to spend some time in the country that [killed all the Jews] ... And when I first got to Germany for the first two or three months I kept ... looking at people on the street and was always wondering 'what did this old woman do during the war?' and I was very, very negative. But the research was so cool and the people that I met over there were so open-minded that they, yeah, I mean three months later I was wanting to learn German. ... [A]ctually, the most surprising thing was that the day I left Germany I actually cried like hell. And the first two or three months I spent here in France was only having regrets of having left too early, in my opinion, because two years is definitely not enough. So first it was a science thing and it very rapidly became a life thing.

So in this case at least, Philippe's judgments about German rules did not prevent him from having a good experience overall. It does imply, however, that there were limits to his ability to see the validity of some of the deeper elements of German culture.

Level of Investment and the Depth of Intercultural Resistance

It may be that Philippe was helped by the fact that his relationships with his German research colleagues (whom he found to be open) were deeper than his relationship with his landlady. The greater the consequences of our interaction with someone from another culture, the more difficult it may be to suspend judgment and see the deeper patterns that underlie the behavior that is so difficult to accept. We can see this tendency in David, a commercial flight instructor who trains student pilots from around the world. One difference between Philippe's interaction with his landlady and David's interaction with student pilots is that piloting errors can have fatal results. The cultural differences that David has found with Asian pilots have led him to some highly prejudicial conclusions about Asians in general:

David: I can feel [cultural] difference when I'm training other-culture pilots. I used to train a lot of [Asian] pilots ... [refers to having trained Chinese]. Never fly with those people. They just don't understand anything, not even what can hurt. I mean if you fly into terrain it's going to hurt! They don't get it, they don't understand it. It's just like, they have no clue what can happen.

Interviewer: Why is that?

David: Indoctrination. ... they have no survival instinct – from what I felt in the training.

David goes on to recount the story of a Chinese student pilot who was supposed to do a round-trip training flight. When he left the weather was good but when he returned it was fogged in and he could not land with the level of training he had received, yet he insisted on landing because his instructor had told him to return to that airport. The traffic controller had to negotiate with him for 15 minutes to land elsewhere. David describes the student pilot's discussion with the air traffic controller: 'But the guy said "my instructor told me to come back", but the guy didn't understand that if he tried to land he would die.'

It is possible, of course, that this particular student was not well suited to be a pilot but David interprets this story in cultural terms. David's general description of the kinds of problems he faced with Asian students matches cultural comparison studies which describe Chinese culture as having high 'power distance' relative to French or European cultures (Hofstede, 1983). Power distance refers to how comfortable people feel with explicit hierarchy. Cultures that score high on the power distance measure of cross-cultural comparison tend to emphasize vertical relationships – respect towards elders, explicit hierarchy in a company or organization and explicit markers of politeness. One interpretation of this story is that the student pilot felt a heavier burden of responsibility towards following the instructor's directive to return to the same airport. In addition, in certain contexts, cultural groups with a more collectivist orientation can give the impression of indecisiveness to people who are more oriented towards the independent decision making valued by individualist thinking. This could have played a role in David's interpretation of Asian student pilot problems as well.

At times, David shows a remarkable *inability* to relativize his experiences with Asian student pilots. Chinese learning to fly in English face a bigger linguistic challenge than Europeans, yet David's comment about language ability was simply: 'Their English sucks, oh man'. He goes on to tell the story of a student pilot doing touch-and-go landings over and over again because he did not understand the air traffic controller:

David: No communication. We'll never know [what they are thinking when they do something like that]. Something would happen and they would not react. And they would let the airplane go, no reaction.
Interviewer: So it's not just language?
David: They're strange people. We lost seven aircraft in a year, belly landings, forgot to put down the landing gear, it's like stupid, I mean [joking] landing with the landing gear up, it's not very practical ... it requires a lot of thrust to taxi ... when the instructor was on board it was marginal, but sometimes when it was the step to make them fly solo, because sometimes it's better to make them do it on their own. Oh my God, flying with Chinese it's just like something that will get you gray hair really quick.

It is hard to say why David draws such denigrating conclusions – such as 'they're strange people' – from his experiences. It is possible that these reactions were built upon pre-existing prejudices against Asians and that difficulties with students exacerbated them. At the same time, David was dealing with highly stressful situations and life and death consequences. If someone's behavior is 'irrational' in these situations, it is a short step to drawing highly negative conclusions. It is most likely that David's response to his Asian students is a mix of pre-existing negative stereotypes reinforced by cultural difference which seems to justify those negative judgments. In this case, the kinds of cultural differences that may have contributed to these problems (power distance, collectivism versus individualism) function at a very deep level of the self. Deep cultural difference seems more inexplicable because the causes are harder to identify. It just does not *feel* right. In extreme cases, it seems pathological ('they have no survival instinct').

David's response to the demands of teaching students from different countries highlights a seldom-emphasized danger of intercultural experiences. Encountering difference can just as easily reinforce negative judgments as mitigate them. And if, as in David's case, negative judgments are reinforced by lived experiences, it would seem extremely difficult to bring about greater tolerance. Furthermore, characterizing a reaction such as David's simply as *racism* or *prejudice* misses the point; there are systematic differences of values and behavior that create the problems in the intercultural relations that he faces. David's attitude can be seen not so much as a moral failure (or at least not *only* as a moral failure) but rather that of resisting hidden elements of cultural difference which he encountered in high-stress situations.

Finding Neutral Intercultural Terminology

One difficulty for sojourners in talking about their experience is a lack of terminology suited to describing and reacting to cultural difference. Most sojourners, when talking about their experiences abroad, use words better suited to describing personality than culture. When Egyptians are characterized by words such as 'emotional', Japanese as 'shy', Americans as 'friendly', Brits as 'reserved', the descriptors fit personality but not cultural groups. This is because in any group of people, some will be more emotional, shy, friendly or reserved than others. It is this range of variation within a group which gives rise to descriptors for personality. But it is not possible that 130 million Japanese are 'shy' in this sense. Some Japanese are shy when compared to other Japanese, and Japanese may give the appearance of being shy when interacting with people from other cultures due to the particularities of Japanese communication styles, but they are not all 'shy' in any absolute sense.

Another difficulty with these *personality words* is that they tend to be either complimentary or pejorative. For example, most people would rather be called 'friendly' than 'shy'. So, if we use these words for describing cultural difference, we end up favoring one cultural group over another, as in: 'Japanese are shy' and 'Americans are friendly'. And while this may not be a problem when we have positive experiences and want to describe our hosts as 'warm' or 'open', how about when we notice that waitresses in China or Korea often don't smile when serving customers? Does this mean that they are 'cold' or 'unfriendly'? By choosing these words we build a hidden cultural bias into our description because the words are judgmental rather than simply being descriptive.

One advantage to the categories of cultural comparison that we saw in Chapter 3 is that many of them can act as neutral vocabulary for talking about intercultural experiences. Thus, in Trompenaars and Hampden-Turner's terms, we can describe interaction as being either 'affective' or 'neutral' rather than 'emotional' and 'cold'. Learning concepts of cultural comparison such as *universal* (rule based) and *particular* (situation specific) may have helped the Australian students in France recognize that their frustration with administrative 'inefficiency' was, at least in part, a result of cultural difference. It may have also helped Philippe understand that his dislike of German garbage collection reflected his discomfort with a more highly *universalistic* society.

Trompenaars and Hampden-Turner's categories of cross-cultural comparison are particularly well-suited to use as neutral descriptors because the contrasting qualities are described in terms that make them neutral relative to each other. This seems somewhat less true for Hofstede's categories. His category of *power distance*, which refers to the level of autocracy or paternalism in a cultural group including fear of those in positions of authority, does not seem as neutral as Trompenaars and Hampden-Turner's category of *achieved status* (status is conferred based on what people do) versus *ascribed status* (status is conferred explicitly and based on who people are). High power distant countries, for example, are associated with a high level of political violence. Likewise, Hofstede's category of uncertainty avoidance – fearing the unknown and feeling threatened by otherness – implies that certain cultural groups are fundamentally less tolerant than others. While this may be true, it is probably better to have neutral descriptors when talking about these issues.

Finally, it would seem that we need a way to describe the negative reactions that sojourners may have to their experiences without resorting to words such as *prejudice* or *ethnocentrism*. No matter how naturally tolerant or flexible one is, when interacting in a new cultural environment for a long time it seems inevitable that there will be elements of one's experience that are hard to accept or which provoke a negative reaction. This work uses the word *resistance* to refer to these negative reactions. This word is seen as relatively neutral – allowing sojourners to say of their own reactions to cultural difference that they *resisted* elements of their experience. Philippe could use this word to describe his reaction to the German garbage collection system without implying a criticism of Germans in general. This would allow him to recognize that he made a negative value judgment because of cultural difference but that this is a normal part of cultural learning.

As will be discussed in more detail in the description of the Deep Culture model of intercultural learning later in this book, *resistance* can be contrasted with *dislike*. Resistance is seen as a negative reaction accompanied by a negative value judgment, whereas dislike is seen as a negative reaction without a negative value judgment. This distinction is necessary because we may accept the value of what we find in a new environment without necessarily wanting to adopt it ourselves. A simple example of this distinction would be a visitor to Korea who finds *kimchi* (spicy fermented cabbage) not to their taste, while at the same time recognizing that those who are used to it find it delicious. This would be *dislike*. Someone who, on the other hand, criticizes Korean food by declaring that it is too spicy and has no subtlety is going beyond the personal reaction of not enjoying eating it. He or she is making a negative value judgment that says, in effect, that there is something wrong with Korean food. This would be *resistance*.

Negative Reactions are Normal

As the distinction between *resistance* and *dislike* shows us, not all negative reactions to cultural difference imply a lack of intercultural sensitivity. Likewise, while making negative judgments about a new environment may be a *normal* part of deep cultural learning, it does not mean that it is a desirable reaction to intercultural experiences. Examining the experience of sojourners shows us that some people manage to recognize that their negative reactions to cultural difference are a result of their cultural background or personal preference and they largely avoid making negative value judgments. Rieko, for example, a Japanese woman who spent a year in the United States had trouble getting used to American individualism.

She recognized, however, that her reaction was at least in part cultural so she was on the lookout for her own negative judgments:

> When I had the feeling that Americans were selfish, I had trouble knowing whether that was something related to Americans in general, or that person in particular. It was hard to tell what was cultural what was personal.

It is Rieko's fundamental recognition that American values are valid for Americans that allowed her to recognize her personal reactions for what they are.

We can contrast Rieko's experience with Adele, an American doing her doctoral dissertation in Japanese literature while living in Tokyo. Her negative reactions are absolute. She describes Japan as a 'very unhealthy country', and goes on to say:

> I'm dedicating my life to this country, but as I walk thought the streets I think, 'Why here?' And I don't share the value system that I see here. In the states there's an opposing faction, but in the streets in Japan I'm overwhelmed by all the bad 'isms' of modernization. ... And here people look at you semi-suspicious. Women look at me and look away, and men look at me in this scuzzy scary-monster way.

Unlike Rieko, Adele doesn't seem to accept the fundamental validity of Japanese values, communication styles, etc. Her negative reactions aren't mitigated by the acceptance of difference that Rieko manages. So while both Rieko and Adele may have negative feelings about their intercultural experiences, one can't help but conclude that the ability to dislike something, but not judge it, is an important marker of successful intercultural learning.

Among sojourners who are the most successful in learning to live in new intercultural environments, the ability to dislike elements of their experience while at the same time suspending negative judgments is a recurring theme. Consider Mayumi, a Japanese woman married to a Korean husband. She found getting used to the role of a housewife in Korea to be extremely stressful, partly because of the need to maintain close relationships with her husband's family and fulfill duties normally expected of a Korean wife. In spite of this stress, she manages not to make negative judgments about her in-laws:

> My mother in law could come to my apartment unannounced. I left Korea a couple of times that I got stressed out. When I wasn't there my

mother in law would go and clean up for me, making me feel like a failure when I returned. She even bleached the teapot. Of course she felt she was being kind, and I didn't take it as an offense, and I felt a bit angry at my husband for letting her do it. Don't get me wrong, I really love his parents. I don't think I could live with them, because of the differences in customs. I have lots of complaints against their son but not them.

Considering that Mayumi was so stressed that she had to leave Korea, it is remarkable that she managed to accept as fundamentally valid the cultural expectations that she reports were largely at the root of her discomfort.

Something similar can be said about Paul who was raised in Nepal but grew up all over the world. In speaking of his reactions to intercultural learning, he clearly makes a distinction between his possible negative reactions and any judgment he might make about the cultural environment which might engender that reaction.

When you go somewhere, the way that people do things is simply the way people do things and so you adapt to that. Of course it doesn't mean that you don't judge, or that you like it, but you adapt. It also has to do with the environment that you are used to. When things are different it might create some internal tensions, but you adapt.

When Paul refers to 'internal tensions' he seems to be referring to his personal reaction to his environment, which he recognizes but doesn't use as a justification for making absolute negative judgments about other cultural environments.

This chapter has argued that negative reactions to a new cultural environment are a natural but not necessarily desirable response to a new intercultural environment, and that these reactions are often the result of differences in deep culture. It has highlighted the fact that simply coming into contact with cultural difference can, in and of itself, constitute a demand for change since sojourners inevitably attempt to make sense of their new environment. The reaction to that demand has been argued to be a key component in the cultural learning process. It has also been argued that negative reactions are not all equal and that dislike of an environment is not the same as resisting it with negative value judgments.

If it is true that a certain reaction to a new environment is more desirable than another, it raises the question of how to define successful intercultural learning. This is an area that has been studied in great detail and which will be examined in the next chapter.

Chapter 5
What is Successful Cultural Learning?

I must have learned something.
Jack

I think one thing that I have learned is that I really like the United States and I'm glad that I was born there.
Adele

I learned that although I wanted to prove [to] the world that I can become 100 percent Japanese and feel very much at home there, that I preferred [going back to Switzerland and] being myself.
Andre

I discovered that I was a butthead.
David

Defining Intercultural Success

While the previous chapter examined how deep cultural difference can trip up sojourners as they try to get used to life abroad, this chapter looks at the question, 'What is a successful intercultural experience?' When talking to sojourners, it becomes clear that there isn't a single standard by which they measure the success of their experiences. We have met Philippe, the French researcher, who rants about German rules for separating garbage. While he has complaints about certain elements of German culture, overall he has many positive things to say about his experience abroad. He has learned German and made many German friends. So how can we conceptualize his success as an intercultural learner? As with other aspects of the intercultural learning experience, the goals of intercultural learning have been studied by specialists in different ways and for different purposes. This chapter will try to make sense of these different approaches and come to a definition that fits the lived experience of long-term sojourners and which takes into account the challenges of dealing with deep cultural difference.

It can be more difficult to define a successful intercultural experience than one might expect. The fact that sojourners report a positive experience, for example, doesn't guarantee that they have learned much about their new environment or that they have had a particularly deep experience. The quote by Jack, above, may be a case in point. He has lived in Japan for 14 years and is very happy with his life there, yet he doesn't speak Japanese, has few Japanese friends and seems content to remain in an expatriate bubble. Yet the ability to speak the language, learn about the country, make friends, and so on, can be deceiving as well. Adele (also quoted above) speaks Japanese and has a doctorate in Japanese literature, yet makes extremely negative and ethnocentric judgments about her host community.

Intercultural education goals versus intercultural adaptation success

The professional literature in this area can be roughly divided into two areas. The first is the field of *intercultural education*, which includes intercultural communication training, language education and global issues education. Broadly speaking, the goals of intercultural education involve fairly abstract measures of success such as an increase in intercultural sensitivity or increased intercultural competencies. A second view of successful intercultural learning outcomes is based on research into *intercultural adaptation* – examining the characteristics that are shared by people who learn to function well in a new cultural environment. It is possible to examine the factors, both external and internal, which contribute to this process. As we will see, this approach tends to be more empirical and lends itself more easily to objective measures of success. Both or these areas offer us insights into the sojourner experience.

Neither of these two areas, however, has as a primary focus the deeper elements of cultural learning. In addition to an overview of professional literature, this chapter will also introduce a phenomenological view of successful cultural learning. This will be followed by a look at how we can describe the depth of an intercultural learning experience. We will specifically look at language learning and relationships with members of the host community. The goal of this overview is to identify criteria that can be used to define successful intercultural learning which incorporate the varying depths of intercultural experiences. These ideas will contribute to the model of intercultural learning introduced in Chapter 7.

Intercultural awareness in intercultural education

Until recently, few sojourners had the benefit of intercultural education. Cultural adaptation was largely a question of 'sink or swim' with success measured simply in terms of learning a language, finishing an overseas posting, completing one's studies or sending money back to the family.

Fortunately, there is now a growing body of literature available which is intended to help sojourners and educators deal with intercultural challenges (Barnlund, 1989; M.J. Bennett, 1986; Brussow & Kohls, 1995; Cushner & Brislin, 1996; Gaston, 1984; Hall & Hall, 1987; Hess, 1994; Landis & Bhagat, 1996; Paige, 1993; Seelye, 1984, 1996; Stoorti, 1994; Tomlinson, 2000; Valdes, 1986, 1994). Much of this is meant for sojourners themselves – especially in business – but there is also a focus on university education (M.J. Bennett, 1998; Jandt, 1995; Tomalin & Stempleski, 1993) and language classrooms (Byram, 1997; Byram *et al.*, 2001; Cates,. 1999; Damen, 1987; Gaston, 1984). Although different authors define cultural learning success differently, there are some broad areas of commonality within the literature.

For the most part, the field of intercultural education defines success in terms of internal changes in the learner rather than a measurable external standard of adaptation. The assumption behind pedagogical goals is that intercultural education can encourage sojourners not only to have positive intercultural experiences, but also to gain qualities such as intercultural awareness. Often the pedagogical goals are focused on helping sojourners come to a deeper understanding of (1) the nature of culture, (2) how cultural difference affects communication and human relations, and (3) the influence of culture and cultural difference in specific domains such as business or language learning. Generally, the field is marked by an emphasis on cultural relativism – understanding the limits of one's cultural perspective and appreciating the cultural perspective of others. The underlying assumption behind this approach is that cultural difference has the potential to create conflict and that intercultural understanding is necessary to mitigate this tendency.

One exception to this is *global issues education* (Cates, 1997; Harrison, 1999; Higgings & Tanaka, 1999). This is an educational approach to internationalism that began after World War II in the United States under different names such as International Understanding (1947), Education in World Citizenship (1952), World Studies (1980s) and Global Education (1980s). It calls for us to go 'beyond' culture in intercultural education and focuses on 'an education for a world citizenship', which would allow us to 'develop an allegiance to humanity as a whole' (Cates, 1999). This approach – generally from the field of education rather than from cultural studies – downplays the importance of cross-cultural difference and emphasizes commonality across culture and an appeal to universal values (Shaules & Inoue, 2000). Unlike the materials above, global issues education is generally meant for students studying in their home culture and not specifically as a way to prepare sojourners to go abroad.

There is often not a clear distinction in the field of intercultural education between the pedagogical goals of the classroom and the assumed desired outcomes for intercultural learning. Having a successful experience abroad is often thought to result in an increase in some abstract quality. One that is frequently mentioned is 'cultural awareness' (Gaston, 1984; Hofstede, 1997; Ingulsrud et al., 2002; Paige, 1993; Tomalin & Stempleski, 1993; Tomlinson, 2000; Valdes, 1986). Such qualities are often abstract as can be the description of how those goals are reached. Gaston (1984: 2–4), for example, defines 'cultural awareness' as 'the recognition that culture affects perception and that culture influences values, attitudes and behaviour'. He goes on to describe the process of gaining cultural awareness as having four stages: The first stage is *recognition* – the 'growing consciousness of our own cultural group'. Stage two is *acceptance/rejection*, which he defines as a reaction to cultural difference that is either positive or negative. The third stage described by Gaston is: *integration/ethnocentrism*. For Gaston, this involves beginning to think biculturally or becoming rigidly ethnocentric. The fourth and final stage of this model is *transcendence*, when we are able to 'value and appreciate our own cultural roots' as well as to 'value and appreciate all other cultures as well'. After achieving this final stage, the cultural learner is able to 'transcend culture and see ourselves as a product of culture, but no longer a prisoner of culture'.

Goals like this frequently fall back on descriptions of ideal outcomes such as 'transcendence of culture'. However, there are limitations with this approach. One is that they describe what educators want to happen rather than looking at what actually happens. In real life, sojourners have not only transcendental experiences of increased cultural awareness, but also mixed reactions of increased insights together with resistance to certain parts of their experience. The Australian students who criticized the inefficient French bureaucracy also had many positive insights about French society. We have also seen how experiences abroad can increase prejudices. David (the flight instructor) had insights into cultural differences between Europeans from different countries but was also highly prejudicial towards Asians. These varying reactions, both positive and negative, seem to be a natural part of the deep culture learning process. Gaston's model allows for only one of two overall reactions: (1) beginning to think biculturally or (2) becoming rigidly ethnocentric. And since many sojourners never fully understand resistance caused by deeper cultural difference, we run the risk of concluding that most cultural learners fail since they do not manage to fully 'transcend culture'.

Another problem with idealized outcomes is that they delegitimize possible negative reactions to cultural difference. Sojourners generally know they are *supposed* to respect difference but that's not always easy. Terminology for intercultural success needs to include the possibility of negative reactions to cultural difference as a natural part of the learning process. Or put somewhat differently, it would seem that nearly all sojourners gain some intercultural insights based on their experience. In that sense, perhaps everyone does gain awareness. But sojourners also need to pay attention to their negative reactions since they are an important part of the cultural learning process. And since some sojourners seem to have more negative reactions than others, it should be possible to make this distinction in a neutral way.

Finally, these goals are highly abstract and intuitive. How does one know if one has transcended culture? Is it enough that a sojourner feels that they have done so? Is it possible for someone to successfully adapt to another culture without consciously learning the lessons described by Gaston? This brings us to another limitation to idealized goals: as they deal largely with attitudes, they are not of much use for learners who want to know more specifically the skills that are involved with living abroad. How does greater awareness relate specifically to communicating with people or understanding their society? When focusing a great deal on attitudes, it leaves out more specific skills that are important when going abroad.

Intercultural competencies in language education

In Europe, the field of language education has stimulated the development of more concrete definitions of the skills and abilities that a successful sojourner can hope to achieve. Byram (1987; 1997) and Byram *et al.* (2001) describe the goals of intercultural education as the 'intercultural speaker', one who attains 'intercultural communicative competence'. He makes a distinction between 'intercultural competence' and 'intercultural communicative competence', defining the first as the ability to interact in one's own language with people from other cultures and the latter as the ability to do so in a foreign language. The component elements of these competencies are centered on what Byram calls *savoirs*. These include attitudes (*savoir etre*), dispositions or orientations to act (*savoir s'engager*), knowledge (*savoirs*) and skills of interpreting and relating (*savoir comprendre, apprendre, faire*). Each of these elements is further defined to allow for educational objectives to be formalized. For example, Byram's attitude goal (*savoir etre*) is defined as 'curiosity and openness, readiness to suspend disbelief about other cultures and belief about one's own' (p. 50). This is then broken down into sub-competencies including things such as willingness to engage others in a relationship of equality, interest in discovering other perspectives and willingness to question one's own values.

Byram's contribution is important for several reasons. First, he breaks down intercultural competencies in great detail, making explicit how complex the phenomenon of cultural learning is. Byram also gives a special emphasis to the contextual nature of intercultural interaction, avoiding overbroad idealizations. Thus, when he describes the competence of 'critical cultural awareness', he lists the ability to 'identify and interpret explicit or implicit values in documents and events in one's own and other cultures' (p. 53) as a sub-competency. His knowledge competencies include things such as knowing 'the national definitions of geographical space' and 'the processes and institutions of socialization' (p. 51). Because Byram focuses systematically on a particular intercultural education context – language education – his learning goals are much more concrete than those of many other educators.

This level of concreteness, however, presents its own difficulties. One is that attempting to catalogue a process as complex as intercultural communicative competence produces an unwieldy list of competencies. Byram's five *savoirs* are broken down into nearly 30 sub-competencies. Yet even these smaller categories are immensely broad and include things such as knowing 'the processes of social interaction in one's interlocutor's country' (p. 51). Another difficulty with Byram's goals is that they include things, such as 'the processes of social interaction', which function nearly exclusively out of everyday awareness. It is not clear, however, what Byram's view of the out-of-awareness nature of intercultural learning is. His definition of 'cultural awareness' is the 'ability to evaluate critically and on the basis of explicit criteria perspectives, practices and products in one's own and other cultures and countries' (p. 53). Yet it is precisely the lack of explicit criteria for the deeper patterns of intercultural interaction that makes intercultural learning a challenge. While he has given us a much more detailed set of final goals, and has even suggested ways to plan classroom activities, the process that an individual learner goes through to reach deeper levels of intercultural understanding is not entirely clear. In addition, the possible negative outcomes of intercultural contact – increased prejudice, for example – are not dealt with in detail.

Intercultural success in cross-cultural adaptation research

The previous two sections looked at goals of cultural learning that were developed primarily in response to a need for pedagogy. The goals of *awareness* or a variety of *competencies* were the desired end product of intercultural training or language education. This approach is primarily inductive – one defines the ultimate goal and then considers the steps to bring about that goal. Another approach to identifying success among intercultural learners is more deductive. There is a significant body of research that attempts to identify the salient features of sojourner success – the skills, attitudes and awareness that have helped them adapt. This can broadly be called the study of *intercultural adaptation*.

Unfortunately, among researchers of intercultural adaptation, there seems to be little consensus about the desired outcomes of intercultural experiences. The literature is muddled with terminology that is often interrelated, overlapping, context-specific and vaguely defined. These include: *intercultural competence, intercultural adaptation, intercultural effectiveness, cultural sensitivity, cultural awareness, intercultural performance* and *cultural adjustment*. While all these terms attempt to describe a positive outcome for an individual faced with intercultural contact, they often describe broad ranges of skills, knowledge and awareness and may mean different things in different contexts to different researchers (Hannigan, 1990).

Much research into intercultural adaptation seeks to clarify the factors associated with success in a cross-cultural setting (Dinges & Baldwin, 1996). Yet adaptation is hard to define and research in this area fragments into varying measures of success such as: self awareness and self-esteem (Kamal & Maruyama, 1990), health (Babiker *et al.*, 1980) and mood states (Stone & Ward, 1990). Other researchers have focused on successful relationships (Cushner & Brislin, 1996) or the ability to manage stress (Hammer *et al.*, 1978). Matsumoto *et al.* (2001) focuses on the social psychology of adjustment and defines personal characteristics desirable for adjustment such as emotion regulation, critical thinking and openness/flexibility. At the other extreme, Black and Stephens (1989) define success in more practical terms such as the ability to perform daily activities or work tasks.

As with the field of intercultural education, one weakness of research like this is that it primarily describes an ideal outcome – an ideal set of skills or states of mind. This is partly a product of research methodology, since the intercultural experience must be broken down into measurable components to measure success and then measurable traits must be compared with rates of success. So while this sort of research produces a kind of profile of the successful intercultural learner, it sheds less light on the processes involved in reaching intercultural learning goals. The results of research such as this, which has produced a variety of qualities associated with success or failure, can be represented as a list of 'do's and don'ts' (Table 5.1).

Table 5.1 For an overview see Matsumoto *et al.* (2001) and Hannigan (1990)

To adapt successfully in another cultural environment	
you should:	you shouldn't be:
1. know culture-specific information	1. overly task-oriented
2. speak the target language	2. authoritarian
3. know about and identify with your own culture	3. perfectionist
4. be flexible	4. rigid
5. be realistic about the target culture	5. ethnocentric
6. have organizational skills	6. narrow-minded
7. manage interactions well	7. self-centered
8. be a good communicator	
9. be able to establish and maintain relationships	

Another limitation of goals produced by current research is that they do not help us conceptualize cultural learning from the point of view of the sojourner. How does a sojourner know if he or she is being realistic about the target culture? Or being a good communicator? How can such broadly defined capacities be developed? Also, the generalizations and ideal outcomes of many goals avoid the reality that learners have positive and negative reactions at the same time; may adapt to one element in their new environment but not to another; or function well but only within certain contexts. They state the final goals but do not describe the process of achieving those goals or the varying degrees of learning reached by different sojourners.

A Phenomenological View of Intercultural Success

This work is specifically interested in how sojourners themselves experience the challenges of dealing with deep cultural difference. It has been argued that this happens when sojourners face demands for change from their environment. This demand for change may be behavioral, as with Philippe and his need to sort his garbage, but it is also perceptual. In response to new phenomena in their environment, sojourners must make sense of their experiences and adjust their worldview accordingly. This fits well with the view of early intercultural specialists and linguistic relativists who argue that encountering someone from another cultural background implies an encounter not only with an individual, but with the hidden assumptions of that person's worldview. One must either defend the primacy of one's own worldview at the expense of others, or accept that one's own view is not primary.

If a defining quality of deep intercultural learning is a change in one's worldview in response to the demands for change from a new environment, it is necessary to define a successful learning outcome in terms of how a sojourner's worldview is modified by coming into contact with other worldviews. Bennett (M.J. Bennett, 1993) has developed a phenomenological model which does this. His model, the Developmental Model of Intercultural Sensitivity (DMIS), describes the desired outcome of cultural learning as 'the construction of reality as increasingly capable of accommodating cultural difference' (p. 24), which Bennett refers to as *intercultural sensitivity*. His model is developmental, i.e. it postulates predictable stages that learners go through as their worldview more fully accommodates the existence of competing social realities. According to Bennett, one moves from a natural starting point of ethnocentrism – natural in that it characterizes normal socialization and human evolutionary biology – to 'increasing sophistication in dealing with cultural difference' (p. 22). For Bennett, the desired outcome of cultural learning is a greater ability to construe other cultural realities.

The key organizing concept of Bennett's model is *differentiation*, which is used in two ways:

> first, that people differentiate phenomena in a variety of ways and, second, that cultures differ fundamentally from one another in the way they maintain patterns of differentiation, or worldviews. If a learner accepts this basic premise of ethnorelativism and interprets events according to it, then intercultural sensitivity and general intercultural communication effectiveness seem to increase. (p. 22)

Thus, Bennett's model is cognitive and phenomenological. It sees dealing with the existence of cultural difference as a primary challenge of intercultural competence but does not focus on behavior or how people feel about a particular culture. Instead, it looks specifically at the cognitive ability to construe cultural difference. For someone who cannot construe cultural difference, other cultural worldviews are nonexistent or denigrated. With an increasing degree of ethnorelativism, learners gain the ability to empathize – look at the world through the cultural lenses of others. In doing so, their construal of the nature of culture and cultural difference becomes more sophisticated.

Bennett's model describes cultural learning as progressing from the most ethnocentric stage: *denial*, through *defense*, then to *minimization*, to the ethnorelative stages of *acceptance*, *adaptation* and *integration*. In practice the stage of a learner's development can be determined by evaluating how an individual describes his or her experience of cultural difference. In other words, someone who says 'Well, people in that country are really backward' is manifesting a particular way of construing cultural difference ('backward', i.e. recognizing difference and denigrating it), which can be categorized in discrete ways. The six stages mentioned are his attempt at determining these stages of intercultural sensitivity.

Bennett's conceptualization of intercultural sensitivity fits well with the idea that the defining characteristic of cultural learning is a sojourners reaction to the difference in a new environment. At the cognitive level, this involves integrating phenomena from one's new environment into one's existing worldview. When cultural difference is experienced as a threat to one's worldview, it is denigrated. This can be seen as a form of resistance – resisting the internal realignment that would be necessary to recognize as valid the worldview of a cultural other. In practice, this involves value judgments, such as those by Philippe or Adele, that attempt to uphold the validity of internal cultural standards at the expense of those in one's host environment.

Constructive marginality

Bennett's model provides an explicit description of the desired goal of intercultural learning. In his view, the highest stage of intercultural sensitivity is a person described by Adler (1977) as a 'multicultural man', someone whose 'essential identity is inclusive of life patterns different from his own and who has psychologically and socially come to grips with a multiplicity of realities' (p. 25). The person in this state, which Bennett refers to as *integration*, creates a self in the process of shifting between different cultural perspectives. The individual in this state lives outside of normal cultural boundaries. Referring to this as 'constructive marginality', M.J. Bennett (1993) explains:

> marginality describes exactly the subjective experience of people who are struggling with the total integration of ethnorelativism. They are outside all cultural frames of reference by virtue of the ability to consciously raise any assumption to a meta-level (level of self-reference). In other words, there is no natural cultural identity for a marginal person. There are no unquestioned assumptions, no

intrinsically absolute right behaviours, nor any necessary reference group. (p. 63)

Bennett insists that this does not mean that the cultural marginal cannot make ethical choices or that 'anything is okay'. Rather, the multicultural person evaluates choices contextually with the ability to look at the same situation from multiple perspectives. Ethical choices are informed by this contextualized understanding.

Conceptually, the DMIS solves a number of problems in terms of defining successful cultural learning. The goal is explicitly defined with differentiated stages of development for learners. It is tied clearly to the experience of people's lived intercultural experience. It avoids the subjectivity of defining success in an intercultural setting using difficult-to-define behavioral measures. It also avoids the subjectivity of relying on emotional states or reports of well-being. Bennett has also used this model as a basis for sequencing different kinds of training activities, i.e. he has connected the theory to the practice of intercultural education. For example, according to Bennett, learners who are in the developmental state of *defense* are best served by learning activities which focus on cultural similarity since this can help them overcome resistance to difference. Learners in the state of minimization are better served by activities that focus on cultural difference.

Another strength of his model is that it provides a conceptual framework to evaluate cultural sensitivity. One's stage of development is measured by the way that one perceives, and by extension talks about, cultural difference. Bennett has expanded on this approach to create a psychometric instrument, the Intercultural Development Inventory (IDI), which purports to measure the level of intercultural sensitivity of a particular individual. In this work, sojourners' statements about their intercultural experiences have been interpreted using a phenomenological approach similar to Bennett's. The way they talk about their experience of cultural difference is assumed to reflect how they perceive cultural difference. Not everyone, however, accepts Bennett's definition of cultural learning success, nor the assumption that one's experience of difference is the defining characteristic of cultural learning success.

Critiques of Bennett

While Bennett's model has gained some acceptance and has been used in some studies as a neutral measure of intercultural competence (Olson & Kroeger, 2001), the desired outcomes of his model have been the subject of criticism as well. Sparrow (2000) challenges the ultimate goal of Bennett's model. According to Bennett, the final stage of intercultural sensitivity is that of *integrated marginality*, a state in which one's identity and worldview stand outside any single cultural reality. Sparrow, however, argues against the notion that it is possible to go beyond one's cultural reality in the way that Bennett describes. According to Sparrow, the idea of using a meta-awareness of culture as a goal of intercultural education, articulated first by Adler (1977) and refined by Bennett, represents a 'Cartesian concept of a mind, detached from experience, capable of determining an objective reality' (p. 177) which has recently been brought into question. She argues that social identity theories suggest that an ultimate stage of social development is typically a reconnection to real communities rather than the marginality described by Bennett.

To support her position, Sparrow studied a group of women with high degrees of intercultural experience and integration into host communities. She found that their experiences were characterized by a sense of connectedness to community and investment in relationships and that their descriptions of their experiences did not match Bennett's model. In addition, she disputes Bennett's idea that empathy can be learned as an imaginative, intuitive skill. Rather, Sparrow concludes that true empathy and interpersonal skills rise naturally from relationships with one's own family and communities of origin and from a commitment to interaction with others (Sparrow, 2000). Her point, she says, is not to deny the cultural learning goals by Bennett, but to show that:

> individuals develop in a variety of ways, depending on almost infinite variables, and that their ways of understanding and describing their development can vary significantly. Gender, religion, racial and ethnic backgrounds, socioeconomic status and language competence all interact within specific contextual realities to configure personal and social identities. (p. 96)

Sparrow's points are well taken. There is a danger in defining a particular kind of intercultural competence as *the* intercultural competence, when the lived experience may be much more organic and varied than predicable by a single theory or conceptual model.

Another point raised by Sparrow is what she sees as the difficulty, or impossibility, of ever going 'beyond' one's cultural frameworks in the way that Bennett describes at the higher levels of his model – the 'integration' stage. According to Bennett, at advanced stages of cultural learning, one no longer has a primary affiliation with a single culture, but rather is engaged in a constructive marginality. Sparrow finds this view to be overly intellectualized and to reflect a particularly male, Cartesian view of development as a process of finding an ultimate objective point of view from which to observe reality. For Sparrow, intercultural learning is closely wedded to a feeling of connectedness to particular cultural communities, not the kind of detachment described by Bennett and Adler.

Proponents of either of these views could find support in the experiences of the sojourners interviewed as part of this work. As with Mayumi's accounts of the challenges of adapting to life in Korea and the US, many participants emphasize relationships, describing the process of cultural adaptation as an attempt to gain entry into a community. When sojourners feel shut out they have very negative reactions. A typical comment related to gaining acceptance into a new cultural community was made by Neil, an American living in Japan:

> Once you demonstrate that you have some ability to speak the language, people treat you more as an ordinary person. Maybe you won't get the special treatment, but at the same time you feel more part of the group instead of always being outside.

Adele, the American researcher in Japan, on the other hand, expressed terrible frustration with her inability to connect with Japanese and make friends. When asked about the Japanese that she felt closest to, she talked of a female Japanese friend, but immediately expressed frustration with the relationship:

> What I'm finding difficult is that we don't have a lot to talk about. She invited me out with her friends because then she doesn't have to spend intense one-on-one with me, and her friends are the bimbos from hell. They all carry those live rabbit bags, rabbit fur bags, they wear those bimbo shoes. ... then there was a woman who I tried to study calligraphy with, but then I realized she was using me to meet western men.

Ultimately, Adele blames her difficulties in part on foreigners: 'I've always found that when I live in Tokyo there's such a huge foreign community that you have to work hard to meet Japanese.' Ultimately Adele seeks community among those who she finds that she has the most in common with, saying that her friends 'are nearly all foreign academics here studying in Japan'. Even Jack, who manages to skim along the surface of Japanese culture, seems to have managed this by finding a circle of friends, in his case foreigners, supplemented by his Japanese girlfriend.

So Jack has come to terms with his intercultural environment by limiting himself to a community of his choosing. In a sense, he is a successful cultural learner because he has found a personal equilibrium that has allowed him to live and work in Japan for more than 10 years. At the same time, he hasn't made a connection with deeper levels of community in Japan. He is in the situation described by Neil:

> It's very easy in Japan to find a situation where you can just speak English. There are people who get comfortable in that bubble and never get motivated to study.

It should be pointed out that Jack's Japanese ability is limited and that his comfortable isolation is both linguistic and cultural.

Despite his apparent level of comfort, few people would say that Jack is a truly successful intercultural learner. Sparrow's ideas about connection to a host community seem important here. Regardless of any intellectual acceptance that Jack might have regarding cultural difference, he has not succeeded in forming ties with Japanese and as a result his intercultural experience is more limited. This is also what makes Mayumi's account of adapting to life in Korea and the US impressive. In spite of negative feelings about certain elements of Korean culture and difficulties with language learning and socializing in English, she has managed to form positive relationships, even with people (her mother-in-law, for example) that she finds difficult to deal with for cultural reasons. Mayumi is engaged in an active process of forming relationships and forming community that mark her as a very successful learner in Sparrow's terms.

We should keep in mind, however, that the view of cultural learning as a process of forming relationships with people from a new cultural community does not contradict Bennett's phenomenological descriptions of intercultural sensitivity. Gaining the ability to construe new cultural realities, as described by Bennett, would seem to go hand in hand with entering into engaged relationships with people from the host cultural community. For Bennett, the ability to empathize and not make ethnocentric judgments marks intercultural sensitivity. These qualities are precisely those that help one develop positive relationships. Mayumi does not like her mother-in-law bleaching her teapot but manages to depersonalize this with her understanding that this is a question of custom. In Bennett's terms, Mayumi accepts other cultural worldviews as viable alternatives and this allows her to develop constructive relationships, which in turn defines her experience as successful in Sparrow's terms.

Meaningful versus Deep Intercultural Experiences

In the professional literature there is very little writing that looks at the varying depths of intercultural experiences. Two years in the Peace Corps is clearly a *deeper* experience than two weeks at a beach resort, yet how these experiences can be compared is seldom discussed. As described in this work, *deep experiences* are those that involve *facing implicit adaptive demands that can only be understood through ongoing interactions in a range of different situations.* As for the Australian students in France, only by attempting to function in their French university environment for a year, were these students in a position to have explored the more subtle patterns of information gathering strategies. Yet, how can we judge in concrete terms the depth of an intercultural experience? We have seen with Jack that simply remaining abroad for a long period of time does not insure contact with more implicit demands. We have also seen that the depth of one's experience is not necessarily related to whether one has positive feelings about the host cultural community or not. Deep experiences can provoke both positive and negative emotional reactions.

Before trying to define criteria for judging the depth of intercultural experiences, it is important to make a distinction between an experience that is *meaningful* and one that is *deep*. In this work, deep intercultural experiences are not those that provoke the most emotion; they are those that touch upon the hidden elements of cultural difference. Intercultural learning is often discussed in terms of it being personally meaningful for sojourners. Personal realizations, however, do not necessarily correspond with deep intercultural experiences as described here. Seeing poverty for the first time, or simply seeing that people in other places live very differently from oneself, can be extremely meaningful personally. But this does not mean that one has faced the subtle and systematic demands of interacting with deep cultural difference. The fact that things are so different can be shocking (we can imagine a traveler who sees extreme poverty for the first time), yet being moved by difference and gaining entry into the worldview of that community are different things. A *surface experience* (coming into contact with explicit difference) is not necessarily a *superficial experience* (one that does not have a great impact).

The professional literature has little to say about the varying depths of different intercultural experiences. One of the few specialists who touches upon the subject of deeper intercultural learning is Hanvey (1979). Hanvey describes cultural learning goals in terms of an increased awareness of cultural difference, starting with visible traits and culminating in having an awareness of how another culture feels from the insider's

perspective. Hanvey describes different stages of cross-cultural awareness, the corresponding modes of experience at that stage of awareness
and how learners interpret intercultural difference at these stages. His
model can be represented as set out in Table 5.2.

Table 5.2 Based on Moran (2001)

	I	*II*	*III*	*IV*
Level of Cross-cultural Awareness	Awareness of superficial or very visible cultural traits: stereotypes	Awareness of significant and subtle cultural traits that contrast markedly with one's own.	Awareness of significant and subtle cultural traits that contrast markedly with one's own.	Awareness of how another culture feels from the standpoint of the insider.
Mode	Tourism, textbooks, National Geographic	Culture conflict situations	Intellectual analysis	Cultural immersion: living the culture

Hanvey's conceptualization of awareness recognizes that superficial
intercultural experiences, such as tourism, are substantively different from
the deeper experience of cultural immersion. It also recognizes that shallow
intercultural experiences involve only the explicit – or in Hanvey's terms,
visible – traits of a culture. The highest level of awareness, according to
Hanvey (1979), requires more than simple exposure:

> it is not easy to attain cross-cultural understanding of the kind that
> puts you into the head of a person from an utterly different culture.
> Contact alone will not do it. Even sustained contact will not do it.
> There must be a readiness to respect and accept, and a capacity to
> participate. The participation must be reinforced by rewards that
> matter to the participant. And the participation must be sustained
> over long periods of time. (p. 51)

The participation that Hanvey refers to involves social approval from
members of the culture as a measure of successful intercultural learning.
Hanvey's model also places a cognitive acceptance of cultural difference at
a lower level of awareness than acceptance based on 'subjective familiarity', which presumably includes deeper, more intuitive and more affective
elements of the self.

Hanvey's learning goals deal, to some degree, with different depths of intercultural experiences. A tourist may be impressed by what they see, but experiencing implicit elements of culture require a different kind of interaction. Hanvey makes this distinction by defining tourism and cultural immersion as varying in terms of the depth of the experience. Yet Hanvey's description of the process of attaining intercultural awareness seems overly simple. In Hanvey's model, explicit cultural difference engenders interpretations in which one finds the new culture *unbelievable*, *exotic* or *bizarre*. He seems to equate noticing explicit difference with denigrating it. This seems to overlook the commonsense observation that many travelers simply find the food, architecture and clothing in foreign culture *beautiful* or *interesting*. One would expect that explicit difference which is accepted, liked and/or adapted to – as when one tries and enjoys new food – can also contribute to increased intercultural awareness.

Another difficulty with Hanvey's model is that the stages of the model represent only two broadly defined categories of intercultural experience: (1) shallow ones such as tourism, textbooks and travel magazines; and (2) cultural immersion, living the culture. Yet, there would seem to be important differences between looking at pictures in a magazine and interacting with foreigners in a foreign country – even if one is staying in a resort hotel. And with the pace of globalization, a total cultural immersion is less common than in the past. Many sojourners may be sheltered expatriates, frequent travelers or short-term residents. The level of involvement with a new environment would seem to vary much more than Hanvey's model recognizes. The intermediary stages in Hanvey's model refer to conflict situations and intellectual analysis, which are more properly reactions to the demands of an intercultural experience, rather than degrees of depth of an experience. As for other specialists, although gaining intercultural awareness is typically thought to involve a bringing into awareness hidden elements of culture, there are few models which allow us to compare different kinds of experiences.

Relationships as a measure of cultural depth

One way of understanding the depth of intercultural experiences is to look at the types of relationships that sojourners have in their host environment. Indeed, a number of scholars have emphasized relationships as a measure of successful cultural learning (Brislin, 1981; Hannigan, 1990; Imahori & Lanigan, 1989). Imahori and Lanigan (1989) argue that intercultural competence derives from 'dynamic interactive processes of intercultural relationships' and that intercultural competence 'should lead to an effective relational outcome'. Successful relationships not only show that someone can get along with others and get things done, but that they have confronted a relatively more abstract level of cultural difference.

Relationships with people from other cultural environments create a demand for change. Since communication is often better when we take into consideration the communication patterns, expectations, values and norms of our cultural hosts, we face a pressure to modify in some way those parts of ourselves. Good relationships with cultural hosts are not only an end product of intercultural learning, they can also be seen as a driving force. And in the process of forming deeper relationships, deeper elements of self are brought into play as we develop empathy (the ability to look at things from the perspective of our cultural hosts) and learn to construe cultural difference better. Indeed, Sparrow argues that empathy is a natural by-product of successful relationships, and argues for relationships rather than disembodied cultural awareness, as a measure of intercultural success.

An emphasis on relationship formation reminds us that intercultural learning is an interactive process, one that is context specific and which engages different elements of the self. The work of Pierre Bourdieu provides terminology that articulates the negotiated, relational and contextual aspects of human interaction, including intercultural learning (Bourdieu, 1991, 1998; Bourdieu & Wacquant, 1992). For Bourdieu, human behavior can best be understood as an ongoing process of negotiating desired outcomes. But this process is not conscious or fully under the control of the individual. Our socialization and experiences give us a default setting, or 'habitus', which Bourdieu (1991: 12) defines as 'a set of dispositions which incline agents to act and react in certain ways'. This concept can be compared to the unconscious cultural programming described by Hofstede and others. For Bourdieu as well, the dispositions which make up the *habitus* operate at the preconscious level and influence us as we take action in specific social contexts (in this case, intercultural contexts) called *fields*. For Bourdieu, an individual operates in a variety of fields and accumulates social and material resources – or *capital*. Bourdieu's writings emphasize the importance of recognizing the internal programming that one brings to the infinite number of contextual fields that one operates in. It also emphasizes the recognition that we are motivated by many different kinds of *capital*, both formal and informal. In this view, we can say that forming successful relationships is an important form of capital in an intercultural environment. Cultural learning is necessary because our *habitus* does not fully prepare us for the intercultural fields that we encounter.

Language learning and deep culture

Ability in the host language has been identified as a critical element of cross-cultural competence (Matsumoto *et al.*, 2001; Olson & Kroeger, 2001). It is often assumed that it is not possible to fully know another culture without speaking the language of that culture (Byram *et al.*, 2001; Damen, 1987; Kramsch, 1998). The connection between language and intercultural understanding goes back to the work of linguists Edward Sapir and Benjamin Lee Whorf (J.B. Carrol, 1956; Sapir, 1921) who argued that language shapes our view of the world to such an extent that speaking a different language constitutes a different perceptual world.

Despite disagreement about strong and weak versions of the Sapir and Whorf hypothesis, it is widely agreed that learning to speak a foreign language well implies more than learning a new code to represent already familiar objects and ideas. Language is a symbolic system that represents the conceptualization of the values and worldview of its speakers and speaking a language implies membership – to some degree at least – of a community of speakers of that language. There has been a great deal written about the inclusion of cultural learning in the field of language education (Alptekin, 2002; Browning *et al.*, 1999; Byram, 1987; Cates, 1997, 1999; Clarke, 1976; Damen, 1987; David, 1996; Higgings & Tanaka, 1999; James & Garrett, 1992; Parry, 2002; Valdes, 1986; Yoneoka, 2000). Most of what is written is from the perspective of encouraging the inclusion of more cultural and global content in language classes. It is also a reflection of the recognition on the part of language teachers that cultural learning and language learning should ideally go hand in hand.

Language ability is also closely related to the types of interpersonal relationships that one has in one's host cultural community and the language used in any intercultural relationship is an important measure of who is adapting to whom. In an international company in which a foreign language is the official company language, local employees are required to adapt their communication to the linguistic worldview of foreigners. An expatriate who needs to learn a foreign language in order to speak to colleagues faces a much deeper challenge in cultural adaptation than someone who does not. In this way, language learning is not only indicative of possessing a code that one can use to communicate, it implies having been through the adaptive changes in terms of one's own communication.

Schema for describing the depth of cultural experiences

Shaules (2004a) has used the relationships that one forms in another culture and the language that is used in that relationship to describe the depth of cultural experience. The premise of this approach is that the kinds of relationships we have in a new cultural community are a reflection of our ability to manage increasingly abstract levels of cultural and linguistic difference. He defines a hierarchy of intercultural relationships, from more concrete and predictable to more abstract and context specific. Relationships with one's physical environment are the most concrete, followed by those with people with whom one has fairly concrete interactions. Relationships which touch more on abstract and less easily predictable interactions are seen as correspondingly deeper. One-on-one relationships are seen as less demanding than those in which one must interact in a group. The demands created by these various relationships also depend on whether one uses the host language to engage in them.

In this view, the first, most concrete and most predictable intercultural relationship dealt with by sojourners is that with their physical environment: streets they don't know, food they have never tried and buildings that look different. A tourist is dealing with this level of cultural depth. The adaptation to these differences is relatively concrete and easy to measure: learning to use chopsticks, learning the layout of the city and figuring out which button to push on the elevator. For some tourists, this may be the extent of their intercultural learning. It is important to point out that, simply because cultural difference is extremely concrete, it does not mean that a cultural experience is easy. Eating strange food, being jostled by crowds in a hectic foreign city and sleeping in new surroundings can all be extremely stressful. The source of the discomfort, however, is concrete and relatively easy to identify.

Dealing with people, as opposed to objects, increases the level of intercultural abstraction. The most concrete relationships for sojourners are those that are functional and formalized, such as waiters, clerks in a store and perhaps a receptionist or secretary in a work environment. Cultural difference confronted at this level of interaction is probably related primarily to language difference and secondarily to the style of interaction. That is to say that the goals of the relationships are relatively concrete – to order food, buy something or make copies. The need to use a foreign language in these situations obviously increases the level of intercultural learning. In addition to the need to communicate, the style of interaction such as whether one pays at the table or at the register, may also present challenges. These challenges are still relatively concrete, however, because they tend to be fixed and formalized.

The kinds of relationships described above are probably adequate to meet the needs of short-term sojourners. But longer stays mean deeper relationships. Shaules (2004a) defines non-formalized, one-on-one relationships in a host community as existing at the next-greater level of abstraction. The goals and interaction in relationships with new friends, colleagues and neighbors are less concrete and predictable. We can learn to anticipate what a cashier may say more easily than a colleague we may be having a meal with. Knowledge of the communicative frameworks used in these relationships implies deeper exposure to cultural difference. Of course the language used to develop the relationship is important. An American working with English-speaking colleagues in a foreign country faces a very different challenge than someone who must work in a foreign language. If a sojourner has a relationship in their native language with a host who has learned their language, it is primarily the host who is adapting. If a sojourner is obliged to form friendships in a foreign language, they are forced to adapt more to the worldview of the host cultural community.

An important distinction Shaules makes in defining intercultural relationships is whether they are one-on-one (friends, spouse) or within a group (working for a foreign company abroad). In the former case, each person may be adapting to the other and may have interests or personality types in common which make relationship formation much easier. In the latter case, the group functions with a set of already established cultural expectations and the learner is much more likely to be forced to adapt their relationship strategies in order to get along. For this reason, the deepest intercultural experiences are related to developing relationships within a group of people in a new cultural environment. A student staying in a homestay family needs to adapt to the routines of the family, just as someone working in a foreign company exclusively with host colleagues will have to fit in with others (unless, perhaps, if he or she is the boss). In a one-on-one relationship the host may adapt to the sojourner whereas when the sojourner attempts to function within a host community group, much of that flexibility is lost.

The hierarchy of intercultural relationships can be summarized as in Table 5.3. It is only intended as a general way of categorizing intercultural relationships and not as an absolute measure. It is assumed that intercultural relationships are too contextual to measure reliably. For example, while one-on-one relationships are defined as being less *deep* than relationships in a group of people, certain one-on-one relationships, such as with a spouse who has a different cultural background, may involve a much more abstract and demanding level of cultural adaptation than certain group relationships such as staying with a homestay family. Despite these

Table 5.3 Shaules' hierarchy of intercultural relationships – from surface to deep

Functional relationships (sojourner adapts to highly explicit systematic difference)	Physical surroundings: adapting to streets, food, subway systems, etc. Relationships with people: Short-term, information based, formalized and (relatively) predictable, non-negotiated (waiter, clerk, acquaintance)
One-on-one relationships (more abstract difference – often involves mutual adaptation)	• Involves deeper one-on-one relationships over extended period • One negotiates mutually satisfying relationship • Feels connection that may extend into social network of others • May or may not be in host language • May involve little adaptation on part of sojourner Examples: Friend, spouse, colleague
Group relationships (sojourner is required to adapt to implicit group expectations)	• Requires extended contact to understand group dynamic • One negotiates one's role and desired outcomes • Requires adaptation to norms of the group • Involves use of host language • Requires deeper adaptation to meet expectations of group Examples: Working in foreign company abroad, homestay, getting along with family of spouse in host community, relationship with neighbors

limitations, this hierarchy allows sojourners' experiences to be categorized in a more structured and meaningful way.

From Goals to Process

This chapter has given an overview of different perspectives on the desired outcomes of intercultural learning as well as examined how the depth of intercultural experiences can be quantified. The next chapter will look at different conceptualizations of the process of cultural learning with a particular view in attempting to describe deep cultural learning.

Chapter 6
The Process of Intercultural Learning

My parents came over [to visit me in the US] and told me that I had become Americanized.
Rieko

It took me three years to learn how to slurp [noodles].
Yuko

My friends say, 'Jack's turning Japanese!' ... Actually, my only close Japanese friends have been my girlfriends.
Jack

I've been living abroad for 12 years, but what do you learn about yourself if you never went abroad and were stuck in your own country for 12 years? I suspect you might learn just as much or even more.
Donald

I'm willing to do more to fit into this culture than would many Americans.
Neil

Differing Results of Deep Cultural Learning

Previous chapters have looked at some of the challenges of deep cultural learning and have examined possible learning outcomes, both positive and negative. They have also looked at what it might mean to call an intercultural experience *deep*. They have not, however, examined in any detail the ongoing process of how those different outcomes take place. As we can see from the quotes of sojourners above, sojourners talk about their cultural learning processes in a variety of ways. Unfortunately, it is not always easy to relate them to a cultural learning theory.

Sojourners' descriptions of their own learning raise questions about the deeper processes of cultural learning. For example, is it possible for someone like Jack, who has lived abroad for 14 years yet does not speak Japanese or have Japanese friends, to have achieved a high level of intercultural awareness? If not, why didn't he? And if he's happy in Japan, then isn't that okay? And how about Yuko, who says that it took her three years to properly slurp noodles, or Neil, who declares his willingness to change himself to fit into his host community? Have they learned more about culture than Donald, who declares that he could have learned as much staying at home? What processes have led these sojourners to these varying results?

There are a number of areas that can shed light on the deep culture learning process. We will examine research on culture shock and see that descriptions of the psychological process of going through culture shock can give us insight into why deeper cultural learning can be so difficult. We will then examine the stages of gaining intercultural sensitivity proposed by Bennett to see if they can explain the varying outcomes that are produced by this process. We will see that these perspectives don't allow us to easily take into account the different depths of intercultural experiences implied by deep culture.

Culture Shock and Cultural Learning

Research on culture shock, though somewhat out of favor now, tries to understand the progression through stages of an intercultural experience (J. Bennett, 1993; Ward & Kennedy, 1993; Ward *et al.*, 1998; Ward *et al.*, 2001). It looks at how people *do* react to intercultural environments, as opposed to how educators might *want* sojourners to react. The concept of culture shock was initially described as an 'occupational disease' of those going abroad caused by 'the anxiety that results from losing all our familiar signs and symbols of social intercourse' (Oberg, 1960). It is a widely known term now and commonly used to mean any discomfort experienced by people going abroad; its psychological causes have been described in detail (J. Bennett, 1998; Oberg, 1960; Stone & Ward, 1990; Ward *et al.*, 1998; Ward *et al.*, 2001). A considerable amount of research in this area focuses on one's *emotional* reactions to a new environment, not how one conceptualizes cultural difference.

Descriptions of the culture shock process match well with the implicit models of culture described by Hall (1959; 1976), Trompenaars and Hampden-Turner (1998) and others. Weaver (1993), in an overview of the literature related to culture shock, describes three elements to this process: (1) the loss of familiar cues, (2) the breakdown of interpersonal communication and (3) an identity crisis. He points out that these all occur in any new situation but that in a cross-cultural situation the effects are greatly exaggerated. Although Weaver was not specifically examining the question of out-of-awareness elements of the intercultural experiences, his description of these causes correlate well with the process of dealing with ever deeper levels of intercultural learning demands. His description of culture shock could even be characterized as starting at the outer limits of the cultural onion described by Trompenaars and Hampden-Turner and then progressing towards the inner layers. It is almost as though the demands of an intercultural experience strip away our normal sense of self layer by layer as ever deeper demands call into question more fundamental parts of the self.

The anatomy of culture shock

In a global age, it is easy to forget how traumatic it can be to live in a new cultural environment. This is not necessarily a product of bizarre or distressing features in our environment, it is simply a natural product of disrupting the normal flow of environmental cues which reinforce our sense of self. Humans are creatures of perceptual habits and can be thrown into deep states of disorientation when these habits are interrupted. One example of this can be seen in traffic accidents when, in spite of not being physically hurt, victims go into 'shock'. This can be seen as a temporary incapacity to maintain the victim's ongoing sense of perceptual continuity, which has been violently interrupted by the accident. This interruption of perceptual reality is also evident in culture shock, although the process takes much longer. It is as though both a traffic accident and a deep intercultural experience both give a *shock* to one's sense of how the world works.

While we may recover from the shock of a traffic accident quite quickly, an intercultural experience can force us to fundamentally alter our view of the world. Weaver's (1993) analysis of the stress involved in this process provides us with a clearly articulated description of how being in a new environment can constitute a deep demand for change. This demand may be behavioral, but is described in terms of the perceptions and worldview that underlie our actions. The description starts with a sojourner's reaction to more explicit difference and progresses to more implicit difference. In this sense, it roughly follows Shaules' (2004a) description of ever deeper intercultural relationships and can be seen as a detailed conceptualization of the psychological and perceptual challenges of deep intercultural learning. In terms of Bennett's model it describes, from a phenomenological perspective, the difficulties of learning to construe new cultural realities.

Environmental cues and 'navigational demands'

According to Weaver, the first demand for change involved in cultural learning is a loss of familiar cues. *Cues* are what is most tangible and observable in our environment and correspond well with Trompenaars and Hampden-Turner's description of explicit culture. Weaver (1993: 140) divides these cues into 'physical cues', which include 'objects which we have become accustomed to in our home culture which are changed or missing in a new culture' and 'behavioural or social cues', which 'provide order in our interpersonal relations'. As with Trompenaars and Hampden-Turner's description of explicit and implicit culture, the cues Weaver (1993) describes are the explicit manifestation of symbols that function at deeper layers of meaning.

> Cues are signposts which guide us though our daily activities in an acceptable fashion which is consistent with the total social environment. They may be words, gestures, facial expressions, postures, or customs which help us make sense out of the social world that surrounds us. They tell us when and how to give gifts or tips, when to be serious or to be humorous, how to speak to leaders and subordinates, who has status, what to say when we meet people, when and how to shake hands, how to eat, and so on. They make us feel comfortable because they seem so automatic and natural. (p. 140)

Weaver goes on to tie this directly to the out-of-awareness element of cultural learning:

> When we enter another culture we feel out of sync and, yet, we often do not realize the cause of our awkwardness because we learned our own kinesic, proxemic, and chronemic cues simply by growing up in our own culture. This silent language, or nonverbal communication, is especially important for the communication of feelings (Mehrabian, 1968) and yet is almost totally beyond the conscious awareness of the average person. (p. 141)

According to Weaver, at the most explicit level, 'the very act of changing physical environments causes stress' (p. 141). The immediate result of a lack of familiar cues is a need to pay more attention to our environment and more actively evaluate the environment in relation to our behavior. This may be as simple as needing to look for signs to find the way out of an unfamiliar airport or examine carefully a menu we do not understand. In either case, we can no longer rely on perceptual habits or existing competencies to manage our activities.

It may be that, as some degree of technological convergence takes place globally, the stress caused by changes in our physical environment will be somewhat reduced. Certainly, a German visitor to Shanghai faces a less baffling physical environment than she would have one hundred years ago, if for no other reason than the increased similarity in the technology of everyday life. But at the deeper symbolic levels the adjustment process can still be very difficult. As we have said, this is not necessarily related to the fact that one's new environment is exotic or threatening in some way. It is simply a demand resulting from the lack of internal resources to navigate unthinkingly in our new environment. This 'navigational demand' is faced in any new environment and is greatest when we have little experience to guide us.

Communication and 'interactive demands'

The cues described above are explicit insofar as they correspond to visible physical and behavioral phenomena and how we respond to our environment. The next cause of culture shock described by Weaver is more implicit. It relates to the ways in which our interactions with others are interrupted.

> Identifying a breakdown of communication as a cause of culture shock emphasizes the process of interpersonal interaction and is much less behavioural than the other possible causes. In fact, it approaches humanistic psychology with its emphasis on the psychodynamics of human interaction. A basic assumption in this explanation is that a breakdown of communication, on both the conscious and unconscious levels, causes frustration and anxiety and is a source of alienation from others. (p. 142)

Communication breakdown causes frustration not only because we have difficulty managing everyday tasks, such as buying train tickets or shopping, but also because the deeper layers of our identity cannot be expressed or reinforced. If we want to express our feelings but don't have the communicative or interactive competence to do so we are cut off from others. This isolation can be disturbing in and of itself – we may feel lonely or lost in a new environment – but if the people we would like to communicate with behave in ways we find unpleasant or strange, it increases our stress. We have both a desire to interact and validate our experience with those around us together with a feeling of resistance towards the people whose validation we seek. This interactive demand opens up a gap between our internal values (perhaps cultural and perhaps personal) and the values and communication style of our new environment. The dissonance that this causes may allow us to gain empathy and intercultural sensitivity (accepting difference and perhaps adapting ourselves) or to denigrate those around us (resisting difference and artificially reinforcing the centrality of our worldview). The demands of intercultural learning generate, necessarily, both the possibility for positive change and the possibility of ethnocentric retrenching.

The 'identity demands' of intercultural learning

The final description of the demands of intercultural learning offered by Weaver is as a form of identity crisis. This description corresponds to the deepest, most hidden parts of personality and cultural identity and with it Weaver also provides a bridge between culture shock and cultural learning. He describes the loss of our normal cues as disorienting, but remarks that this same disorientation can free us from our normal way of doing and perceiving. This can make us more conscious of the grip that culture has on our behavior and personality. He goes on to compare the overseas experience to an encounter, or sensitivity group, in that it 'offers a new social milieu in which to examine one's behavior, perceptions, values, and thought patterns' (p. 146). This comparison, which is perhaps not intuitively obvious, emphasizes the degree to which intercultural experiences put our behavior and values into a new perspective. Being in a new environment interrupts the usual flow of stimuli that reinforces our normal sense of self. We must maintain or modify that self-image in the face of our 'encounter' with a different environment.

In Trompenaars and Hampden-Turner's cultural onion, implicit assumptions about reality are at the core of culture. It seems reasonable to say that the kind of deep personal changes described by Weaver would correspond to dealing with cultural difference that resides at these deeper layers of unquestioned assumptions. Put more simply, learning to eat with our fingers (explicit culture, physical cues) probably will not cause us to question our identity, but communicating with and developing relationships with people who have fundamentally different worldviews might. Weaver (1993) emphasizes how difficult this process can be:

> An experience close to psychosis may be required to take one outside the collective pressures and assumptions of our culture. We may discover things about ourselves that allow for great personal growth. Yet it may be an ego-shattering experience. (p. 144)

Weaver's descriptions of culture shock introduce an element of psychology into the attempt to understand cultural learning. It also provides a clear model for understanding why intercultural learning demands can produce both positive and negative outcomes. Finally, it helps us look at intercultural learning as a developmental process which happens over time although the descriptions of the stages in that process are often not delineated in great detail.

Deep and Surface Adaptive Demands

One limitation of Weaver's view of culture shock is that it doesn't account for the fact that different people are more or less open to the demands of a new environment. Jack, for example, seems to have lived in Japan for 14 years without ever having gone through many of the deeper processes that Weaver describes. Likewise, when Steven, who lived in Korea for 6 years without learning Korean, talks about what was hard getting used to, he says:

> [It bothered me that] things were half-assed. ... For example, I bought a mountain bike and after two weeks I was replacing things, and fixing it, and that was just indicative of the quality there. But it wasn't that big of a problem because once you get your lifestyle settled you don't need to be shopping every weekend.

Steven's conceptualization of adjusting to his new life seems focused on the physical objects that he needs to live his daily life. This parallels a statement by Jack, who comments that getting used to life in Japan is easy because things are predictable and you know that your train is going to come on time.

This doesn't mean, of course, that Jack and Steve didn't have a culture shock experience. It does seem, however, that expatriates like these who tend to isolate themselves in expatriate communities manage to stay in another cultural environment avoiding, to some degree at least, change at deeper levels of the self described by Weaver. Neither of them discuss frustration with communication (despite having limited language ability) nor struggles with questions of their identities – elements of the cultural adaptation process which Weaver postulates as involving deeper elements of the self. Compare Jack and Steve to William, who talks about his learning challenges in terms of the stress and isolation engendered by not speaking the host language:

> In Hiroshima I went every Saturday to this all-volunteer class and that's how I learned the basics of Japanese grammar and conversation.

And actually that class pulled me out of my solitude because I met people and made friends there.

William goes on to make an explicit connection between the ability to communicate and the ability to have a satisfying experience:

There was a woman at my university who didn't speak any Japanese and I used her as an anti-role model. I could see how she was seen in the school. She seemed unhappy. She was seen as lazy, and detached and not interested in getting involved. I decided early on that I didn't want to be like her. ... It seems to me that the people who are bilingual are happier, they travel more, their conversations don't dip into a dark zone of complaints and frustrations

Of course, not everyone who doesn't speak the host language becomes frustrated, as in Jack's case. But Weaver's description of communication (and perhaps by extension the ability to form satisfying relationships) seems to fit the process that William has been through.

The third stage of culture shock/cultural learning that Weaver discusses is experienced as an identity crisis. Neither Jack nor Stephen or William discussed this. Perhaps, as English teachers in Asia living a relatively sheltered expatriate lifestyle, they were somewhat removed from the adaptive demands of a more complete integration into society. This can be contrasted with Mayumi, a Japanese woman who spent 7 years in the United States attending university, and then a year and a half in Korea with her Korean husband. Interestingly, she reports that language learning was not difficult for her but the ability to communicate linguistically didn't imply adaptation. She reports: 'I love learning languages, and so my linguistic skills were advanced, but my perception is that I don't have the social skills to match my linguistic skills.' Unfortunately, being able to communicate didn't allow her to feel at ease with the roles she was expected to play. She describes the role she was expected to play with her husband's family in Korea by saying: 'I tried to be accommodating and then got frustrated and finally exploded at the end.'

Perhaps it is precisely Mayumi's ability to communicate well that raises deeper questions of adaptation and identity, since she is being expected to play roles that she may not always find comfortable. Just as Weaver describes, Mayumi has trouble understanding her own identity:

I haven't yet figured out this has all affected my identity. I try to accommodate to the other person, but sometimes that's at the expense of my true identity. If I continue to do that I reach a threshold, but when I got to the point that enough is enough, then I kind of retreated and tried to be more true to myself

In important ways, Mayumi is more integrated into her host society and has faced more adaptive demands than William, Stephen or Jack. She has dealt successfully with communicative demands (unlike Stephen or Jack) and adapted herself to her new environment enough to call her identity into question.

Interestingly, these four sojourners – Jack, Stephen, William and Mayumi – have spent comparable periods abroad. Yet only Mayumi seems to have been through the deepest intercultural learning process as described by Weaver. This can be seen as a response to deeper adaptive demands being made of her (playing the role of the wife in Korea rather than being a relatively sheltered language teacher in an expatriate community). While this is intuitively understandable, it points out a limitation to Weaver's conceptualization of intercultural learning. Weaver's process seems to hold true for some people, but even those abroad for a long time sometimes seem not go through the deeper process as he describes them.

There are two elements to Weaver's model which, when added, may better explain the variety of responses that different sojourners have to their intercultural experiences. One of them is the concept of *adaptive demands*. The simple fact of being in a new cultural environment does not automatically constitute a demand for change. This is why sheltered expatriates sometimes seem to remain detached from their host communities. Intercultural learning is not a product of physical proximity to cultural difference, but rather having to respond to the *adaptive demands* of that cultural difference. If expatriates are not subject to a need to change in order to get things done, communicate daily needs or develop relationships, their cultural learning may stop. In this way Jack, who has spent a longer period of time in Japan than Mayumi spent in Korea, has had a much more shallow intercultural experience. He hasn't had to face a need to change as much as Mayumi.

Resistance, acceptance and adaptation

Another element that could be added to Weaver's conceptualization of cultural learning relates to whether sojourners are willing to accept difference they encounter as valid and reasonable and allow themselves to change in response to that difference. One sojourner may readily accept that the difference found in his or her new environment forms part of an alternative, yet viable system of meaning and therefore be more willing to adapt to that difference. Likewise, if difference is not seen as valid, it may be resisted, leading not only to non-adaptation but perhaps denigration as well. In this way, Jack, who seems comfortable with his life in Japan, has the *choice* of adapting more to his host community, but doesn't. In doing so he may avoid communicative frustration or deeper questions about his identity, but he also remains more or less detached from his host community. The fact that he doesn't seem to denigrate Japanese culture too much would seem to speak to his ability to accept its validity to some degree.

Shaules (2004a) uses the terms *resistance, acceptance* and *adaptation* as labels describing whether an intercultural experience provokes change within a sojourner. *Resistance* describes a (conscious or unconscious) unwillingness or inability to allow for internal change in response to the patterns or expectations of a new environment. *Resistance* is considered to involve denigration or being dismissive of difference as a way to uphold the primacy of one's internal cultural patterns. *Acceptance* implies a willingness to perceive as valid the cultural differences encountered, without necessarily implying a change in order to better align one's internal patterns with those of the environment. *Adaptation* implies a willingness to allow for internal change in response to adaptive demands in the environment. These terms were developed in part to be able to describe reactions to intercultural experiences in a neutral way.

Shaules (2004a) argues that all of these reactions are involved in the intercultural learning process. *Acceptance* is of central importance as it indicates the recognition of the validity of other worldviews. *Acceptance* implies a construal of cultural difference as valid and is thought to encourage *cognitive empathy*, the increased ability to construe other worldviews as valid. *Adaptation*, as defined by Shaules, does not presuppose *acceptance*, as it does in Bennett's schema. Someone may adapt to their environment – changing their behavior or communication style – without accepting that the differences being adapted to represent valid alternative worldviews. And we may resist something at first and then accept or adapt to it later, or perhaps resist certain elements of our experience and accept or adapt to others. That is not to say that these reactions all lead to similar outcomes, or that one might not be preferable to another. As simple descriptors, however, they allow us to describe both 'positive' and 'negative' responses to intercultural experiences using a relatively neutral vocabulary.

The concepts of *resisting, accepting,* or *adapting* to adaptive demands can help explain why not everyone passes through the stages of cultural learning described by Weaver. In some cases, the adaptive demands may not constitute much of a challenge to expatriates, since they may have the choice of remaining in a sheltered expatriate community. This would explain not only how cultural learning can be deeper and engage ever deeper parts of the self – as described by Weaver – but also why some sojourners don't seem to go through this whole process. It would also make it easy to compare the intercultural experiences of tourists or short-term visitors and longer-term sojourners. A short-term visitor will face adaptive demands at an explicit level and *resist*, *accept* or *adapt* to them, while a longer-term sojourner may face deeper adaptive demands. They are both going through an intercultural learning process, but they are doing it at different depths. It would also explain how long-term sojourners can remain so aloof from their host community. If they are able to isolate themselves from adaptive demands, their experiences end up being like long-term tourists rather than host community residents.

The Stages of Cultural Learning

Weaver's description of the intercultural learning process involves stages of culture shock engaging ever deeper parts of the self. There have been other attempts to identify a progression or stages in which culture shock takes place and different authors use a variety of phases to describe it (J. Bennett, 1998). These include the 'U curve', which describes an initial high, or honeymoon period, followed by a sharp emotional downturn and then finally an emotional upswing as sojourners get adjusted. Often this adjustment corresponds with making a friend in the foreign culture (Weaver & Uncapher, 1981). A variation of the 'U curve' is the 'W curve' which includes an element of culture shock and adaptation upon return to the home culture. But not all research finds the same patterns and some research finds that some people do not experience high levels of stress when adapting to life abroad (Lewthwaite, 1996; Ward *et al.*, 1998).

In terms of trying to understand the details of deep intercultural learning, the curves postulated by research into culture shock are crude markers. Many of them use a sojourners sense of emotional well-being as a measure and simply represent the fact that one feels stress in new environments, which decreases over time. M.J. Bennett (1993; 2004), using a more cognitive approach, has described in detail what he sees as universal stages that sojourners go through in the process of gaining intercultural sensitivity. Because of the importance of those claims, and because he claims research to back them up, his proposed stages and the research to justify them will be looked at in some detail.

Bennett's six degrees of intercultural sensitivity

As we saw in the previous chapter, Bennett proposes that intercultural learning happens in discrete stages as sojourners become increasingly capable of integrating the existence of cultural difference into their cultural reality. The stages that Bennett proposes are: *denial, resistance, minimization, acceptance, adaptation,* and *integration.* He conceptualizes the first three stages as different degrees of ethnocentrism, while the second three consist of differing degrees of ethnorelativism.

The ethnocentric stages

Denial

The first stage posited by Bennett is denial. In the stage of denial, learners simply do not recognize that cultural difference exists. This stage is based on ethnocentrism, defined by Bennett as 'assuming that the worldview of one's own culture is central to all reality'. Someone in denial lives in physical or psychological isolation and the reality of other cultural viewpoints does not exist at all. Difference is simply not recognized. According to Bennett, people in *denial* use wide categories for cultural difference. This can lead to the 'stupid question' syndrome, such as when someone asks a Japanese visitor about Samurai or asks an African visitor about wild animals. These questions betray the fact that the person asking the question has extremely simple perceptual categories for the concepts of 'Japanese' or 'African', e.g. 'there are Samurai in Japan' and 'there are lions in Africa'. These kinds of benign stereotypes mask a more insidious side to the stage of denial. When a cultural group in denial feels threatened by another group, the response can be to dehumanize them and in extreme cases commit genocide.

Defense

Bennett describes the stage of *defense* as a 'posture intended to counter the impact of specific cultural differences perceived as threatening' (p. 34). Cultural difference poses a threat to one's identity and by extension to one's cultural reality. In *denial* cultural difference is ignored – its existence is amorphous. In *defense,* the threat is recognized and specific strategies are created to counter that threat. Someone at this stage of development might respond to cultural difference with statements such as 'well, people in that country are lazy' or 'at first people seem polite, but you later realize that they are being phony'. In these cases, real cultural differences are perceived, but they are evaluated negatively. The evaluation of these observed behaviors as 'laziness' or 'phoniness' upholds the central position of the cultural values of the speaker. Three kinds of *defense* are described by

Bennett: *denigration, superiority* and *reversal. Denigration* is one in which negative evaluation is focused on some aspect of cultural difference, such as in the examples above. *Superiority,* on the other hand, is a positive evaluation of one's own culture. Finally, Bennett describes the state of *reversal,* which involves someone denigrating one's own cultural background and believing in the superiority of another. Bennett mentions Peace Corp Volunteers who disavow American values and instead try to adopt the values of their host community. A statement that might indicate *reversal* might be, 'I did not realize how screwed up my country was until I started to live here [in this foreign country]'.

Minimization

The final ethnocentric stage for Bennett is *minimization,* which involves 'an effort to bury difference under the weight of cultural similarities'. Cultural difference is recognized, but it is seen as less important than certain cultural universals. Put more theoretically, 'one finds superordinate constructs that place previously polarized elements onto one side of a larger construct' (p. 41). *Minimization* can be seen in the 'golden rule' of 'do unto others what you would have them do unto you'. This assumes that people share the same fundamental characteristics and therefore one can use one's own experience as a guide for interacting with others. Bennett describes two forms of *minimization: physical universalism* and *transcendental universalism.* He describes *physical universalism* as corresponding to the assumption that people everywhere share a fundamentally similar physical biology, which reflects a similar set of needs and motivations. The second form of *minimization* described by Bennett is *transcendental universalism.* This is parallel to *physical universalism,* except that the universal qualities that someone at this stage relies on are related to some transcendent law or principle. Examples of this are religious thinking such as 'we are all children of the same god' or assertions of psychological or sociological imperatives, such as 'all humans have the same emotional needs' or Marxist theories of class struggle. This stage of development may recognize that cultural difference exists and even give it great importance. Ultimately, however, this difference is always seen as less important than the overriding principle. An example of this thinking might be a missionary who understands the need to learn the customs and language of a community to be better able to bring them his message of 'truth'.

The ethnorelative stages

Acceptance

M.J. Bennett (1993; 2004) describes acceptance as marking a fundamental shift in how cultural difference is dealt with. No longer is cultural difference something that is denied or denigrated. From an ethnorelative standpoint, cultural difference is not seen as good or bad, just different, and particular behavior is understood to exist within a cultural context. Someone dealing with cultural difference from the *acceptance* stage of development might say something like: 'Well, everyone has their own way of doing things that works for them.' Bennett describes acceptance as 'crossing the barrier' from ethnocentrism to ethnorelativism and describes two forms, respect for behavioral difference and respect for value difference. Respect for behavioral differences refers to the recognition that how people act reflects deep-seated differences in culture. An example given by Bennett is language. Someone operating from the perspective of *acceptance* will recognize that learning a foreign language means more than learning new words to express the same ideas, it reflects an entirely different view of the world which is separate, but as valid as one's customary view. Bennett sees the acceptance of other values as more difficult than the acceptance of behavior. Because sooner or later values will be found which are personally offensive, a learner at this stage must understand that even these must be viewed in a cultural context and must be seen as an ongoing process of assigning meaning.

Adaptation

At the stage of *acceptance* the framework of appreciating cultural difference is created, while at the stage of *adaptation* skills for functioning within the cultural viewpoints of others are developed. These skills are seen as an additive process, in which new ways of communicating and looking at things are added to a learner's personal repertoire. In *acceptance* learners develop the ability to shift among multiple perspectives. He describes two kinds of cultural frame shifts for the purpose of communication: empathy, which involves temporary and intentional shifts of a frame of reference and pluralism, which may be unintentional and tied to more permanent frames of reference. These frame shifts allow for people to develop relationships and share more fully in the worldview of someone else. Someone at the adaptation stage might make a statement such as 'let me explain it from the German point of view'.

M.J. Bennett (1993: 55) describes pluralism as reflecting a 'philosophical commitment to the existence of a "multitude of irreducible and equivalent ultimate wholes, ideas, values and value scales, as well as experiences in which they are tested."' By this, he means that cultural differences must be understood 'totally within the context of the relevant culture' and that by extension, one's understanding of that culture must come from actual experience within that cultural frame of reference. Pluralism is the general category that Bennett puts 'biculturalism' and 'multiculturalism' in. Someone operating from a pluralistic standpoint experiences multiple perspectives as a normal part of themselves. They may have an 'Italian self' and a 'Greek self', which functions within those relative worldviews.

Integration

Bennett describes the state of *adaptation* to be 'good enough' for most intercultural settings, but as we have seen, he defines one final stage beyond the ability to shift into different cultural points of view. As we saw in the previous chapter, integration is described as a state in which a sojourner goes *beyond* cultural difference in the sense that their cultural identity and criteria for behavior go beyond the ethnocentric assumptions of any single cultural framework. Individuals have the capacity to raise any question of behavior, values, norms or belief to a meta-level based on an intuitive understanding of the meanings that those things have in differing environments. Cultural identity is *constructed* within the context of being both marginal and integrated in one's view of one's environment. One is marginal in the sense that one doesn't completely share the perceptual frameworks of that environment, but one is integrated in that those frameworks are understood and don't pose a threat to one's identity or sense of well-being.

Validity of the DMIS

The previous chapter looked at some of the strengths of Bennett's model, including the fact that it provides a clear criterion for determining a person's level of intercultural sensitivity and that it doesn't rely on behavioral or subjective emotional measures. In addition, the stages are described in detail, giving us clues as to how best to interpret the intercultural learning experiences of sojourners. Since Bennett claims that these processes are cognitive processes that can be measured objectively, it is important to look into research claims of this model's validity.

Bennett and others have undertaken studies to show the validity of his model (M.J. Bennett, pers. comm. 2003; Hammer, Bennett & Wiseman, 2003; Paige *et al.*, 1999). The fundamental premises of Bennett's model are relatively simple:

(1) 'The phenomenology of difference is the key to intercultural sensitivity. Intercultural communication behaviour is treated as a manifestation of this subjective experience.' (2) 'The construing of difference

necessary for intercultural sensitivity is that of ethnorelativism, whereby different cultures are perceived as variable and viable constructions of reality.' (3) 'Ethical choices can and must be made for intercultural sensitivity to develop. However, these choices cannot be based on either absolute or universal principles. Rather, ethical behaviour must be chosen with awareness that different viable actions are possible.' (p. 66)

While the general approach of Bennett's model seems intuitively obvious, the particular stages and sequencing of learning as described by Bennett seem less obvious. He describes six stages, but why six? Couldn't it be five? Or perhaps it is simply a cumulative process without identifiable stages. And are these stages valid for people of all cultures?

Bennett's approach to measuring intercultural sensitivity is to treat an individual's description of the experience with cultural difference as a manifestation of the individual's ability to conceptualize cultural difference. In other words, how one talks about cultural difference gives evidence for one's degree of ethnocentrism or ethnorelativism. One method for doing this is to have a conversation with someone and ask opinions about cultural difference. Those statements are then analyzed based on the DMIS to determine the level of intercultural sensitivity. In the course of his work as a cross-cultural trainer, however, Bennett has also developed a written multiple-choice instrument – the Intercultural Development Inventory (IDI) – designed to measure intercultural sensitivity. The IDI consists of a series of statements regarding the respondent's view of cultural difference. Respondents mark their level of agreement with the statements and based on their responses a profile of their level of intercultural sensitivity is created. Bennett claims that the IDI is a valid and objective measure of intercultural sensitivity. The IDI is proprietary and is used in Bennett's intercultural communication consulting and training work. The right to use the IDI is reserved for people who have been trained in its use.

Bennett's work has been subject to different studies to test the ideas behind the DMIS (Hammer *et al.*, 2003; Paige *et al.*, 1999; Yamamoto, 1998). The largest studies, however, focused not on the DMIS directly, but on the IDI. The items on the IDI were created using the six categories of the DMIS. A series of interviews were done in which 40 people with experience abroad were asked to talk about their ideas regarding cultural difference. A set of open-ended questions, intended to elicit responses associated with the six stages of the DMIS, were asked. Based on the answers to these questions, Bennett created a list of statements which typified responses from each of these categories, such as: (1) People from our culture are less tolerant compared to people from other cultures (defense); (2) Our common humanity deserves more attention than culture difference (minimization); (3) I have observed many instances of misunderstanding due to cultural differences in gesturing or eye contact (acceptance/adaptation). The items generated from this study were refined and expanded on and then further refined. The end product was a multiple-choice questionnaire based theoretically on the DMIS and which was subsequently studied.

In two studies intended to examine the empirical structure of the IDI, Hammer *et al.* ran a variety of statistical tests to see if the distribution of responses on the IDI clustered in the way predicted by the DMIS (Hammer *et al.*, 2003). A first study done on an initial version of the IDI did factor analysis to test the validity of the categories and the results suggested that the factors identified were not highly stable. The finding suggested that rather than six categories as predicted by the DMIS, answers were more reliably explained when other categories were used. Three of these dimensions were identified: a Denial and Defense category, a Minimization category, and an Acceptance and Adaptation category (Paige *et al.*, 1999). Based on these results, a further refined version of the IDI was also then subject to a large scale study to test the validity of the categories (Hammer *et al.*, 2003). Confirmatory factor analyses, reliability analyses and construct validity tests were run. This study validated five main dimensions of the DMIS: Denial/Defense, Reversal, Minimization, Acceptance/Adaptation and Encapsulated Marginality.

These studies indicate that rather than six categories as predicted by DMIS, subjects' responses grouped into the five categories above. Denial and defense seemed to be essentially a similar experience. Reversal seems to be a different experience than other kinds of defense; minimization seems to be an experience of its own; acceptance and adaptation are similar to each other; and the marginality which typifies the integration portion of the model is seen as a separate category. The DMIS and the results of the study of the IDI can be compared using the diagram in Table 6.1.

Bennett and the other authors of this study claim that they are not trying to use this study to test the DMIS. Rather, they are testing the IDI – the test instrument created based on DMIS. Somewhat contradictorily, they also say that based on the findings of this study the DMIS model has been largely supported by testing (Hammer *et al.*, 2003). The results of this study, as well as the contradictory claims of validity, raise some doubts about the ability to describe intercultural learning in a fixed series of six distinct stages as predicted by the DMIS.

Table 6.1 Developmental model of intercultural sensitivity

Developmental model of intercultural sensitivity					
Denial	Defense	Minimization	Acceptance	Adaptation	Integration
Categories validated by Hammer's IDI study					
Denial Defense	Reversal	Minimization	Acceptance/ Adaptation	Encapsulated Marginality	

Validity across cultures

One important issue for Bennett's model is whether it works equally well for people from different cultural milieus. Bennett is from the US and his educational background and training experience are centered on the United States. It is reasonable to question whether this model works better for Americans than for people of other countries, particularly non-Western countries. As for the national origin of the subjects in these studies, the interview-based study which produced the statements used to create the items for the IDI was conducted with 40 subjects, almost 40% of which were American (15/40). Another 25% were from western and northern Europe (11/40) and the remainders were eastern Europeans (3/40), central Asians (2/40), South Americans (1/40), Africans (2/40) and East Asians (6/40). Although this group is culturally diverse it is heavily weighted towards US Americans and Europeans (26/40 = 65%). It should be pointed out that three of the American subjects were from ethnic minorities (Hammer *et al.*, 2003). The largest quantitative study done to test the validity of the IDI was done with a much larger sample (591 respondents). The subjects, however, were weighted even more heavily towards the US (87%, with 13% from 37 different countries)

One study done in Japan raises questions about the category of *minimization* as it applies to Japanese. Yamamoto (1998) did a series of qualitative in-depth interviews of Japanese university students studying in the United States. Data were analyzed according to the categories proposed by Bennett. Then, emergent categories were identified which typified students' experiences. In the first analysis, Yamamoto found many instances in which students' descriptions did not fit the DMIS, and in particular were not consistent with either the physical universalism or the transcendent universalism predicted for the *minimization* stage by

Bennett. Rather, students' descriptions of their experience were 'closely related to Japanese cultural values and perception of reality' (p. 77). An example was that students simply described difference and indicated a relative level of comfort/discomfort with difference. They did not talk about their experience in terms of *acceptance* or *respect*. Regarding the use of Bennett's model in Japan, Yamamoto (1998) concludes that:

> These results suggest that the definitions of each stage may need some modification to understand intercultural sensitivity in the Japanese context. It might be possible to say that what Japanese perceive as differences/similarities or how they deal with differences/similarities are different from or not included in the stages of the model. These aspects need to be considered and added to the model in order to modify it to apply in the Japanese context. (pp. 77–78)

One other consideration for this study was that unlike Bennett's initial quantitative study which used questions based on the categories of DMIS theory, Yamamoto's study asked open-ended questions in a qualitative interview model designed to avoid inadvertently leading interviewees to the researcher's conceptual categories.

M.J. Bennett (pers. comm., 2003) has commented on the results of Yamamoto's study and feels that the stage of minimization for cultures like Japan's may refer to cultural absolutes other than physical universalism and transcendent universalism, yet still follow the same developmental stages predicted by the model. This point of view has not been elaborated on in detail by Bennett in his writing and is therefore difficult to evaluate.

The DMIS and 'mixed states'

One important distinction made by Shaules (2004a) is that Bennett's categories are meant to categorize general levels of intercultural sensitivity – an overall generalization – and may be less useful for describing the individual reactions that sojourners have to particular experiences. According to Shaules, many sojourners have differing and contradictory reactions to their experiences, seeming to accept and/or adapt to a certain kind of cultural difference, but denigrate others at the same time. Shaules refers to this as a *mixed state* and questions the ability to describe intercultural sensitivity in terms of a single discrete stage of intercultural development. In this work we have seen this with David, the French man who went to the United States to learn to be an airline pilot. After living several years in the US he got a job back in France as a flight instructor. David's work brings him into contact with students from all over the world. While he is accepting and coolly analytic about certain differences among certain people, he is extremely judgmental and prejudiced about certain others.

On the one hand, David seems to recognize, at least intellectually, that cultural difference represents differing yet viable ways of viewing things or getting things done. For example, after describing the things that he does and does not like about American and French culture, he concludes by saying: 'I would take the best of both worlds. There's pros and cons on each side. There's no perfect system.' This would seem to indicate *acceptance* in Bennett's terms. This is echoed in other statements as well. When speaking about human relations with people, he says 'we don't feel the same things the same ... we're not exactly on the same page. For people that travel the world it's easier to understand that people can react "whoops"'. He seems to be saying that intercultural experiences make you anticipate cultural difference. Regarding his realization of the importance of cultural difference in human relations, he comments: ' ... it was like, this is weird. Culture is a big barrier to people's relationships. I'm not saying it can't work, but because if you want to make it work it's going to work.' So, apparently, he recognizes the importance of cultural difference and seems to accept the need to work around this.

In addition, based on his experience as a flight instructor, David articulates patterns of cultural difference that he has discovered using very neutral terminology – in almost the same way that intercultural researchers do. And while he may be guilty of overgeneralizing, he seems to see both sides of some cultural questions in neutral terms:

> One thing about the difference between the Latin culture and the English culture – in the English culture you have procedures and you follow them and they work all the time. If there is something that is not in the procedure and the system people tend not to make any decisions to make it work – to circumnavigate the problem – it would just block the system. On the Latin side, there would be some procedures but nobody will follow them, so of course everything that is out of the loop or unexpected or unforeseen will work because they will make it work.

David goes on to elaborate on the cultural differences he found in dealing with systems and procedures much in this vein, saying that if one has a cultural predisposition to accept rules and procedures (described by Trompenaars and Hampden-Turner (1998) as a *universalist* orientation, as opposed to a *particularist* orientation, which focuses more on the needs of a particular situation or context) there is the danger of overreliance on procedures and lack of creative thinking in a crisis situation. This is clearly an issue for commercial pilots like those David was training. On the other hand, someone with a more particularist approach is creative in a crisis situation but sometimes has problems created by *too much* improvisation and ignoring rules that should be followed.

If we use Bennett's terminology to describe David's interpretation of his experience, we might use the terms 'acceptance' or 'adaptation' to show that David has realized the validity of cultural variation in terms of decision making. Yet Bennett's terminology is meant to describe an overall state, not a particular reaction. In fact, further discussion with David reveals that he also makes highly ethnocentric statements about cultural difference when talking about people from other cultural communities. For example, when talking about Asian pilots, a very different picture emerges:

David: I can feel the difference when I'm training other-culture pilots. I used to train a lot of eastern-country [Asian] pilots ... [refers to having trained Chinese] Never fly with those people. They just don't understand anything, not even what can hurt. I mean if you fly into terrain it's gonna hurt! They don't get it, they don't understand it. It's just like, they have no clue what can happen.

Interviewer: Why is that?

David: Indoctrination. ... they have no survival instinct – from what I felt in the training.

The degree to which David's varying reactions to his intercultural experiences is typical, points to a difficulty with the DMIS. The DMIS posits that the ability to conceptualize cultural difference as a viable alternative worldview defines intercultural sensitivity. Seen in these terms, David's mixed state is more than simply a question of liking or disliking certain cultural characteristics. It is David's conceptualization of cultural difference itself that is in question. Does he accept alternative cultural realities or not? The DMIS presupposes that learners' cognitive ability to conceptualize cultural difference clusters around a particular point on a singular linear axis of intercultural sensitivity. This may be true in a general sense, but Bennett's model does not easily give us the ability to describe someone, such as David, who has mixed reactions to cultural difference. This does not necessarily mean that the fundamental premise of the DMIS

– that cultural empathy can be used to measure intercultural sensitivity –
is wrong, it simply implies that an individual's particular reactions to the
demands of intercultural learning may not be adequately described using
Bennett's linear set of labels. Without discarding the premise that construal
of difference is an important indicator of one's overall level of intercultural
sensitivity, the experiences of the participants interviewed for this work
seem better modeled using concepts which allow for contradictory and
complex reactions to intercultural experiences.

Intercultural sensitivity and deep culture

One question raised by Bennett's conceptualization of intercultural
sensitivity relates to how the depth of a cultural experience affects the
ability to gain intercultural sensitivity. Can a tourist learn to be ethnorelative by passing through the predicted stages of DMIS in spite of a relatively superficial intercultural experience? M.J. Bennett (1993) does not
address this question in detail, but implies that someone with limited
experience living abroad could conceivably reach the *acceptance* level of
intercultural sensitivity. According to Bennett, the nature of cultural
empathy is such that it does not depend on the depth of the experience.
From the point of deep culture, however, it would seem that unless one
has confronted more implicit cultural differences, it would be difficult for
sojourners to even discover the deeper elements of cultural difference.
How can something that hasn't been discovered yet be accepted?

The experiences of the sojourners interviewed for this work suggest an
alternative to Bennett's discrete-stage linear view of cultural learning. It
seems that not only do cultural learners develop views of reality that are
progressively more capable of conceptualizing difference (cultural sensitivity), but that this process also entails an increasingly *deep* sensitivity –
that which corresponds to the more hidden elements of intercultural experience. This view rests on the premise that one can only accept or adapt to
the degree of cultural difference that one has experienced. A tourist may
accept the cultural difference they find, but this does not mean that they
would continue to accept the deeper elements of cultural difference if they
stayed longer. Seen in this way, intercultural sensitivity, rather than developing along a single axis, develops both in terms of the degree to which
difference is accepted and adapted to, and the depth of the experiences.
This can be represented visually in the way described in Diagram 6.1.

We can maintain Bennett's definition of intercultural sensitivity as entailing
the increasing recognition of difference as a viable alternative construction
of reality. This is represented by the horizontal axis. The experiences of

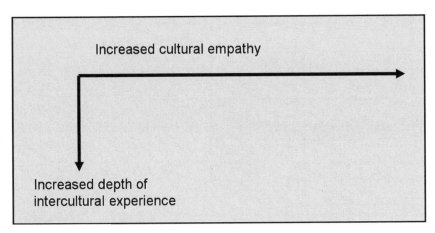

Increased cultural empathy

Increased depth of
intercultural experience

Diagram 6.1

sojourners indicate, however, that explicit levels of cultural difference are relatively easier to accept than deeper ones. After all, it is not generally food or architecture or clothing that creates prejudice or negative judgments. Deeper cultural difference such as differing values, norms and underlying belief systems are not so easily integrated into one's worldview.

As mentioned earlier, Shaules (2004a) maintains that an individual's reaction to the demands of intercultural environments can be described using the terms *resistance, acceptance* and *adaptation*. These three reactions were said to involve the degree to which the adaptive demands of the new environment are allowed to affect the internal state of the sojourner. *Resistance* implies a rejection or denigration of difference, *acceptance* implies a validation of difference without necessarily changing oneself, and *adaptation* implies a change taking place inside the sojourner in reaction to the demands of the intercultural environment. Adding these three reactions to the above diagram of intercultural learning, we can model a variety of reactions to the sojourner's intercultural environment.

This model makes it easier to understand the reaction of someone who might quip: 'I love France. It is just the French I can't stand.' Presumably, 'France' for this person is the food, the wine, the monuments, etc. – all highly explicit; and 'the French' refers to attitudes, values, communication styles etc. – more implicit. This person, therefore, has achieved only a 'shallow' acceptance of cultural difference and this statement represents a mixed state of cultural empathy. This can be shown as in Diagram 6.2.

In this diagram, the statement 'I love France' represents the fact that this sojourner has adapted to (indeed likes) some explicit elements of his intercultural experience – the more concrete elements of French food or

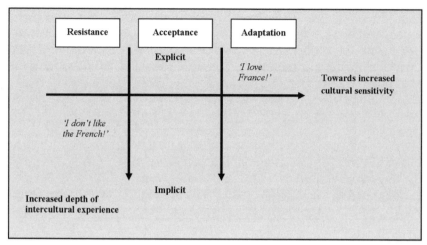

Diagram 6.2

fashion. This is an adaptation to an explicit difference and is placed in the upper right hand corner of the diagram. The statement 'I don't like the French' on the other hand, represents the sojourner resisting the more implicit patterns found in France. This deeper resistance may not prevent the sojourner from adapting to surface elements of French cultural communities but may well prohibit a deeper progression towards intercultural sensitivity. This way of describing intercultural learning allows us to distinguish between the intercultural experiences of, say, a tourist, from those of a long-term resident abroad. The tourist may accept or adapt to cultural difference, but only at explicit levels such as enjoying the food or appreciating architecture. This also gives us a tool to view the relative depth of the experiences of different sojourners.

The view of cultural learning represented by the diagram above incorporates some important elements of the DMIS. In particular, it accepts Bennett's fundamental assumption that an increased ability to construe cultural difference lies at the core of the intercultural learning process. In addition, it sees intercultural learning as developmental with sojourners having the potential to achieve higher levels of intercultural sensitivity over time. It also shares the assumption that sojourners may not themselves be aware of their own level of intercultural sensitivity and that intercultural learning is a process which takes place independently of sojourners' opinion of their own intercultural learning. Some of the terminology, too, seems similar, with this work using the terms *acceptance* and *adaptation* as does Bennett. The intercultural learning process as conceptualized in this work is built on the fundamental insights of Bennett's phenomenological approach.

Despite all of this, there are important distinctions between the intercultural learning model presented here and the DMIS. Most importantly, these two models are attempting to describe fundamentally different aspects of the intercultural experience. While the DMIS is attempting to define overall stages of intercultural sensitivity, this work attempts to describe the way in which one's reactions to adaptive demands encourage (or don't) the development of intercultural sensitivity. Bennett's model describes where the sojourner is along the road to an overall intercultural sensitivity, while this work tries to describe the experiential engine that drives that learning. In this way, the DMIS has a much great emphasis on defining discrete stages of learning – a sojourner is thought of as being at *minimization* or *acceptance*. This is not a reference to the reaction to a specific experience but rather an overall progress report. Because this work attempts to model intercultural learners' reactions to particular adaptive demands, it allows for reactions that are contradictory. In this model, a sojourner may adapt to one element of his or her experience while resisting another.

As we have seen, Bennett has developed a psychometric instrument, the IDI, which intends to measure an individual's overall level of intercultural sensitivity. The *deep culture model* presented in this book seems less suited for this sort of intercultural 'report card'. It is intended more to allow sojourners and educators to describe intercultural experiences in neutral terms – such as *resistance* (as opposed to *defense*). The assumption behind this choice of words is that intercultural education needs terminology that is not evaluative, which a single linear model like Bennett's might be perceived as being. While Bennett's lower stages of *denial*, *defense* and *minimization* are seen as less desirable stages of intercultural sensitivity, the *deep culture model* assumes that all reactions to adaptive demands, *resistance*, *acceptance* and *adaptation* are normal parts of the intercultural process.

The terminology of these two models, while sometimes similar, has important differences. While both models refer to *acceptance* and *adaptation*, the DMIS assumes that these are discrete stages of intercultural learning. A person who is at the *adaptation* stage is expected to exhibit certain cognitive characteristics related to their stage of development. In the present model, the meaning of *adaptation* is much simpler. It implies only that one has allowed oneself to change in some way due to an adaptive demand. As will be explicated more fully in the chapters to come, this may or may not imply a high level of intercultural sensitivity. *Adaptation* to explicit cultural difference, such as different food, may not lead to much increased intercultural sensitivity. In addition, one may adapt (change surface behavior, for example) while at the same time resisting deeper cultural differences. This mixed state could even be considered psychologically unhealthy. In this way, *resistance, acceptance* and *adaptation*, as described in this model, are simple descriptors and don't indicate an overall level of intercultural sensitivity.

Diagramming Intercultural Learning

As stated above, the DMIS attempts to describe an overall state of intercultural sensitivity, while the model presented in this book attempts to describe the ongoing process of reacting to adaptive demands. This gives us a means to visualize differing depths of intercultural experiences. For example, Jack seems to have avoided deeper contact with Japanese and is focused on the most explicit elements of cultural difference. Speaking of whether adjusting to life in Japan was difficult, he says:

No. ...Once I got here and I was set up it wasn't too bad ... Japan is predictable. Lost of times that's a good thing. I know my train's going to come on time. I know I'm going to get good service. I was in the States a few weeks ago and some of the people behind the counter were pathetic.

Naturally Jack recognizes obvious cultural difference and seems to be relatively accepting of it. He sees both a positive and negative side to Japanese politeness, for example, mentioning the good service above, but also saying:

The Japanese ability to be patient has rubbed off on me. ... They are attuned to other people's feeling, but a lot of times they limit themselves too by being too concerned with what other people think, and so they don't express themselves or do what they really want, 'cause they are too worried about how other people view them.

Jack expresses acceptance of cultural experiences with Japanese and satisfaction with his life in Japan. But one also gets the impression that Jack, despite having spent 14 years in Japan, is accepting cultural difference only at the most explicit levels. His ambivalence towards Japanese values is evident in how he pairs his positive statements about Japanese cultural values with negative ones. For example, he says 'The Japanese ability to be patient has rubbed off on me' and 'They are attuned to other people's feelings' but then goes on to make negative comments which mirror his positive comments: 'A lot of times they limit themselves too, by being too concerned with what other people think' and 'they don't express themselves or do what they really want' (see Table 6.2).

Table 6.2

Positive	Negative
'The Japanese ability to be patient has rubbed off on me'	'[T]hey don't express themselves or do what they really want'.
'They are attuned to other people's feelings'	'A lot of times they limit themselves too, by being too concerned with what other people think'

We can see that Jack is talking about the same qualities but is expressing a fundamental ambivalence produced by his inability to see cultural difference as neither good nor bad, simply another valid alternative. Jack seems to be stuck by a need to pass ethnocentric judgment.

As mentioned earlier, he seems to avoid deeper engagements with Japanese and states clearly that he is not interested in going any deeper than he already has.

> I have the feeling that it's not really possible [to adapt to Japanese culture], so I haven't really tried. ...Japanese society as a whole will never fully accept me. There's a sense that there's a barrier there. I didn't feel, it wasn't even worth trying to break that barrier down. I'm happy on this side. If the culture was accepting and open, and not this 'us vs. the outsider', then I'd be more apt to get closer to them, because I'd feel wanted.

Intellectually Jack accepts difference, yet chooses not to engage more deeply. Compare this to Adele. As we have seen, she has overwhelmingly negative things to say about her experiences:

> And here people look at you semi-suspicious. Women look at me and look the other way, and men look at me in this skuzzy scary-monster way ... I'm dedicating my life to this country but as I walk thought the streets I think, 'Why here?' And I don't share the value system that I

see here. In the States there's an opposing faction, but in the streets in Japan I'm overwhelmed by all the bad 'isms' of modernization. I don't like the young people, their self-centeredness ... I never thought it was a healthy society to be a part of. I'm not a group person in general. ... I've come to realize that this current modern Japan ... I don't like, I don't like the neolism, the selfishness of young kids. Yesterday I was walking [at university] and there were four individuals all talking on their cell phones at the same time. That represents what I can't stand about here. There are some things that are easier now, but unfortunately the things that make living here easier, represent Japan losing its culture. I wonder how long it will be until you have to travel to the ends of the earth to see Japanese architecture.

It is not clear precisely what Adele is referring to when talking about Japan 'losing its culture' but it seems more related to the explicit, artistic elements of Japanese cultural phenomena. As for the implicit elements, she has only bad things to say. In spite of this, she has learned Japanese, gives presentations in Japanese at academic meetings and has Japanese friends that she speaks to only in Japanese (though she expresses great frustration with these relationships). Either as a product or as a cause of her frustration, Adele seems to resist both the more explicit elements of her experience (the Japan's 'loss' of culture) and her disagreement with Japanese values (Diagram 6.3).

Diagram 6.3 shows how we can represent the intercultural learning process of both Jack and Adele. Adele has adapted to the challenge of learning to speak Japanese. She has not, however, fundamentally accepted Japanese values and worldview as valid. Thus, in terms of both adaptation and resistance, Adele's intercultural experiences are deeper than Jack's. Unfortunately, forcing herself to learn the language spoken by people whose values she cannot accept has been very difficult for her. The cognitive dissonance of both *adapting* and *resisting* at the same time has led Adele to be quite bitter about her experience. Jack, on the other hand, has never adapted at a deeper level to any of the demands of living in Japan. In this way, he can take advantage of the fact that trains run on time and that he gets good service without troubling himself to change at the deeper levels of himself that would be required to learn more Japanese, form more relationships with Japanese or integrate more fully into Japanese society. Having said this, Jack seems to exist in a sort of happy isolation. His experience has been shallower than Adele's, but perhaps psychologically easier.

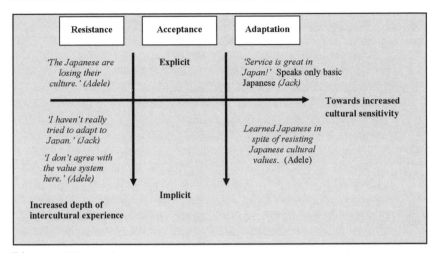

Diagram 6.3

The discussion of intercultural learning up to this point has introduced a number of ideas meant to make understanding the differing depths of intercultural experiences more understandable. These ideas have been visualized, at the end of this chapter, in terms of a diagram of intercultural learning that incorporates the concept of *depth* into the intercultural experiences. We have seen some examples of how this can be used to model the learning processes of particular sojourners. The ideas that went into this conceptualization, however, have been introduced piecemeal over five chapters and have not been integrated into a clearly delineated learning model. Starting from the next chapter, those ideas will be synthesized more completely in order to give a clearer idea of how the various insights examined up until now can be formed into an overall view of intercultural learning.

Part 2
A Model of Cultural Learning

Chapter 7
The Deep Culture Model

Even if I felt some trouble, I thought: 'Well, that's American culture.'
... [But] when I had the feeling that Americans were selfish, I had
trouble knowing whether that was something related to Americans in
general, or that person in particular. It was hard to tell what was
cultural and what was personal
Rieko

The Deep Culture Model of Cultural Learning

Previous chapters have outlined the theoretical background of current models of intercultural learning with a particular focus on *deep culture learning* experiences. This chapter will synthesize these ideas into a new model of intercultural learning. Because of its emphasis on how intercultural learners react to the implicit adaptive demands of longer sojourns, it will be referred to as the *Deep Culture Model* of intercultural learning. This model is phenomenological and focuses on cultural learning as an ongoing process of responding to the adaptive demands of a new cultural environment. A general overview of the model will be given in this chapter with subsequent chapters looking in more detail at particular elements of the intercultural learning experience.

In the quote above, Rieko gives us a snapshot of the intercultural learning process. She finds herself in a new cultural environment – university study in the United States – and faces adaptive demands in her new environment. She must learn a new language, form relationships in a new way, communicate in a new way and generally make sense of her experiences. At times, she has trouble telling what is cultural and what is personal, i.e. she's not sure how Americans would interpret particular behavior. In order for her to understand she has to come to an understanding of how behavior is perceived by Americans. That requires an ongoing interaction with her new social environment in order to enter more deeply into the perceptual world of her hosts. This ongoing interaction with an environment and our reactions to the adaptive demands of *cultural difference* are at the center of the process of cultural learning, defined as an *ongoing process of responding to the adaptive demands of a new cultural environment.*

Definition of terms

Culture can be conceived of in many different ways. For the purposes of this model it is defined in a way which emphasizes the shared frameworks of meanings that sojourners must learn about as they deal with adaptive demands. Culture is *the shared products and meanings which act as the interactive frameworks in a given community*. *Products* refer to the objective output and visible elements of a community. They may include things such as food, music, churches and architecture but also cosmologies, language and so on. These products are not seen as static but rather evolve in conjunction with the ongoing changes and development of the community. Products are said to be 'objective' because they have an existence that can be demonstrated in a way that can be observed by all. This doesn't mean that these products won't be interpreted differently but that they exist independently of any individual interpretation of them. Products may be physical (food) or conceptual (cosmology) or behavioral (language and ceremony) but in all cases they exist in reified form and can be subject to explicit analysis. Food can be tasted, cosmologies are written down or described explicitly, language is reified into dictionaries and grammars, and ceremonies are defined and prescribed.

Meanings refer to the shared sense of how products are interpreted. This includes, most obviously, the way that words are used, the importance of certain objects, the meaning of ceremonies, ideals and so on. This also includes relatively stable patterns of meanings used to interpret behavior, such as expectations about how to greet people or what kinds of behavior are considered formal or informal. Behavior is interpreted contextually but that doesn't mean that behavior is interpreted arbitrarily. There are layers upon layers of contextual frameworks that people use to interpret the meanings of given behaviors, objects and concepts. A crucifix that is used as part of a Catholic Mass may be interpreted differently than one that is used as part of an avant-garde work of art, and individuals may choose one interpretation over another, but the frameworks that are used to create meaningful interaction are based on a repertory of shared meaning that forms the fabric of interaction.

Individual variation in a cultural community is seen as an emphasis on one particular interpretation over another. Thus, while one person may see a sports car as a sign of success, another may see it as a waste of natural resources. These competing interpretations do not imply that the individuals who make these interpretations do not share the same cultural frameworks, but that they emphasize certain meanings over others. Both share the more concrete concepts of waste, success, nature and so on, but emphasize and prioritize them differently. Values are seen as a shared sense of which meanings should be used to interpret behavior. A shared emphasis on community, for example, implies an overall orientation towards the multiple frameworks of meaning: cooperation, mutual support, a feeling of in-group, etc.

Meanings are seen as existing at different levels of abstraction, or *depth*. Depth refers to the extent to which meaning is limited to a single, explicit interpretation. The meanings of single words which refer to physical objects, for example, are highly explicit and thus provide relatively little room for individual interpretation. More abstract or *deeper* meanings, on the other hand, require contextual interpretation that is abstracted over a wider range of situations. Whether a piece of fruit is an 'apple' or not can be examined with little difference in interpretation. The deeper concept of 'justice' on the other hand, must be given meaning in relation to other meanings and patterns of meanings. A particular product can have both concrete and deep meanings. A flag can be both a piece of cloth and a symbol of national pride. Because more abstract levels of meaning require a great deal of contextual interpretation, and call upon a large number of other meanings in order to have significance, there is potentially significant disagreement within any given cultural community over deeper meanings.

Despite this possibility for disagreement, cultural communities share common meanings which act as frameworks for interaction. When someone asks 'Are you a sports fan?', the shared understanding of which activities constitute sports (how about billiards?) or expectations about the level of interest which constitutes being a 'fan' (does watching a match on television occasionally qualify one as a 'fan') are an underlying framework which allows the question to have meaning. In this way, the simplest of interactions are often built upon many layers of unspoken assumptions and shared frames of references. Every individual prioritizes their meanings in their own way and thus, even in very tight-knit communities, different individuals will have differing views of a particular phenomenon. But it is the shared frameworks that allow that individual to justify or defend his or her particular point of view when communicating with those who share frameworks of meaning.

Cultural difference refers to the ways in which a sojourner's knowledge of his or her environment is inadequate in systematic ways – that is to say, sojourners must deal with not only new facts but also new systems of meaning. They must learn not only 'things' but also 'how things work' and 'what things mean'. Cultural difference is experienced as incompetence, since there is a gap between a sojourner's internal competencies and the demands of their environment. As sojourners (hopefully) learn new systems of meaning, their new environment becomes more predictable and they develop a higher functional fitness in relationship to their environment. At the most explicit level, for example, a tourist who learns how to use the subway system undergoes a process of cultural learning. Once these systems are understood and internalized a traveler can function more freely and can more fully express their individual predilections. Concrete demands of intercultural learning such as these are perhaps not easy but they are at least easily defined. Learning the subway system can be done consciously and in a relatively predictable way. Guide books are designed to help precisely with this kind of cultural learning. The more subtle and difficult elements of intercultural learning, however, exist at the hidden level of values, norms, implicit beliefs and assumptions. Cultural differences at this *deep culture* level are considered to be the most fundamental challenge of intercultural learning.

Intercultural Success – Intercultural Failure

Successful intercultural learning is marked by an increase of *cognitive empathy*, which is defined as an *increased ability to differentiate cultural phenomena*. *Differentiation* refers to the ways in which one creates meaning from the perceptual phenomena in one's environment (M.J. Bennett, 1993). One's worldview becomes more differentiated by increasing the perceptual categories used to make sense of one's experiences. This allows for the construction of varying yet valid interpretations for a given phenomenon. This is experienced in a number of ways. Foremost, sojourners gain empathy, the ability to view the world using new perceptual frameworks. There is also a cognitive ability to examine the cultural differences encountered on the meta-level – that is to say, it is understood that one's point of view is a product of one's experience. This overall ability allows a sojourner to more easily enter into the worldview of others even if the details of that worldview are not known.

Cognitive empathy does not imply an absence of value judgments, personal values or a sense of right and wrong. It does imply, however, that value judgments are relative rather than absolute. Relative judgments allow for the possibility that the meaning of a given phenomenon could reasonably be construed differently. This does not imply that 'anything goes' since the ability to construe varying interpretations of a phenomenon does not imply that one isn't responsible for the affects of one's actions on others. The relativism implied by cultural learning is not a moral relativism but a cognitive relativism. The distinction between these two can be seen, for example, in the ability to hate racism without hating racists. Moral relativism might excuse a racist, while cognitive relativism recognizes that a racist's viewpoint is cogent from the point of view of the racist. Cognitive relativism recognizes that one's own view, as well as those of other people, is built upon one's experiences and thus potentially changeable.

Intercultural contact sometimes fails. Intercultural failure is defined as a *decrease in cognitive empathy in response to adaptive demands*. This involves a sojourner's worldview to become less differentiated relative to his or her experience. When a learner is faced with a competing interpretation for a particular phenomenon the existing interpretation is given primacy while a competing interpretation is ignored or denigrated. Relative to the sojourners total cultural experience, there has been a decrease in the perceptual categories used to differentiate phenomena. It is assumed that all sojourners have some capacity to accept cultural difference as valid and that all sojourners have limits to their ability to accept difference. In that sense, intercultural learning is never a failure or a success in an absolute sense. Everyone learns from their intercultural experiences and there is no end to the intercultural learning process. However, ongoing experiences with intercultural difference generally push sojourners either more towards an expanded perceptual view or more towards a defensive retrenching of existing views.

From the sojourner's point of view, intercultural failure is not necessarily perceived as something bad. It is often experienced as a reaffirmation of what they had previously understood of the world. When Adele says that what she learned made her glad that she was born in the United States, she is finding reaffirmation of the American values that lead her, at least in part, to draw such negative conclusions about Japan. Of course, it isn't American values themselves that cause Adele to make these judgments; it is her inability to interpret Japanese cultural phenomena as valid. Adele's reactions are not an indictment of American culture but rather express her rejection of cultural difference using the implicit values she has gained growing up in the United States. Having said this, although rejecting cultural difference may reaffirm one's values, it creates a form of cognitive dissonance. It requires an artificial insistence on one's own cultural interpretations in the face of contact with people who don't subscribe to one's worldview.

Deep and Demanding Intercultural Experiences

The *depth* of an intercultural experience refers to *the degree to which an experience touches upon the implicit cultural differences of values, norms, implicit beliefs and hidden assumptions*. Few sojourners among those interviewed during the development of this model expressed difficulty adapting to the explicit elements of intercultural experience. When they did, such as when Philippe complained about the trash collection system in Germany, the complaints were focused on the symbolic elements of those cultural products. Another example is Adele's distaste for how Japanese young people use their cell phones – she felt that a love of technology reflected a loss of Japanese culture. More concrete problems, such as difficulty eating food, were barely mentioned and seemed not to be a primary cause of long-term adjustment difficulties. This reinforces Hall's (1959) view that dealing with differences in implicit culture is the primary challenge of intercultural learning. It seems that the greater the depth of an intercultural experience, the greater the potential for increased *cognitive empathy*.

This work has highlighted the ways in which the experiences of short-term travelers and longer-term expatriates are different. A short stay generally only allows for a kind of 'surface learning' based on experiencing the most explicit elements of culture which includes visiting temples, eating new food and visiting markets. Someone who spends a year traveling to 52 different countries will gain a lot of cultural knowledge but most of it will reflect the most visible elements of a society's values and lifestyles. A second person may spend that same year in a rural village of a foreign country learning a new language and participating in village life. The experience will be less varied but much deeper. That is not to say that one learns more by staying in the same place. Rather, what is learned is less obvious.

The distinction between these two types of learning highlights the difference between intercultural experiences that are *demanding, meaningful* and *deep*. A demanding intercultural experience is one that *requires a high degree of change and adjustment* on the part of a visitor, while a meaningful experience has *personal significance* for a sojourner. A deep intercultural experience is one that *involves adaptive demands at the deeper levels of implicit culture*. In this way, a college student from Spain who hitchhikes for six months in rural Africa may have an extremely demanding experience requiring great flexibility, curiosity and openness. Still, the experience probably won't involve learning a new language, developing close ongoing relationships with local residents or adapting to the deeper values of the communities visited. The experience may be very meaningful for that traveler but the elements that make these experiences meaningful are particular to the individual. Experiences need not be deep to be very meaningful. Having said that, demanding experiences and deep experiences tend to be meaningful if for no other reason that they involve responding to high levels of intercultural demands and facing any difficult challenge tends to be meaningful.

There is anecdotal evidence that American expatriates working in Britain have a surprisingly high rate of early return, that is, they give up and return home before completing their assignment. The demands that Americans face in terms of explicit cultural difference are not that great. Language, shopping, transportation and the routines of everyday life are not radically different from what Americans are used to. With a longer stay, and as Americans attempt to integrate into life in the UK, however, powerful implicit differences emerge such as differences in: communication styles, e.g. the value placed on openness versus discretion; social relations, e.g. the ways people make friends or socialize; and expectations related to hierarchy, e.g. the level of formality required at work. These deeper differences are deceptive because they are not apparent until one has tried to participate more fully in relationships and social expectations in the UK. In spite of the short cultural and linguistic distance between the US and the UK (relative to some other cultural settings), an American in this situation may have an extremely *deep* intercultural learning experience. The fact that deep change may be necessary to function effectively and the differences encountered are so abstract and difficult to define, it may create a much higher than expected level of stress.

The most challenging intercultural experiences are *demanding*, *meaningful* and *deep*. Many studies of culture shock have focused on Peace Corps volunteers because they often found themselves in cultural learning situations that required great change not only at the explicit level of food and daily life but at the deeper levels of language learning, relationships and values. Meeting these challenges often required an extreme personal transformation. As communication and transportation technology brings about greater interconnectedness and technological convergence, short-term stays in new cultural environments are becoming steadily less demanding. The demands of deeper intercultural experiences, however, are similar to what they have always been except that globalization has allowed for more long-term sojourners to avoid these challenges.

The Inevitability of Intercultural Learning

Responding to the adaptive demands of a new cultural environment is at the center of the intercultural learning process. Human experiential reality is so closely related to perceptual interaction with one's environment that responding to adaptive demands is an inevitable result of intercultural experiences. In some sojourners, of course, it seems that little has changed in their intercultural experiences. Among those interviewed for this work, Jack seemed one of the least touched by his years of living abroad. Yet Jack seems unchanged precisely because he responded to his intercultural demands by isolating himself. This is typical of one of the most common responses to adaptive demands: *resistance*. Resistance implies that the cultural difference which creates the adaptive demand is denigrated or ignored. Isolation prevents contact with more cultural difference than is necessary and helps to maintain an existing ethnocentric worldview. The refusal or inability to change constitutes a response to adaptive demands.

It is perhaps counterintuitive to think that an environment can demand change of a sojourner. After all, the sojourner has the freedom to act as she or he sees fit. Yet environments demand change on at least two levels. At the level of more concrete cultural phenomena there is a need for internal change to satisfy simple survival needs, e.g. use of the subway requires an understanding of how to buy tickets and which platform to stand on. What was easy back home – ordering in a restaurant or knowing which detergent to buy – becomes energy-consuming abroad. It is not the exotic elements of a cultural environment which are creating these demands but simply the act of everyday living. A particular sojourner's response to these explicit demands constitutes his or her intercultural learning. One may find the challenge of adapting to new foods and learning a new city exhilarating while another may complain constantly. These differences imply different responses to an unavoidable adaptive demand.

The second, more abstract demand that a new cultural environment places on us is perceptual. Humans live not only in the physical world but also a social world of human relations and meanings. Stevick (1980) refers to this phenomenon as an inborn human need to feel that one functions in a 'world of meaningful action'. He argues that language learners feel great stress due to limitations in their sense of having a viable social self in a foreign language. At a more fundamental level, our social self is upheld by participation in a *perceptual world* in which we share the frameworks of meaning with those around us. Accordingly, we need for the world to 'make sense' and when faced with inexplicable phenomena we need to find or create perceptual categories to fit these new phenomena into. *Ethnocentrism involves using pre-existing categories to judge phenomena while ethnorelativism involves the creation and integration of new perceptual categories.*

Use of the word 'judge' when referring to the processing of perceptual phenomena can be misleading, however, because it implies a conscious evaluation. The ongoing creation of meaning in our perceptual world is so automatic and powerful that we seldom notice it and have difficulty trying to control it. Castaneda (1972) refers to our *internal dialogue* – the sequence of thoughts, reactions and judgments that more or less continually runs through our conscious mind – as being the pillar which upholds our construction of meaning. Stopping this process, which Castaneda refers to as 'stopping the world', can completely upset our normal sense of perceptual reality. The Buddhist tradition of meditation also presupposes that one's thoughts serve largely to reinforce the centrality of the individual in the experience of reality. Recognizing that such fundamental elements of human perceptual processes are brought into play for intercultural learners can help us understand how powerful intercultural experiences can be. It also explains why some sojourners prefer to isolate themselves from deeper levels of cultural difference.

Cultural Learning Dilemmas and Orientations

The above view of cognition and perception implies that, in general, intercultural learners feel a need to keep oneself (and by extension one's habitual system of meaning) central to one's experience. According to Shaules (2006), the fact that a sojourner is interacting in a new environment, however, creates intercultural learning 'dilemmas' related to how best to deal with adaptive demands. He has identified varying 'orientations' towards cultural learning and developed a psychometric learning instrument to identify these orientations. These adaptive demands:

> have both an internal and an external element. Externally, a sojourner must function in an environment that is less predicable and less understood than usual. The need to take action in the face of the unknown is seen as a fundamental external dilemma of cultural learning. In addition ... sojourners face an internal dilemma – a loss of clear internal criteria for making decisions and anchoring one's identity. In effect, the conceptual universe that sojourners use to interact with their environment is less functional than usual and needs to be adjusted.

These external and internal adaptive demands are described in terms of dilemmas because in practice sojourners are caught between two contradictory choices: (1) externally, in the face of the unknown, should one take action sooner (and experiment) or later (and avoid risk) and (2) internally, should one first look outside of oneself (seeking external criteria) or inside oneself (clarifying one's internal criteria) when modifying one's conceptual universe?

[C]*hange vs. stability* (orientations) relate to how intercultural learners react to the uncertainty resulting from changes in their external environment. A change orientation is defined as *a preference for taking action as a way of dealing with the unknown*. Change strategies involve a 'trial and error' approach to intercultural learning – seeking out new experiences to help deal with uncertainty. *Stability* strategies are defined as *a preference for reducing uncertainty as a way of dealing with the unknown*. They involve a 'look before you leap' approach to intercultural learning – knowing where we stand and learning about our new environment helps to make it more predictable.

Inner-referenced thinking implies clear internal values and standards. Knowing oneself is the starting point for intercultural learning. *Outer-referenced* thinking, on the other hand, implies a recognition of the need to take into account the values and standards of others. Knowing others is the starting point for intercultural learning. (p. 71)

Shaules' description of intercultural learning dilemmas can shed light on what this model proposes to be the central dynamic in the cultural learning process: the conscious or unconscious choice to *resist*, *accept* or *adapt* to the adaptive demands found in a new cultural environment. *Resistance* implies an attempt to maintain internal standards as valid while denigrating or ignoring external standards. *Acceptance* implies recognizing that neither the internal nor external standards are primary – they are both valid and viable in their own right. *Adapting* to the demands of one's environment can either be constructive if it is done from the standpoint of *acceptance* or destructive if attempted while still resisting cultural difference. Acceptance of difference, then, allows the sojourner to resolve the internal versus external reference dilemma described above.

The Cultural Learning Process

Any model of intercultural learning must recognize that the goals that each individual brings to a sojourn are different – adventure, language learning, making money and so on – and involve both concrete things and more general 'life goals'. In this sense, the goals of cultural learning are highly personal as is the process through which each person accomplishes these goals. Each person must decide for him or herself if their experience abroad has been satisfactory. But the experiences of the sojourners interviewed for this work remind us that the process of responding to the adaptive demands of an intercultural experience takes places independently of all these other goals. A sojourner may be highly satisfied with his or her experience, yet have gained little *cognitive empathy*. And while the differing responses to the demands of an intercultural experience – *resistance, acceptance* and *adaptation* – are all 'normal', they are not all equal and they do not lead to equal outcomes.

This model supports the idea suggested by many intercultural educators that cultural learning is developmental (Adler, 1977; M.J. Bennett, 1986, 1993; Candlin, 1991; Goldstein & Smith, 1999; Hammer *et al.*, 2003; Hanvey, 1979; Kim, 2001; Tomalin & Stempleski, 1993; Ward *et al.*, 1998; Weaver, 1993). Though different researchers and educators describe this process in different terms, this model follows Bennett's premise that cultural learning progresses (or has the potential to progress) from ethnocentrism to ethnorelativism and increased *cognitive empathy*, following fairly predictable processes. This model also accepts Sparrow's (2000) assertion that this most often goes hand-in-hand with developing satisfying relationships with people in host communities. (Diagram 7.1)

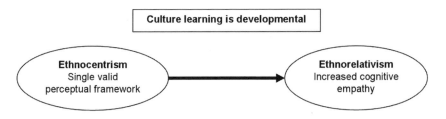

Diagram 7.1

Not everyone, however, progresses smoothly or in the same way towards ethnorelativism. The demands of intercultural experiences provoke different reactions in different sojourners. This work has characterized these reactions as: *resistance, acceptance*, and *adaptation*. In practice, most people have all three reactions – resisting some things, while accepting and adapting to others. For example, tourists often experience some of the more obvious elements of cultural difference like new foods, clothing, architecture, etc. The reaction to this may range from resistance, 'Raw fish? That's gross!' to acceptance, 'Well, sushi is okay, but I'm not really used to eating fish that isn't cooked.' to adaptation, 'I tried everything! You should see how good I am with chopsticks now!' Deeper elements of cultural difference – e.g. an expatriate business person

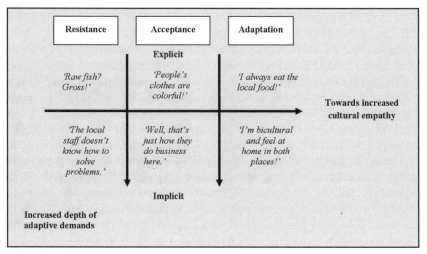

Diagram 7.2

working with local staff may encounter cultural difference in communication styles, values and worldviews – can also be resisted, accepted or adapted. It is not uncommon for sojourners to accept superficial elements even as they resist deeper ones: 'I love Korean culture but the people there are really pushy.' In the same way, it is possible to accept deep differences ('Well, that's just the way things are here.') without necessarily adapting to them.

As we have seen, this process of cultural learning can be represented visually in this way (see Diagram 7.2). The top three statements in Diagram 7.2 all represent reactions to explicit cultural demands such as might be heard from a tourist or short-term visitor. The first statement ('Raw fish? Gross!') represents *surface resistance* and involves denigration of explicit cultural difference implying that raw fish is not something that is normal to eat. The second statement, 'People's clothes are colorful', is a simple descriptive reaction and implies a recognition of explicit difference without any negative judgment attached. It doesn't imply that this person will change the way he or she dresses. The third statement, 'I always eat the local food', implies that this person has changed his or her eating behavior in response to the environment. This change, however, remains at the explicit level.

The bottom three statements in Diagram 7.2 represent reactions to deeper adaptive demands. The first one, about local staff not being able to solve problems, implies that the sojourner has had ongoing interactions with staff and that he or she hasn't been able to work within the problem-solving mindset of the host community. This inability to make things 'work' has led to a denigration of host community standards for how things get done. The second statement, 'Well, that's just how they do business here', implies that deeper cultural patterns have been discovered in the course of doing business and that they have been accepted uncritically – even if this person doesn't want to change how he or she does business. Finally, the statement 'I'm bicultural and feel at home in both places' implies that a sojourner has had deep, transformative reactions to cultural difference which have provoked change at deep levels of the self.

Based on what the participants in this study have said about their experiences, as well as the ideas that have informed this work, we will now look in more detail at some common patterns of cultural learning that have been identified. The next three chapters will focus individually on the primary reaction to intercultural demands – *resistance, acceptance* and *adaptation*. Subsequent chapters will look at some of the factors that seem to influence why individual sojourners respond so differently to similar intercultural experiences. They will also examine the question of whether it is possible to ever go 'beyond' cultural difference.

Chapter 8
Resistance to Change

> *I'm dedicating my life to this country, but as I walk thought the*
> *streets I think, why here?*
> Adele

Resistance

Resistance is one of the primary ways that sojourners may react to adaptive demands. *Resistance* is defined as an *unwillingness to change in response to the adaptive demands of a new cultural environment*. This doesn't mean that one doesn't change, but that if one does so it is done unwillingly. The need to eat with chopsticks, take off shoes before entering a residence, learn a new subway system – these are all explicit adaptive demands. At the level of explicit adaptive demands, someone who *resists* an intercultural experience feels that they shouldn't need to change their behavior – or at least not very much. It may seem like too much trouble to learn to use chopsticks or 'dirty' to eat with one's fingers. The subway may be avoided because it seems 'inefficient' and less convenient than the one back home. While these behavioral demands may create problems for some sojourners, the more important demands are perceptual. Sojourners must *make sense* of their experience and find explanations for their physical environment, the behavior of the people, and so on. The streets may seem dirty or clean, the people loud or quiet and the sojourner attempts to interpret these things. For these *interpretive demands, resistance* makes a sojourner feel that they already have the criteria necessary to judge what they see and hear. One's ignorance is not recognized and one's pre-existing standards are reinforced. The streets may be 'dirty' because there's no 'civic pride' or people may talk loudly because they are 'aggressive'.

It is possible to be in a new environment and be oblivious to cultural difference. M.J. Bennett (1993) refers to this overall state as *denial* and argues that it implies a simple lack of perceptual categories for cultural difference. Yet not noticing cultural difference may be due to contextual reasons as well. A business person traveling from country to country, going from hotel to hotel, meeting to meeting, may pass through different cultural communities without noticing much difference. Of course, most people recognize a great deal of cultural difference and this *recognition of difference* creates adaptive demands. The recognition of cultural difference, however, need not be conscious. Sojourners may feel vaguely threatened or uncomfortable with things they find in their new cultural environment. A French visitor to Japan recounted that seeing Japanese bow to each other left him feeling uneasy although he couldn't identify the cause. With time, he came to the conclusion that in France bowing tends to imply an uncomfortable or unjust level of servitude, an association with roots in the history of the French aristocracy and social values influenced by the French revolution. He felt uncomfortable seeing such frequent expressions of apparent 'servitude' and only later became aware that bowing for Japanese did not imply servitude in the way that he had initially thought. He had been influenced by his French cultural background without having been fully aware of it. The fact that he felt uncomfortable, however, implies that there was recognition of cultural difference at some level and thus a corresponding demand for change – at least in the sense that he reacted affectively to Japanese bowing.

From the sojourners point of view, *resistance* is experienced as a need to avoid, judge, denigrate, explain away or take offense to elements of their experience. This may involve something as simple as a criticism of the local food, or the conclusion that ugly buildings or dirty streets are somehow a reflection of some deficiency of the people who live there. At a more subtle level, it could involve feeling that the people in a new environment are somehow backwards, inefficient, unsophisticated, aggressive, immoral, subservient or unenlightened. *Resistance* can be at the root of prejudicial or racist attitudes as well, insofar as the difference felt in those groups is perceived as a threat.

Resistance versus dislike

Resistance involves not recognizing that a negative reaction is caused in part by one's own expectations rather than by the phenomenon itself. One's conclusion that a people are 'loud' comes from one's expectations about how people 'should be'. *Resistance* is more than simply a negative reaction to something one finds unpleasant. The food that one finds in a new environment can seem bizarre or hard to eat without necessarily making the sojourner critical of it. This could better be referred to as *dislike* – a negative reaction to difference that does not involve a negative value judgment. *Resistance*, on the other hand, involves an ethnocentric judgment, such as 'the bread here isn't nearly as good as that back home' or, 'you can't trust people there'. The difference between these two statements is not always obvious especially to sojourners themselves. *Dislike*, however, tends to provoke descriptive reactions – saying the way things are; while *resistance* provokes more critical reactions – expressing how things should be. That difference may be as subtle as feeling that (1) 'Many of the dishes were too spicy for me to eat' (descriptive) and (2) 'The food there is way too spicy' (critical – implying that the food is unreasonably spicy).

An intellectual commitment to respecting cultural difference does not preclude *resistance*. As we have seen, those who draw ethnocentric conclusions about their new environment often feel that they are simply 'reporting the facts' and usually don't see their reactions as involving denigration of difference. Linda, a British woman who lived in the US, is typical in telling her story about 'snobbish' Americans: 'Everyone said Americans are so open, it will be great, but ... they had such a snobbish attitude. It was unbelievable. I detest things like that.' When asked why she had come to this conclusion, she explains:

> It was a very closed environment ... [and] they just didn't like outsiders, especially the English. [I could tell] by the fact that no-one would speak to me. Even when we moved in, the one neighbor came with a bottle of wine, but after that I didn't meet anyone for nine months. Later, I decided to have a party together with that neighbor, and we invited everyone in the whole neighborhood, and they came, and they said 'Oh, I'm sorry, I should have come.'

One sign of the denigration that typifies resistance is the fact that Linda makes blanket statements about all of her neighbors. She doesn't speak about individuals but the whole community as 'snobbish'. Her conclusion that people had a special dislike of the English seems based on nothing more than the fact that her neighbors didn't seek her out in the way she would have liked. Interestingly, Linda herself admits that people's reactions to her were partly her responsibility:

> Some of it was my fault. There was a group of people that had coffee and I was supposed to go and do that with them, a kind of coffee klatch, but I hate that kind of thing. I hate having to forcibly go and meet people. It was partly my state of mind because I didn't really want to be there. Things got better after that, but I was still doing things I didn't want to do just to survive.

Here, Linda understands clearly that this community has a different type of social interaction than she would prefer – she doesn't like 'coffee klatches'. In the face of this demand she resists adapting to her new environment ('I hate having to forcibly go and meet people'). In the end, she seems to have adapted herself to some degree in order to be part of the community and admits that things improved. Still, her resistance is evident in her statement that she 'was still doing things I didn't want to do just to survive'. She didn't accept the need to change as valid.

Nowhere in Linda's account are there statements which relativize the neighbors' behavior. It is probably true, for example, that many small communities (as this was) have very close relationships between neighbors and that they are often not easy to gain entry into. The problem was not 'American snobbishness' but a natural condition of having moved into a small community. Her admission that she was part of the problem seems not to have allowed her to see her neighbors' behavior as valid. Linda wanted to have good relations with the neighbors but she didn't want to change in order to do so. Ultimately she did adapt to some degree but even her improved relations with her neighbors didn't mitigate her sense that they were 'snobbish' and that she had been unjustly treated.

Linda's negative reaction was largely transformed into denigration – she defines the problem as being the neighbors fault. For a more positive counter example, a strong negative reaction that did not engender denigration, we can revisit the case of Mayumi, the Japanese who found the stresses of being the wife of a Korean man in Korea extremely difficult. Her adaptive demands seem immeasurably more than Linda's as she was learning a new language (Korean) and had to deal with the strain of integrating herself into her husband's family life. Her frustration is palpable:

[T]here were subtle differences which were hard to accept, and I tried to be accommodating and then got frustrated and finally exploded at the end. [There were] very close family relationships, and I had to call my mother in law every day, and I was nervous talking to her in Korean without knowing what to say. My husband was working late and we had a lot of things we had to do with the family. In American I didn't really have to hide my Japanese-ness, but in Korea I felt I really shouldn't talk about Japan. Also, when I went to the US I could converse enough not to feel like a child, but in Korea I only knew the alphabet and to say hello. I also couldn't eat spicy food, and so my mother in law prepared food for me and my nephew, and the only thing I could do was take care of him.

Yet, despite this adaptive pressure and having 'exploded at the end', she never criticizes Korean culture or the expectations of her Korean family members. Indeed she says:

> My mother in law could come to my apartment unannounced. I left Korea a couple of times that I got stressed out. When I wasn't there my mother in law would go and clean up for me, making me feel like a failure when I returned. She even bleached the teapot. Of course she felt she was being kind, and I didn't take it as an offense, and I felt a bit angry at my husband for letting her do it. Don't get me wrong, I really love his parents. I don't think I could live with them, because of the differences in customs. *I have lots of complaints against their son but not them* [emphasis added].

What a difference between Linda's blaming of 'snobbish Americans' and Mayumi's having affection for her in-laws despite the stress of adapting to life with them. She relativizes her challenges by saying that the problem came from the 'differences in customs' but that she has no complaints against the parents themselves. We can see clearly that Mayumi may *dislike* the customs she needed to adapt to but she didn't denigrate them and fall into *resistance*.

Among sojourners interviewed for this work, the most typical strategy to deal with feelings of *resistance* seemed to be *avoidance* – isolating oneself from adaptive demands. *Avoidance* doesn't mean that sojourners don't spend time with people from the host community, it means they avoid putting themselves in situations in which they need to adapt themselves to the host community. We have seen Jack, of course, and his ability to live in an expatriate bubble in Tokyo. His relationships with Japanese are all in English (meaning they adapt to him, rather than the other way around) and he feels no interest in integrating further:

> Japanese society as a whole will never fully accept me. There's a sense that there's a barrier there. I didn't feel, it wasn't even worth trying to break that barrier down. I'm happy on this side. If the culture was accepting and open, and not this 'us versus the outsider', then I'd be more apt to get closer to them, because I'd feel wanted. I don't accept the fact that they are not accepting.

And while Jack is not nearly as critical as Linda, he seems to be more protected by his membership in an expatriate community. It is interesting to consider the possibility that Linda, an English woman in the United

States, faced deeper adaptive demands than Jack, an American living in Japan. Like Linda, Jack seems to want Japan to welcome him without him having to change. The fact that he accuses Japan of being a closed culture without ever having learned Japanese, shows the difficulty he has relativizing his experience. According to Jack, his isolation from Japanese society is the fault of Japanese, not his lack of adaptation. The inability to accept adaptive demands as legitimate is a sign of resistance.

Sojourners like Jack live primarily in an expatriate community and some report great satisfaction with their experiences. They are, in effect, limiting their experience to more superficial and often less demanding challenges. They are able to do this because their position in the host community brings with it the status and resources to allow them to hold themselves apart from the expectations of the host community. There is nothing inherently wrong with this approach but as the length of the sojourn increases isolation can lead to frustration and negative judgments. There are other sojourners, however, who seem to adapt readily to their environment and feel little resistance to the changes they make. They may be fascinated by the differences they find or even feel more at home in their new home.

Resistance and rapport

Some people who report little resistance to their new surroundings seem to feel a special *rapport* with their new environment. They may find that the expectations of the new environment somehow match their personality or values. This kind of rapport often leads to a positive intercultural experience and very little *resistance* to adaptive demands but it can also be a mixed blessing. In some cases, an initial feeling of rapport gives way to disillusionment as the deeper levels of cultural difference come into play. This happened with Andre, a Swiss who was enamored by Japanese culture, yet who became disillusioned and ended up returning to Switzerland and Adele, who studied Japanese literature and loved traditional Japanese culture, yet found little to relate to among the Japanese that she discovered in Japan. In this case, a rapport based on unrealistic images of another cultural community can bring about *resistance* later on.

Some people who feel little or no *resistance* in their new environment have deeply satisfying experiences in a new environment, sometimes with little desire to return to their cultural roots. Neil, a well-adjusted English teacher living in Japan, commented, 'I feel at home here'. This may come from a simple match between a person's personality and their new environment. Neil describes himself as being less 'aggressive' than many Americans and says that he was somewhat of a misfit in the rural town where he grew up. He feels at ease with the collective values and reserved communication style he finds in Japan. It is important to recognize, however, that sojourners who report these feelings about their environment may be sheltered from deeper levels of intercultural demands by an insulated status as foreigners. In Neil's case, if he was forced to live and work exclusively in Japanese, for example, rather than being an English teacher who is not expected to have a deep understanding of Japan, his reaction might change. *Rapport* is quite common and will be examined separately in Chapter 11.

Reversal

Though there weren't sojourners in this study who fell in this category, based on anecdotal evidence, there may be another disadvantage with avoiding all *resistance* in one's new environment. One danger is *reversal*, in which a sojourner feels such rapport for their new environment that they denigrate their original cultural environment. This can involve 'going native' and adopting the prejudices of the new cultural community or simply feeling that the new cultural community is better than the old. This has been described as a relatively common experience among Peace Corps volunteers who sometimes return to the United States decrying its materialist, selfish, capitalistic, shallow, etc. values and lifestyle (M.J. Bennett, 1986). Ultimately, *reversal* is a form of *resistance* since it involves denigrating cultural difference, although what's being denigrated is one's home cultural environment rather than one's host environment. The root cause is a lack of acceptance of the validity of a particular worldview. Reversal can be represented visually as shown in Diagram 8.1.

Surface Resistance

For newly arrived sojourners initial adaptive demands are often the simple result of being in a new physical environment. Someone used to the damp, quiet streets of an English country village may find themself in the hot, clanging bustle of the streets of Calcutta. It can be shocking to find just how different things are when abroad. An American traveling for the first time in Mexico was struck by the fact that among the different types of potato crisps in a bus station snack bar, none of them were familiar: rather than 'sour cream and onion' flavored crisps, for example, he found 'lime and chile' flavor. Some travelers are struck by the fact that MacDonald's menu the world over vary according to local tastes and countless travelers have been disappointed by ordering an item from a menu which doesn't match their expectations of the 'real thing' back home. Having to eat food

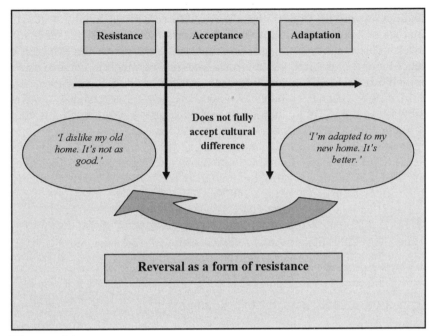

Diagram 8.1

that is different from what we expected is a significant demand for change. If we seek the familiar in a new cultural environment we may easily be disappointed.

The let-down of things not being what we want or expect does not, in and of itself, constitute *resistance. Surface resistance* involves passing negative judgments on these explicit parts of an intercultural experience. Noticing that the fish and chips served in a beach resort in Thailand differ from those at one's pub back home slips into *resistance* when the chips at home are used as the standard for the 'real thing'. Of course, there is no 'real thing'; people eat different foods in different places and it is only the fact that we have unconscious expectations about what constitutes normal which make us react this way. In a sense, if we seek the familiar in making our choices when abroad, we stand a much greater chance of being disappointed than if we seek the unfamiliar. We can judge unfamiliar food, for example, on the qualities that it has rather than the qualities that we expect.

Sometimes, *surface resistance* results from the 'inefficiency of the unfamiliar'. A Swiss who attempts to buy train tickets in a train station in

Beijing may find the train station chaotic. If he concludes that the system is 'inefficient' because things don't work in the way he is used to, he experiences a form of *surface resistance*. In fact, efficiency is in the eye of the beholder and those that understand a system generally find ways to use it to their advantage. This does not mean that hitchhiking, for instance, as a form of public transportation – as is done in Cuba – is as predictable as the subway system in Tokyo. It does mean that Cubans have evolved a system of public transport in keeping with their circumstances and that those who understand the system well can use it more effectively. Tourists and travelers are often not able to take advantage of local systems, not because of any absolute inefficiency, but because they are incompetent. Recognizing this mitigates the negative reactions that a Japanese traveler in Cuba might feel and leads a sojourner toward *acceptance*, rather than *resistance*. The Swiss traveler may realize that his inability to read the Chinese destination names above the ticket windows makes him, the traveler, inefficient. It doesn't mean that the system itself is inefficient – at least not for the Chinese as the system was created by and for them.

Explicit demands and symbolic significance

Perhaps the most challenging aspect of superficial intercultural contact is that explicit cultural products have symbolic significance. Philippe's experience with the trash collection system in Germany is a clear example of this. In Philippe's case the trash system bothered him not for what it *was*, but for what it *represented*. The actual demands of separating trash into separate categories and putting them out on different days was probably not a great burden in terms of time spent. Yet the need to change the way he dealt with his garbage offended Philippe at some deeper level. It is as though he took the need to separate garbage personally. This may be exacerbated by the fact that since Philippe may not have clearly understood the precise expectations, he needed to spend more time and energy than he was used to dealing with the issue of garbage. This impingement on his personal sense of competency may have made him react more strongly. It can be surprisingly difficult to simply 'do as the Romans do' and often sojourners react not only to the surface phenomenon but to the perceived significance of that phenomenon.

This can be seen when explicit phenomena represent deep differences in cultural values. A Swedish woman, accustomed to a society that makes relatively few social distinctions based on gender, may visit Saudi Arabia, a society that makes many social distinctions based on gender, and find gender roles unfair or offensive. The veils many women wear could represent an affront to deeply held values related to egalitarianism and gender equality. In this case, the adaptive demand she faces is not that she needs to wear a veil; it is the need to make sense of a society in which women wear veils and where there are strong divisions based on gender. It is a short step from the negative associations one may have to a particular phenomenon, to developing a powerful resistance. And it takes a strong commitment to set aside personal judgments to avoid this.

This is not a form of moral justification nor does it imply that one changes one's values. Rather, a sojourner who finds things in a new environment 'unfair' or 'immoral' may recognize that at least part of his or her reaction comes from cultural conditioning and not an absolute standard of good and bad. The Swedish sojourner could seek to understand how gender roles are experienced from the point of view of Saudis. This would contextualize Saudi cultural expectations and allow for a more nuanced view of Saudi gender roles. One British woman in Saudi Arabia was shocked when a Saudi woman, rather than seeing herself as a victim, expressed pity for her single British guest in her 30s, saying that it must be difficult not to have the support and care of a husband and male relatives. While the British visitor saw owning her own home, supporting herself and not being married as a sign of her independence, her Saudi host perceived this as a very isolated existence.

The experience of a conservative Muslim from Tunisia visiting the United States illustrates a similar dynamic in the opposite direction from the British visitor to Saudi Arabia. This traveler saw American society as self-evidently dysfunctional. Provocative (by his standards) clothing among women, combined with his knowledge of the divorce rate and the limited (by Tunisian standards) family life of Americans, convinced him that Americans had no respect for women or families and that many women seemed to have little respect for themselves. Like the Swedish woman in Saudi Arabia, if he returned to Tunisia without trying to learn how Americans view gender or families, his resistance could easily harden into a self-fulfilling set of negative judgments.

Negative reactions to cultural difference in deeply held values can be especially difficult to suspend judgment on because, as pointed out before, sojourners often don't recognize the cultural underpinnings of their reactions. The Tunisian man in the United States reports the 'facts' of life there – the divorce rate, the kind of clothes women wear, the number of children born to unmarried families – and draws self-evident conclusions. In the same way, the Swedish visitor to Saudi Arabia reports on institutional gender segregation, expectations about what constitutes appropriate attire, the fact that women are not permitted drivers licenses and also draws self-evident conclusions. These reactions are complicated by the fact that the ideals that these visitors use to justify their reactions are not, in and of themselves, ethnocentric. Americans agree that family life is important and some do criticize American 'immorality'. Saudis believe that respecting women is important and some do criticize gender segregation. The difference between an American who criticizes American immorality and a Saudi visitor who does so, however, is that the American better understands the full range of American values that lead to American behavior. Likewise, the Saudi who criticizes gender segregation in Saudi Arabia has a better understanding of the Saudi values that underlie those social practices. Our Swedish visitor may find Saudis that agree with her judgments about Saudi society. Yet simply finding someone to agree with one's judgments doesn't mean that one's criticisms are based on absolute truths.

These examples remind us that while an intercultural experience may be short or superficial the effects can be profound. A disadvantage of short sojourns is that one does not have the opportunity to explore more deeply the point of view of people in the host environment. Worse yet, deeply rooted judgments based on superficial experiences are often not recognized for what they are – intercultural experiences. The Swedish woman in Saudi Arabia and the Tunisian man in the United States risk returning home with – in some ways at least – less tolerance than before they visited, since their brief experience has confirmed that the other place was backward, unjust or immoral.

Deep Resistance

Interviews with sojourners suggests that *resistance* to explicit cultural difference that is *not* connected in significant ways to deeper cultural values are rarely the primary cause of stress for longer stays abroad. The food that we eat, the buildings we live in and the transportation systems that we use are different in obvious ways and expatriates soon gain competence in these areas. None of the expatriates who were interviewed for this book expressed serious adaptive trouble because of food or physical surroundings. Their longer stays, however, did bring them into contact with deeper adaptive demands and showed that implicit adaptation constitutes a much deeper challenge.

These sojourners provided evidence that staying longer in a new environment implies, but does not guarantee, a deeper intercultural experience. Life abroad is more convenient than ever and expatriates increasingly have the possibility to create a cocoon of familiarity in the midst of a new cultural world. This is particularly true of expatriate professionals working abroad. The accouterments of everyday life back home can often be found abroad and there may be little need to learn a foreign language when local staff already speaks English or another shared tongue. In spite of this, more prolonged contact and deeper relationships generally confront expatriates with cultural demands that they did not notice or felt only intuitively when they first arrived.

Deep resistance is characterized by an *absolute judgment* in which a group of people is found lacking based on a principle that the sojourner assumes to be universal, yet which is based on ethnocentric assumptions. Values like this are deceptive because while they appear to represent stable concepts, they often embody deeper assumptions about reality. One example given in the business world is of an American company attempting to introduce a system of pay based on performance in a Latin American subsidiary, arguing that it was 'fair' and 'motivating'. Local staff, however, complained that this was neither 'fair' nor 'motivating' since it implied that one had to compete with one's colleagues (which local staff felt distinctly unmotivating) and it wrongly assumed equality. One may work hard yet still not perform at the level of a more experienced or talented colleague.

The hidden assumptions that form the basis of deep resistance are often those that function at the deepest level of the self and which are least conducive to dispassionate analysis. Sojourners who are unable to accept that some of their deepest feelings and values represent a predictable cultural response rather than insight into some absolute reality, run the risk of stressful intercultural experiences. This can lead to cutting short an expatriate assignment, cynicism, resentment or deeply rooted prejudice. David, the Frenchman who as a flight instructor for commercial pilot's license worked with many Chinese students, found them impossible to teach. Communication difficulties and reactions which he found bizarre (e.g. insisting at great risk on following instructions rather than breaking procedure) led him to conclude that 'those people don't have any survival instinct', something which he explained by their cultural 'indoctrination'.

His use of the word 'indoctrination' gives a hint that he finds their behavior less than human. This is the biggest danger of deep resistance. When one dehumanizes people from other cultures they simply become objects to be dealt with and lose the normal consideration afforded to those we feel more of an affinity with. This doesn't imply that one is incompetent in dealing with members of the other culture. One can learn to predict behavior even while denigrating it. This could be referred to as the 'animal trainer' style of intercultural adaptation. One learns how to manage relations to get what one wants without ever accepting the fundamental equality of the people one is dealing with. Given the violence and conflict frequently engendered by cross-cultural contact it seems that this reaction may be less rare than one would hope. Transcending this response requires the willingness to 'bracket' or set aside one's response, attempting to discover the hidden assumptions that make something difficult or offensive. Acceptance of the validity of alternative views is the central requirement of this more constructive approach.

Resistance versus defense

M.J. Bennett (1993) uses the term *defense* to describe someone who denigrates cultural difference as a way of upholding their own ethnorelative viewpoint. Bennett's concept of *defense*, however, can be contrasted with this model's conceptualization of *resistance* in important ways. An obvious difference is that these terms are attempting to describe different things. *Defense* describes a stage of intercultural development that is passed through on the way to greater intercultural sensitivity. In Bennett's view, once one has passed the state of *defense* into the less ethnocentric stages of *minimization* and *adaptation*, one will presumably no longer denigrate cultural difference. This represents a fundamental shift in one's development of intercultural sensitivity and implies that one has gone beyond the need to make ethnocentric judgments to uphold one's worldview.

Resistance, on the other hand, describes the reaction to a particular intercultural experience and not an overall state of intercultural development. It is assumed that sojourners with different degrees of *intercultural sensitivity* (the term used by Bennett) may experience *resistance* to cultural difference. This assumption rests on the fundamental premise that intercultural learning takes place at varying *depths*. Thus, as an intercultural learner's experience brings him or her into contact with deeper adaptive demands, cultural difference may be *accepted* on one level and *resisted* on another. We have seen that David accepted cultural difference he found among European student pilots but made highly ethnocentric judgments about Asian student pilots. The ability of the *Deep Culture Model* to describe these mixed reactions is an important characteristic that distinguishes *resistance* from Bennett's concept of *defense*.

In addition, while the Bennett's Developmental Model of Intercultural Sensitivity (DMIS) assumes that it is possible to go beyond ethnocentric judgments once a certain degree of intercultural sensitivity is developed, the *Deep Culture Model* assumes that even the most developed interculturalists may not always be able to relativize their experiences. Even extensive experiences abroad may not bring one into contact with important deep elements of cultural difference and sojourners may find themselves resisting those elements in spite of past success in accepting difference. These contrasting views do not, however, represent an absolute contradiction. The DMIS allows for intercultural learners to have unresolved 'issues' (M.J. Bennett, pers. comm., 2003) in previous stages of intercultural development. This implies that even advanced intercultural learners may make ethnocentric judgments as they integrate new elements of cultural difference into their world view. The *Deep Culture Model* also assumes that intercultural learning is developmental and that those who have developed a high level of *cognitive empathy* will largely go beyond the need to defend their worldview with ethnocentric judgments.

One disadvantage to viewing intercultural learning in a linear fashion consisting of distinct stages, as the DMIS does, is that the lower stages of development can be seen as less desirable than higher stages. One's own level of intercultural development becomes an object of evaluation that can be compared with that of other people. In that sense at least, *defense* as a category could be seen as less neutral than *resistance* as a reaction to adaptive demands. In the same way, the term *resistance* can be used by interculturalists to describe their own reactions to their experiences without implying some overall failure of intercultural development.

Resistance, Ethnocentrism, Racism and Prejudice

Resistance must be distinguished from other words that are used to describe negative attitudes towards ethnic, racial or cultural difference. Racism has been defined as 'a belief that race is the primary determinant of human traits and capacities and that racial differences produce an inherent superiority of a particular race' and more broadly as 'racial prejudice or discrimination' (Merriam-Webster). Unlike ethnocentrism, which is the normal (though not desirable) tendency to judge one's experience from one's own cultural viewpoint, racism constitutes a learned attitude of superiority or denigration towards particular groups. This distinction is important because while racism may be minimized by not teaching it to children, ethnocentrism is such a built-in part of human perceptual reality that it is difficult or impossible to ever avoid completely. *Prejudice*, on the other hand, refers more generally to the irrational belief in the superiority of one thing over another and may or may not be inculcated. It implies an inclination to see something as better even when it is not. Prejudice may be a result of an inculcated attitude of superiority or of an ethnocentric reaction to an intercultural experience, or both.

In intercultural education, it is sometimes assumed that prejudicial attitudes can be avoided by emphasizing commonalities across cultures and ethnic groups. As mentioned previously, this approach is common in the field of Global Issues Education (Cates, 1997, 1999) which emphasizes going *beyond* cultural difference and the use of universal principles of shared humanity and global awareness (Shaules & Inoue, 2000). In this view, ethnocentrism is seen as a limited view that assumes the superiority of one's own cultural community over others. If defined in this way, *ethnocentrism* is very similar to *racism* or inculcated prejudice. Yet as we have seen from sojourners, judging things based on one's own cultural experience – ethnocentrism as used in this work – seems to be an unavoidable starting point for intercultural learning. It is, in the broadest sense, simply using one's learned perceptual framework to make sense of the world. This implies a sense of superiority only in the sense that one's own cultural experience is the standard used when judging cultural difference.

The concept of *resistance* implies that in order to go beyond ethnocentrism and avoid prejudice or racism, one must experience difference and learn to see it as valid. It is not enough to have a philosophical commitment to tolerance or an education which emphasizes acceptance of different cultural groups. Those things may help but ultimately it is the process of responding to adaptive demands that allows for the development of a more inclusive view of the ethnic or cultural difference. This process is complicated if, in addition to cultural differences which might provoke *resistance*, one has learned specific prejudicial attitudes about a particular group. In addition, since racial and ethnic difference is often marked by visible characteristics – the color of skin, type of clothing, language spoken and so on – it is normal to perceive other ethnic or racial groups as different. They are different though not inferior.

The ideology of racial inclusiveness can complicate cross-cultural understanding. To say that we shouldn't judge someone by the color of their skin reflects an important truth – judging things as inferior simply because they are visibly different is wrong. At the same time, to say that all humans are similar despite the color of their skin, or despite different beliefs or cultural practices, ignores the reality that cultural difference is real and needs to be understood. It cannot be overcome by saying that it doesn't exist. The ideology of inclusiveness can also lead us to confuse racial difference with ethnic or cultural difference. Many black Americans, for example, grow up in different cultural communities than white Americans with differing speech, values, communication styles and so on. There is a cultural divide between different ethnic and racial communities as well as a racial one. To say that we should overlook difference risks delegitimizing it. The experience of the sojourners we have looked at here shows us that culture's influence on how we view the world is deeply rooted and cannot be overcome with simple goodwill.

Resistance is perhaps the most natural reaction to an intercultural experience. Human evolutionary biology dictates that humans form cultural communities which cooperate in order to ensure the survival of the group. Deeply internalizing and feeling personally invested in those practices allows group members to coordinate their activities and protect the group from external threats. Ethnocentrism seems to have a great survival value and in that sense trying to gain greater intercultural empathy involves going against our evolutionary heritage. This is not an excuse for racism or a reason to accept xenophobia. On the contrary, recognizing the deep roots of resistance to demands for perceptual change can and should inform education and social policy and may help us not to underestimate the difficulties of pluralistic societies. The fact that ethnocentrism is natural doesn't imply that it is desirable. The fact that acceptance of cultural difference is desirable does not mean that it is a superior reaction in any absolute sense.

Chapter 9
Acceptance of Difference

When you go somewhere, the way that people do things is simply the
way people do things. ...Of course it doesn't mean that you don't [have
negative reactions] or that you like it, but you [accept it]. It also has to
do with the environment that you are used to, when things are
different it might create some internal tensions, but you adapt.
Paul

Acceptance

One common thread that runs though the sojourner experience is that acceptance of cultural difference is an essential ingredient of successful cultural learning. The way that Paul (above) puts it, is: 'When you go somewhere, the way that people do things is simply the way people do things.' This fundamentally neutral stance towards cultural difference – seeing other people's perceptual realities as valid – is the core of acceptance. As used in this model, acceptance is defined as *perceiving as valid alternative interpretations of the cultural phenomena that one experiences.* Stated as a definition or an ideal, acceptance of cultural difference is neither abstract nor difficult. But acceptance as an ideal and acceptance as a response to intercultural challenge are two different things. While a philosophical commitment to acceptance may be desirable it does not guarantee an accepting response to actual experiences. As we will see, while most sojourners accept many explicit elements of cultural difference, deeper acceptance is much rarer.

Acceptance implies an ability to *relativize* an experience – to look at the contextual reasons that influence one's experience of it. This often leads to a perceptual *decentering* as standards for judging a given phenomenon shifts away from oneself and moves to larger frames of reference. At the level of explicit difference one may recognize that, for example, a local dish seems unpleasant because one is not used to particular ingredients. One sees one's distaste in relative terms – as a result of a lack of familiarity – not absolute terms such as there being something wrong with the food itself. Different greetings or behavioral customs are seen as appropriate and valid (a natural product of the community that uses them) and not simply 'exotic' or 'quaint' (relative to what one is used to). Seeing greater modesty in public, a sojourner does not conclude that 'people are modest here like they used to be back home', but that differing standards result from the worldview of that community. One German sojourner reported that as he learned how to bargain in the marketplaces in Morocco, he began to see it as a valid way to express the relationships between buyer and seller rather than what he had initially thought – an attempt to take advantage of ignorant tourists.

While acceptance doesn't require that we change our own behavior to fit new standards of perception, it means that if we choose to do so, we will likely do so without feeling somehow untrue to ourselves. When we experience the perceptual frameworks of others as fundamentally valid, adapting our behavior to those frameworks becomes simply a question of choosing how best to communicate, build relationships or get things done. If we choose not to change our behavior it won't be because of a knee-jerk reaction to *resistance*. It will be a choice based on a fundamental knowledge that there are other reasonable standards at work. The fact that cultural standards are reasonable, of course, does not mean that all actions have equal merit.

For some, the idea of *acceptance* sounds suspiciously like a moral relativism in which 'anything is okay'. This reaction, while a misconception of *acceptance*, is understandable. In many parts of Western Europe and North America ethical choices are framed in terms of choosing one behavior over another, and adopting someone else's standards is the equivalent of losing one's moral compass. Yet *acceptance* does not involve the adoption of someone else's ethical standards. It involves increasing the number of conditions that must be kept in mind when making ethical choices. Ethical choices are made by gauging the effects or significance of one's actions. We don't, for example, say things that we know to be hurtful because we understand the consequences of our behavior. The ethical imperative of *acceptance* involves an attempt to understand the ethical standards of others without assuming that they are inherently inferior. Indeed, *acceptance* implies that we cannot fully understand the ethical standards of others if we start from the assumption that they are inferior. In this way, ethical behavior requires that we don't assume our standards to be superior.

In practice, this line can be difficult to draw. Sojourners sometimes find themselves unable to tell whether the behavior of a particular individual in the host community is reasonable *by the standards of the host community*. We have seen that Rieko, the Japanese exchange student in the US, was sometimes unsure about whether particular behaviors were normal for Americans or particular to that individual. In this sense, Rieko's suspension of judgment about particular behaviors can make her own value choices difficult. Yet this difficulty is caused primarily by an ignorance of host community standards, and as those standards are understood, one's choices become clearer. Yuko, a Japanese woman raised abroad, is an example of someone who had to deal with these issues. As someone raised in an international environment who had returned to Japan and started working for a Japanese company, she found the behavior expected of women at odds with her upbringing. She resolved this by first immersing herself in Japanese standards and then coming to her own conclusions on how to react to them:

> It's a give and take – being Japanese [when the] situation asks for it. Since my name is Japanese, I'm Japanese and [people at work] expect a very submissive person. The salespeople think they can get their way with me because I am young. But I can yell when I want to, or speak up when I want to, when the situation calls for it. But at the same time it doesn't mean that I don't know what the manners are. I just choose.

We can see that Yuko has not lost her moral compass. She has multiple frameworks for evaluating the appropriateness of behavior and makes choices accordingly. If anything, it has made it stronger by giving her a solid foundation for making choices.

Like versus acceptance

It is easier to accept as valid cultural difference that appeals to us personally. But we must make a distinction between difference that we *like* and that which we *accept*. It is possible to dislike some element of cultural difference, yet still accept it as a valid alternative for others. We may prefer, for example, to be told directly if someone is angry with us, yet understand that some people prefer communicating through a third party to avoid an awkward confrontation. We can also like an element of cultural difference without accepting it as valid. We can see this in Jack's description of his Japanese student attitudes towards him as a teacher. In Chapter 2 we saw that he refers to the 'adoration' that his students treat him with. He seems to like this but goes on to say that he's not sure how much of it is 'legit'. Although Jack *likes* the increased status he seems to enjoy as a teacher in Japan (as opposed to what he might expect to receive in the United States) he finds it rather suspect. It may be that some cynical or jaded expatriates do this because they *like* the increased status or money that results from living abroad without ever finding its source completely legitimate. This puts them in the awkward position of being dependent on a cultural community whose values or worldview they are denigrating.

Surface Acceptance

Nearly everyone, it would seem, is accepting of difference to some degree. Difference that is not threatening is easy to accept and recognize as valid. This is why exotic food rarely creates prejudice. Yet increased adaptive demands make acceptance more difficult. The food that tasted exotic the first week of a trip may have lost its appeal by the second week and this increasing degree of demand may push someone who initially reacted with *acceptance* to shift to *resistance*. As we have seen, the incompetence of sojourners themselves is often largely responsible for this stress. Bus service may be confusing because one doesn't know where to get off and restaurants may seem disorganized because one doesn't know how to place an order. The inability to use a local language may turn the smallest of daily tasks into a powerful demand for change. Dealing with adaptive demands can be extremely stressful but *acceptance* implies the ability to recognize and accept one's own ignorance in these situations without blaming one's environment for one's difficulty. It is easy to respond to stress by becoming critical, slipping into *resistance* in spite of the intellectual intention to enjoy the adventure of it all.

Surface acceptance with deep resistance

Among those sojourners interviewed for this work, many made statements that showed they accepted cultural difference at the surface or explicit level. Jack says that 'Japan is predictable. Lots of times that's a good thing. I know my train's going to come on time. I know I'm going to get good service.' Likewise, Steven describes getting settled in to life in Korea by saying that '[cultural adaptation] wasn't that big of a problem because once you get your lifestyle settled you don't need to be shopping every weekend'. It seems that many sojourners don't have serious problems getting settled in – they learn how to shop, navigate around their city or neighborhood, and take care of life tasks. This can give the impression that these sojourners are well adapted to their life abroad. Yet, there is a big difference between those who stop at this level of acceptance and those who go deeper.

Some sojourners continue to react to their intercultural experiences only with *surface acceptance* even though their sojourn may go on for years. This implies that in addition to this *surface acceptance* they are also engaged in a *deep resistance* of cultural difference. This could be described as a *long-term tourist* phenomenon. This may be managed by isolating oneself from deeper adaptive demands like hanging out with expatriates, speaking primarily to those who know one's language and relying on media from

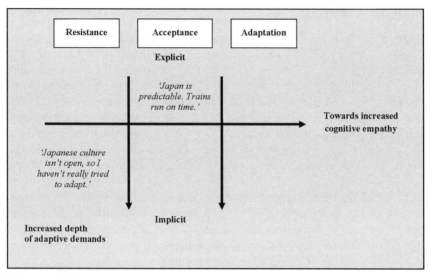

Diagram 9.1

back home. This means sojourners have been unwilling or unable to confront the deeper adaptive demands of viewing the host community from an insider's perspective. For their part, sojourners often don't recognize their own limitations. Jack, for example, hasn't understood that the Japanese language offers him a way to look at the world as Japanese do. When he is asked whether learning Japanese is an important element for understanding Japanese culture he says, 'I can learn about Japanese culture through English'.

We have said that isolating oneself from deeper adaptive demands is a form of *resistance*. Jack's *deep resistance* combined with *surface acceptance* can be diagrammed as shown in Diagram 9.1.

Jack's resistance is characterized as *deep resistance* because the cultural differences that he is isolating himself from are the deeper ones of values, communication styles, and so on. He has not fundamentally accepted the Japanese worldview which creates these deeper cultural elements as valid.

Minimization versus mixed states

M.J. Bennett (1993) refers to the stage of intercultural learning of someone who recognizes that cultural difference exists, yet who downplays its significance as *minimization*. According to this view, while significant difference may be perceived, it is interpreted as being less important than principles which are thought to serve as a universal measure of the human experience.

Bennett uses the example of the religious belief that 'we are all children of the same God' or the idea in biology that all humans are subject to the same drives and instincts. These 'superordinate categories' (Bennett's term) invalidate the importance of cultural difference. We have seen this with the Australian students who found the French 'inefficient', yet who failed to recognize that the idea of 'efficiency' was not a universal quality beyond cultural influence.

Using the present model, it would be possible to characterize this kind of reaction to adaptive demands as *surface acceptance* combined with *deep resistance*. Indeed, this is how Jack's intercultural learning has been illustrated in Diagram 9.1. As we have seen in Chapter 6, a reaction in which certain elements of an intercultural experience are accepted or adapted to and others are resisted can be referred to as a *mixed state*. In Jack's case, this involves a *surface acceptance* with *deep resistance*. In the case of the Australian students, it seems that there was acceptance or adaptation to many elements, yet a deep resistance to certain others. In the case of David, the pilot instructor, he seemed to have a fairly deep acceptance of cultural differences he found in Europe but was strongly resistant to those he found among his Chinese students. It seems fairly clear that when reacting to particular adaptive demands, sojourners manage to relativize certain elements of their experiences even as they fail with others.

Intellectual acceptance versus deep acceptance

Having a mixed reaction with *surface acceptance* and *deep resistance* does not preclude, however, a sojourner from having a sophisticated intellectual understanding of the society that they are living in. Steven, for example, talks about the need for intellectual knowledge in order to understand Korean culture:

> For me, learning a culture starts with their history. To me the history will give lots of clues to current behaviors, customs and values, and trying to learn how the local people think and behave. ... [Learning about Confucianism and Buddhism] helped me understand why things worked the way they did. For example if I wanted to see someone, and I was told that I couldn't, it helped me understand that it was because of their status. It even helps with body language. Once I was in a restaurant sitting with my back to the door and suddenly everyone stood up and bowed. What gave me the clue was that it was a very deep bow. That let me know that the person who entered the room was very important.

One interesting point about Steven's account is his intellectualization of things that are, for Koreans, simply intuitive common sense. Bowing deeply does, in fact, indicate a high level of deference but it is not necessary to have read about Confucianism or Buddhism to understand this. Steven sounds like someone who doesn't participate in Korean society and he seems to be looking for an historical 'explanation' for behavior that he finds remarkable. From the Korean point of view, however, bowing to show deference is no more remarkable than an American who wears a necktie to a job interview or calls someone by his first name to show friendliness. While it is possible to seek historical explanations for these phenomena, they are not critical to accepting them as normal or valid.

It is significant that Steven speaks little Korean even after having spent six years there. He does profess an acceptance of Korean culture, saying 'Well, [I] accepted [cultural difference]. That's just the way that it's going to be, whether I like it or not.' Yet, at other times he refers to the way Koreans do things as 'half assed' and says that they 'don't plan ahead'. In fact, his statement that he accepts things 'whether (he) likes it or not' may imply that he doesn't like it but that he's had to change his behavior anyway. This implies that he has adapted his behavior without fully accepting the values behind the adaptive demand. His cultural learning could be diagrammed as shown in Diagram 9.2.

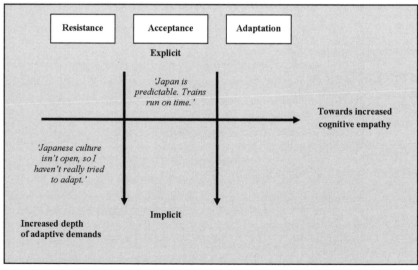

Diagram 9.2

In telling a story about his difficulty getting used to his university grading policies he says:

> One of the hardest things for me when I went there was grading. At my university they gave me a piece of paper that said most of our students will get a B grade. And with my western way of thinking, I thought 'No, I don't give anything. The grade you get is what you earn.' But seeing things from their perspective helped me rationalize and say 'I can do this'. For example they were saying at the beginning of the semester that so many students are going to get a 'B', whereas in the States many teachers grade on a curve, so it's basically the same thing.

Notice that Steven doesn't say that he learned a new cultural perspective in coming to understand the grading policy. Instead, he finds a way to equate the Korean system to the American system that he was familiar with. It is also telling that he talks about the need to 'rationalize' this expectation. Deeper acceptance implies seeing how implicit values and expectations work from the inside, not a rationalization based on external standards. Steven doesn't, for example, say that the grading system helped him understand some of the deeper values in Korea. Steven's perceptions seem fundamentally based on his own cultural standards and he hasn't been able to step into a Korean worldview. This shows that an intellectual attempt to understand behavior is not equivalent to the ability to step into that worldview. Koreans themselves probably rarely talk about Confucius when discussing grading.

If the sojourners interviewed for this work are an indication, deep acceptance of cultural difference is still relatively rare, even among the highly educated, experienced and successful interculturalists in this study. This is not because people are willfully prejudiced, but because (1) one can't accept cultural difference at a deeper level until one has engaged with it. Many people who have extended experiences abroad are not required to face deep adaptive demands – this is the case of many of the expatriates interviewed for this work. In addition, (2) when there are deep adaptive demands, sojourners often have the ability to 'pick and choose', enjoying the parts of their experience which they like and criticizing those that have been inconvenient or difficult to deal with. We found this in the experiences of the Australian students who participated in a study of cultural adaptation during a year abroad in France (de Nooy & Hanna, 2003). We saw this with Philippe and his ability to have very meaningful experiences in Germany – to the point of helping him get rid of prejudicial images he had of Germans – without him ever being able to accept the broad, deep differences embodied by German garbage collection. We also saw this with David, the flight instructor, who managed to have extremely prejudicial attitudes towards Asians even as he accepted cultural differences between Europeans.

It is important to point out that these sojourners overwhelmingly described their experiences in positive terms. They certainly learned a lot about the cultural communities they participated in. But they also walked away with embedded negative judgments about certain elements of their experience. This seems typical of the mixed nature of intercultural experiences. We react differently to different elements of our experiences. Herein rests a fundamental challenge of deep acceptance of cultural difference. The act of recognizing that something is cultural is often more difficult than might be expected and requires a deep-seated understanding that there are different systems in play. In order to discover these differences, we must not only have the willingness to set aside our judgments, but also the longer-term experience of having grappled with a new way of doing things.

Deep Acceptance

Deep acceptance requires not only the ability to see individual elements of cultural difference as valid, but to accept the fundamental premise that other worldviews have a consistent internal logic which, once understood, can be operated within. This implies more than simply learning what to do to get the things that one wants. The Australian students often learned techniques to get what they wanted but they weren't able to see the internal logic of French information gathering strategies. Their understanding of French culture was more piecemeal and didn't allow them to look for answers to their difficulties within a French worldview. Likewise, Steven learned how to meet the requirements at his university for grading, but seems to have only been able to rationalize it, rather than relativize it.

The process of coming to grips with the internal logic of other worldviews is illustrated well by Gunter. Gunter is a German who spent three years working as a manager of a team of Japanese engineers. He had few German colleagues and worked primarily with this team of Japanese engineers as well as Japanese customers. At first, he had a lot of trouble understanding his colleagues:

At the beginning I had really big problems at work ... to understand how [my colleagues] think, how they do their jobs, for example. I had to ask them ... it was not clear for me if they understood what they had to do or not ... I did not know that I had to give this information in a totally different way from in Germany, where you explain something to someone and they give you the feedback if they don't understand .

Gunter is referring to the fact that he would give instructions to his team of engineers assuming that they understood what to do. Only later would Gunter find out that they were having trouble. Gunter felt he wasn't getting any feedback and it made it very difficult to deal with the technical problems that needed to be solved for customers. Since both his team of engineers and his customers were Japanese, Gunter had to adapt himself to a Japanese way of communicating and solving problems. He found himself baffled by his customer's reactions to technical problems – one which focused on gathering a lot of data about the problem:

When we had a problem they were asking for detailed investigations. It was completely incredible for me and for my colleagues in Germany. We couldn't understand why Japanese people need so much information to solve problems.

It seemed to Gunter that his customers and engineers had no plan for solving the problem but they simply were mindlessly collecting information in the hope that somehow things would work out.

Gunter's cultural learning challenge is of a different magnitude than the travelers mentioned in the previous section. Whereas short-term visitors may draw conclusions about things of symbolic importance before returning home, Gunter had to stay and continue working with people who were relying on a different framework of values and communication styles. With time, however, he came to see the communication and problem-solving styles of his co-workers, not as an aberration but as one piece of a larger system of shared meaning that, with effort, he could enter into. As for his communication with his engineers, he reports:

I had to get used to the behavior that they don't really tell you what they don't like. They don't really speak openly ... and it was a completely different way of how to get the information ... This was a big problem at the beginning but at the end it was no problem at all.

So it seems that Gunter learned how to better interpret the communication styles of his engineers. His assertion that in the end communication was 'no problem' hints that he was able to learn to read subtle behavioral clues and interpret them accurately. In order to do this, he had to have ongoing contact – practice doing so – and undertake that learning with the fundamental assumption that once he understood the system he would be able to make it work for him.

Likewise, Gunter struggled to understand the approach to problem-solving that he found. As with the differences in communication styles, Gunter managed to work out the underlying logic. In explaining what he learned, Gunter gives a concise descriptive explanation of two different, yet functional, approaches to solving technical problems:

> Japanese people were trying to collect details as much as possible. If they wanted to solve a problem, they collect details, details, details, and they ask questions, never-ending questions. Then when they have the details they start to think about how to solve the problem. In Germany it's just the opposite. No one is interested in the details. Basically they come from the other side – they try first to get an overview and then maybe go to the details later.

Gunter's deep acceptance is indicated not only by the fact that he was able to make differing implicit systems work, but that his fundamental conclusion wasn't that a particular system was better – though he saw advantages to the Japanese approach – but that they were complementary. He says:

> After a few months working with them, I thought that it was good that they tried to get so much information to get a good conclusion in the end. ... I could never say the German way is better or the Japanese way is better. Both have advantages and disadvantages, I think we need both, definitely.

Gunter's experience of differing approaches to solving problems reflects Trompenaars and Hampden-Turner's view of cultural difference as dilemmas whose solutions mirror each other.

It is striking, when examining Gunter's cultural learning experience, that he doesn't talk about a philosophical or moral commitment to tolerance or cultural relativism. His interest is in coming to a systematic understanding of how things work so that he can be effective in his work. It involved trial and error and depended on good relationships with Japanese who acted as cultural informants. It was not something that could be easily understood through intellectualizations – it had to be experienced. We can sense from his description that, even with the best of intentions, it took time and involved frustration and missteps. Developing a close and trusting relationship with one of his engineers seems to have been important:

> I started working with him a little bit more than a half a year after I went to Japan. In that time I had already learned the basics, at least by trial and error. But afterwards with him we could at least discuss things that were strange for me, [that I] really thought were strange. I could ask him 'What do you think about that?' ... I would say after [a] half year of making errors I didn't have the really basic problems any more. Mainly I would say I learned how to handle Japanese customers. I got used to how they behaved. This is the main thing I learned from him.

So it took Gunter a year and a half to 'learn the basics' by trial and error, and then at least another six months of working closely with a Japanese colleague to no longer have 'basic problems' when dealing with customers. With Gunter's matter-of-fact description it is easy to overlook that a fundamental and firm stance of *acceptance* must have been necessary to maintain a positive attitude in the face of the isolation and stresses of his working environment.

Deep acceptance and language learning

One reason that Gunter's experience is unusual is that he managed to come to understand quite implicit levels of cultural difference without ever having mastered Japanese. This is unusual. By and large, the sojourners who managed to look at their host communities with *deep acceptance* are those that integrated themselves more fully into those societies and who used a foreign language to do so. Since use of a foreign language implies an adaptation of the conceptual framework of a host community when communicating, this seems understandable. Gunter's experience hints, however, that it is not language ability itself that is necessary for this level of cultural learning, but rather having grappled successfully with the integration of other systems of thought and behavior into one's worldview. While Gunter didn't step into a Japanese linguistic worldview, he stepped into an approach to doing things which had its own previously alien logic. This integration of new systems of meaning is a strong indicator of successful *deep acceptance*.

The sojourners who seemed to stay at the *surface acceptance* level had quite different attitudes towards language learning than those who better understood the worldview of their host communities. Jack recognizes intellectually that he would understand Japanese people better if he spoke Japanese, though this doesn't seem to be his primary concern. He says:

> But I do think I'm missing out on a lot ... there's a lot of chicks [laughs] . ... I have this buddy and he speaks Japanese and he gets more chicks. He's got a larger population to choose from. Probably [I miss out] how they think. I learn how they think in English and I'm sure I miss out a lot because they're speaking in their second language.

And while Jack's comments about missing out on 'lots of chicks' may seem insensitive, his tone was one of joking self-deprecation. He seemed to assume the role of the womanizing foreigner (he was, in fact, in a stable relationship) in order to avoid the uncomfortable reality that his experience was shallow. His comments did suggest, however, that his primary perception of language was instrumental – something that allows one to carry out particular tasks.

> I'm limited in vocabulary and grammar. I know more terminology and vocabulary that's work related than if I tried to explain what's wrong with my motorcycle. I don't feel confident if I had to ... if there's an emergency. I don't think I can even make reservations. Well, I could probably do more than I think I could. My grammar would probably be atrocious. I've surprised myself on the phone a couple times I was able to get things across. ... I don't use it. I went to the post office today. They said 'sign' and I said 'hai' [yes]. I really don't have the opportunities. I would have to create opportunities. For example I could go to the store, even though I don't need tuna fish I could ask for the tuna fish. I could call a department store on the phone and ask for something. ... I could go days without using Japanese, I'm sure I have.

As for Steven, he doesn't seem to think that learning Korean would help him understand Koreans, though he recognizes that many people would disagree with him. When asked if language learning is necessary for understanding a foreign culture he says:

> There's a lot of people who say that if you are foreigner there's always a limit. It's a question of degree. I'm sure that being fluent in the foreign language would help. But there are also other ways of getting that information, like how I did.

So Steven seems satisfied with his ability to understand Korean culture without extensive language skills. Of course his conclusion is neither right nor wrong since there is no absolute standard to judge how one *should* go about cultural learning. The point here is that those who react to adaptive demands with *shallow acceptance* are not able to see how individual instances of cultural difference – including language – are only one piece of a larger puzzle. If language learning is viewed instrumentally by the tasks it helps one carry out, rather than holistically as representing a valid system of meaning that it is possible to gain entry to, one's view of its importance is reduced. Indeed, Steven explains his limited language ability by saying that 'it wasn't absolutely necessary. I had the survival skills, the functional skills. Those things were highly needed. Beyond that [there was no need]'.

Acceptance and adaptation

We have examined *acceptance* as a cognitive reaction to demands for change. This has been considered separately from *adaptation* to demands for change because they are seen as fundamentally different processes. One can accept cultural difference as valid, yet not adapt one's own behavior. Likewise, one can adapt one's behavior without accepting that the demand that one is responding to is valid or reasonable. The next chapter will examine *adaptation* with an eye to making this distinction clear.

Chapter 10
Adaptation and Cultural Identity

> In the beginning I was trying to act like Americans but I wasn't very comfortable. ... I try to accommodate to the other person, but sometimes that's at the expense of my true identity.
> Mayumi

> You are as many people as languages that you speak. When you speak a different language your thought patterns change and your gestures change.
> Paul

> I think living in Japan definitely has [affected me] but that probably has to do with reinforcing things that were already there. ... You cannot become a snowman by pouring flour over your head.
> Donald

> When I go back to Senegal, I put on my Senegalese glasses.
> Abdou

Adaptation

Adapting to a new environment requires change on the part of the sojourner. Mayumi (above) talks about 'trying to act like Americans', yet feels that changing too much may come at the expense of her true identity. Paul (above), the son of a diplomat who grew up all over the world, seems comfortable with adaptive change, almost to the point of being a different person in different places. Donald (above), on the other hand, seems to deny the possibility for deep cultural change since you 'cannot become a snowman by pouring flour over your head'. For his part, Abdou (above), a Senegalese living in France, describes the perceptual changes which he makes – putting on his 'Senegalese glasses' – in response to being back in Senegal. Each in their own way, these sojourners have dealt with the question of adaptation: How do I change in response to the demands of my new environment?

For the purposes of this model, adaptation is defined as *allowing for change in oneself as a response to adaptive demands from a different cultural environment*. To some degree, change is forced upon sojourners since their normal way of doing things simply may not work in a new environment. If no one speaks your language, survival dictates that you change how you communicate. If you don't know the layout of a city or the names of food on menus, you must learn them (learning being a form of change) in order to function. This kind of *adaptation* is not conditioned upon the sojourner's acceptance of the legitimacy of the adaptive demands being faced – the sojourner has little choice. At the other extreme, *adaptation* is limited by a sojourner's capacity or desire for change. It is extremely rare, for example, for an adult language learner to ever acquire native-like proficiency in a foreign language, no matter how determined a student he or she is. One can never totally 'go native'. And a desire to change may not be accepted by members of a host community. This *enforced resistance* can mean that even when a sojourner tries to *adapt*, that he or she is excluded. This is the situation of Abdou. As a black African living in France, he encounters prejudice which makes it more difficult for him to be accepted in important parts of French society, regardless of how well he may want to adapt himself.

Adaptation can be enjoyable. We go on vacation because we want to escape our life routines and a certain amount of adaptation is often stimulating, for instance when we try out new phrases in a foreign language, see new sights and so on. In the short term, adaptation does not imply permanent change as a sojourner can go back to their familiar environment soon enough. As time goes on, however, choices must be made about the degree to which one integrates changes into existing life patterns. Travelers who start to crave familiar foods and habits confront this challenge. Short-term sojourns allow a visitor to 'bracket' their change – suspending their normal way of doing things in the expectation that they will soon be back home. Longer-term sojourners need to acquire new routines, not simply new behaviors. Sooner or later, nearly everyone reaches the limits of their ability or desire to adapt. The exception to this, of course, is children for whom meeting the demands of their environment is simple part of growing up.

Adaptation is largely beyond our conscious control. We rarely say to ourselves: 'Oh, I'm adapting now!' Rather, we are caught up in the stress or the stimulation of being someplace new. We may not even notice much in terms of cultural difference ('the people there are pretty much like people back home') even as we learn to navigate in a new environment. After an extended period, deep cultural adaptation may raise questions of identity or even make a sojourner feel lost or alienated when they return home. But adaptation is fundamentally an additive process. It does not imply 'replacing' one's 'culture' with a new one but rather adding to existing knowledge, skills and perspectives. Just as learning a new language doesn't mean losing one's first language, cultural adaptation involves learning to do and see things in a new way without ever giving up the competencies that one has. This doesn't mean, of course, that the process is never disconcerting.

Adaptation itself is neither positive nor negative, it simply implies that change has taken place in response to the adaptive demands of one's environment. If one changes in spite of a desire not to, the outcomes of adaptation can be negative. Cynical or sheltered expatriates, aliened immigrant communities, tourists who feel superior or critical – all of these outcomes can be traced to a need to adapt oneself to an environment that one cannot truly accept. If, on the other hand, one changes while accepting the validity of difference encountered, adaptation leads to increased cognitive empathy. If it goes on long enough, and in enough situations, adaptation can lead to a new way of looking at the world, biculturalism or even a state of integrated cultural marginality in which a sojourner goes beyond single cultural frameworks. Adaptation can be a marvel or a horror, or barely noticed at all. It is as subtle, powerful and fundamental as change itself.

Norms and values – the 'rules' of a new community

For many sojourners, adaptation implies learning to deal with the norms and values of a new cultural community. Norms (expectations about what should be done or how things should be done) and values (standards used for defining good and bad) exist at both the explicit and implicit level. Explicit norms are the laws and formal rules and etiquette of a society. This includes things as mundane as traffic regulations and as serious as criminal laws (which vary considerably from country to country), but also explicit behavioral expectations like taking one's shoes off before entering a home. Explicit norms usually involve very little ambiguity and can be explained clearly. They don't imply a need to interpret, only to follow the rules. They involve questions of 'do's' or 'don'ts' such as 'don't eat using your left hand' or 'say 'bless you' when someone sneezes', 'don't drive over 100 kilometers an hour on the expressway' and 'don't litter or you may get fined'. This doesn't mean, of course, that everyone always follows these norms, but explicit norms themselves are unambiguous and easy to understand.

Implicit norms are the unspoken expectations about the way that things should be done. They are often more difficult to define clearly and can be related to expectations about a seemingly endless list of different things, including use of time (If a dinner party starts at 8:00 p.m. is it rude to arrive at 8:30 p.m.?), proxemics (How much touching is acceptable in what circumstances? How close do you stand when you talk to someone?), body language (eye contact, facial expressions, use of gestures), social expectations (when or how to compliment, how to deal with conflict), status markers (wait for the host to begin before starting to eat) and use of language (when to use someone's given or family names, use of varying linguistic forms such as *vous* and *tu* in French). Trying to make a complete list of implicit norms would be impossible. Implicit norms are judged contextually, not as straightforward rules. It may be possible to give pointers or guidelines ('*tu*' is more informal than '*vous*') yet successfully applying these guidelines depends on an intuitive understanding of how behavior will be judged in context.

As opposed to norms, values are the criteria that people use to evaluate the goodness or badness of a particular behavior or to make choices between different alternatives. When a politician talks about the importance of democracy or a priest talks about the need to 'Love one's neighbor', they are appealing to widely accepted explicit values. Proverbs often reflect cultural values. Whereas 'the squeaky wheel gets the grease' implies that standing out is an effective way to get what one wants, '*Deru kui ha utareru*' (The nail that sticks up gets hammered down) is a Japanese expression which implies the opposite. If we don't like the food that someone has prepared for us we may face the choice between competing values (Should we be kind and compliment the food or be honest and say we don't like it?). Because an understanding of values requires the interpretation of behavior relative to a shared standard, it can be difficult to fully understand the values of a host community. These shared standards are contextual as well. The standards of politeness among young people may not entirely overlap with those of their elders.

For sojourners, it is relatively easy to understand the explicit values and norms of a host community, but much more difficult to deal with adaptive demands related to implicit norms and values. In Mayumi's case, the importance of the family in Korea (a value) led to the unspoken expectation (an implicit norm) that she should call her mother every day, even if she could barely speak Korean. Values related to gender roles (the woman's role as caregiver) led to expectations about her taking care of her husband and led Mayumi's mother-in-law to take care of her son when Mayumi was not in Korea. Having to figure out what these hidden expectations are (which happens often by trial and error) and trying to respond to them, all while maintaining one's own feelings of personal worth, can be a tremendous challenge.

We have seen that Mayumi, in spite of the difficulties, deeply accepted that the adaptive demands she faced were a natural produce of cultural difference and didn't blame her mother-in-law or her husband's family personally. Yet accepting the validity of cultural value difference does not automatically make the adaptation process easy. In describing cultural difference between Korea and Japan, Mayumi effortlessly produces a list of things that she seemed to find difficult.

> The family gatherings [were hard to deal with]. The fact that it's the wife's job to make the phone call to the mother. Also, a sense of privacy. In Japan you don't open someone's refrigerator. They do that in Korea. They might look at your photo album without asking or open the closet. Also they tend to be very straightforward compared to Japanese and show anger much more easily. Sometimes it's scary because they shout at you or scream at you in the street. We were parking somewhere we shouldn't and my husband left me for a few minutes, A person came up to me and started yelling at me and I didn't know what to say and how to handle that situation. In Japan people might ask you, but there he just started shouting. There's that tendency. In Korea waitresses don't smile, because that's seen as cheapening the woman. They seemed very unfriendly. Or, for example, taking off your shoes. In Japan, for example you turn the direction of the shoes of the guests and put them in order. In Korea you don't ever change the direction or straighten them up. They might take offense. Now that I think of it, there are lots of differences, like how to pay. Even the eating habits. They use spoons to eat the rice. My mother-in-law could come to my apartment unannounced. I left Korea a couple of times that I got stressed out. When I wasn't there my mother-in-law would go and clean up for me, making me feel like a failure when I returned. She even bleached the teapot.

The stress that Mayumi felt in Korea is palpable and when we see the degree to which Mayumi had to change her behavior, communication style and relationships, it is not so difficult to understand that deep adaptation can be a traumatic process. It is also easy to see why many sojourners never adapt to this deep level.

At deeper levels of adaptation we may have to reevaluate our own values: what are my values and how much should I change myself? Mayumi seems to have felt that her identity as an independent woman was under attack. This created a conflict between her desire to accept as valid the cultural expectations she found in Korea and her values both as a Japanese (with different gender values than in Korea) and as an individual woman who had made individual value choices. As we will see in Chapter

12, some sojourners seem to manage to resolve the seemingly contradictory desire to accept as valid value differences, yet remain true to their self. This is accomplished largely by integrating the understanding that values do not exist independently as a sort of absolute guide to right and wrong. Values have meaning in the context of the experiences and worldview of the people that share them. Based on this understanding, we can make choices about behavior contextually without losing sight of our personal integrity.

Enforced adaptation – adapting because we have to

Choice is an integral part of the adaptation process and having to change against one's will is difficult. Linda – the British woman who found Americans to be 'snobs' – went abroad as a trailing spouse in an unhappy marriage and explains that adapting to life in the United States was made more difficult because she didn't want to be there. *Enforced adaptation* compels a sojourner to change in spite of psychological resistance. Linda describes this situation as 'doing things I didn't want to do just to survive'. Some sojourners are in the opposite situation, having chosen to go abroad and feeling very attracted to the idea of adapting to their new community. Andre, a Swiss who went to study in Japan, says he 'tried to be more Japanese than the Japanese themselves'. Sojourners such as Andre will be discussed in more detail in Chapter 11.

Enforced adaptation involves being obliged to change, though not always by external sources. It is defined as *adaptive change that is undertaken in the face of resistance*, meaning that at some level a sojourner does not perceive of demands for change as being legitimate. This lack of legitimacy may be a result of the coercive nature of the demands, but is also inextricably linked with *acceptance* of cultural difference itself. Adele, the American scholar of Japanese literature, was not coerced in her decision to come to Japan (although her first choice was China). As a student of Japanese literature, she was both pursuing a personal interest and choosing to do so by coming to Japan to live and do research. Yet, her fundamental inability to accept the validity of Japanese values led her to being at cross-purposes with herself. On the one hand, she needed to learn about Japan, learn to speak, read and write the language, develop relationships with Japanese and understand Japanese society. On the other hand, she disliked Japanese cultural values and resisted modifying her values in response to her intercultural experiences. She had her own view of what was valuable in Japanese traditional culture but she found that the Japanese themselves did not value those things as highly as she did.

Table 10.1

Adele's reactions to life in Japan.	*Adele's adaptation and motivations for being in Japan.*
Here people look at you semi-suspicious. Women look at me and look the other way, and men look at me in this skuzzy scary-monster way.	I do a lot of writing in Japanese. My reading is very good.
My friends are nearly all foreign academics here studying in Japan. (With my main Japanese female friend) what I'm finding difficult is that we don't have a lot to talk about. She invited me out with her friends, because then she doesn't have to spend intense one on one with me. And her friends are the bimbos from hell. They all carry those live rabbit bags, rabbit fur bags, they wear those bimbo shoes.	I have to start looking for a job as a professor of Japanese literature. I'd like to work in a small New England college town.
	I never wanted to come to Japan. Actually I wanted to go to China, but came here.
	Well, Japan is a job for me, and all of my friends and I have come to that realization.
Then there was a woman who I tried to study calligraphy with, but then I realized she was using me to meet western men.	Coming to Japan is about finding a job and none of us are enjoying our lifestyles.
It's a very unhealthy county.	I speak Japanese well enough to get around and get my work done, and I can watch TV and enjoy it.
I'm dedicating my life to this country, but as I walk thought the streets I think, why here? And I don't share the value system that I see here. In the States there's an opposing faction, but in the streets in Japan I'm overwhelmed by all the bad isms of modernization. I don't like the young people their self-centeredness, I've come to realize that this current modern Japan ... I don't like, I don't like the me-ism, the selfishness of young kids.	I go to a lot of (research workshops) and hear people speak (in Japanese).
	I was taking Japanese classes but I gave that up. I'm in a weird zone where the Japanese classes are not challenging for me.
I think one thing I've learned is that I really like the Unites States, and I'm glad that I was born there.	

Enforced adaptation can be extremely stressful and involve a great deal of cognitive dissonance. We can see this as we juxtapose Adele's statements related to her motivations and the degree of adaptation she has achieved with her reactions to cultural difference (see Table 10.1).

So *resistance* makes change difficult or painful, yet in the case of *enforced adaptation*, one is compelled – sometimes by one's own goals or desires – to change anyway. Common examples of those facing this challenge include immigrants who must learn a new language and adapt to life in a place simply for the sake of supporting a family back home. Another example involves well-paid expatriates who dislike their surroundings but loath to give up the money and prestige that returning home would entail. Psychological stress and cognitive dissonance are engendered to the extent that sojourners *adapt* to adaptive demands without *accepting* the validity of cultural difference itself. This can be represented as shown in Diagram 10.1.

In this way, *enforced adaptation* can engender the worst of all possible intercultural learning outcomes. Sojourners make little progress towards deeper cultural empathy because they are unable to relativize their experiences. In addition, their negative judgments become entrenched by their lived experience. Even sojourners who isolate themselves in an expatriate community in order to avoid deeper adaptive demands end up feeling less negative about their experiences than those who are forced to adapt. When Jack, who lived an isolated but happy expatriate lifestyle, was asked what he had learned from his experience abroad, he wasn't sure what to answer. This seems understandable because he hadn't engaged with cultural

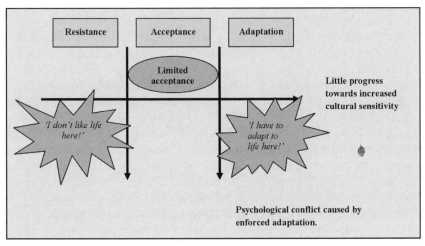

Diagram 10.1

difference that deeply. Adele, when asked the same question, concludes that she was glad to have been born in the United States.

In practice, of course, few people ever reject absolutely a new cultural environment and intercultural learning usually involves a mix of different reactions to intercultural demands, *resistance, acceptance* and *adaptation*. The sojourners interviewed for this work, however, remind us that adaptation to the demands of a new cultural environment leads to a positive outcome when it is founded on an acceptance of difference. The deeper the acceptance, the easier it is to accept the change entailed by adaptation. In that sense, adaptation in and of itself does not represent a measure of intercultural learning success. We may behave in a way which allows us to function in our new environment, but if that behavior is not freely chosen and doesn't recognize the validity of the demands that we are adapting too, the results can be worse than if a sojourner had never left home.

Surface adaptation – explicit learning and symbolic meanings

Surface adaptation refers to having changed something about oneself to better match the explicit adaptive demands of one's environment. Surface adaptation can be thought of as the explicit learning of a new environment. Learning to eat new foods and becoming familiar with the streets of a new city are examples of this. Sometimes, surface adaptation simply implies a new way of doing things, for instance when we must use toilets we are unfamiliar with or learn to use a mosquito net. The adaptive demands that drive surface adaptation may be related to simple survival (food and shelter) or may involve learnings related to our new environment such as when we study the history of the country we are visiting. The act of reading a guidebook explanation while traveling is a form of surface adaptation, since it involves changing ourselves through the taking in of information as a response to our desire to understand our environment. To say that someone has had an experience of *surface adaptation* does not mean that they have had a superficial experience. A *surface* intercultural learning experience does not imply a lack of thoughtfulness, it simply means that one has not been subjected to the implicit adaptive demands that come with longer stays and more involved interaction. A tourist from a small town in England visiting India may see cattle wandering the streets and be very impressed by cultural difference, but these are *meaningful experiences* that are not necessarily *deep* in terms of implicit cultural patterns.

The ceremonies and objects that have a great deal of symbolic importance for people in a particular community – e.g. a cross in a community of Christians or a flag in a community of patriots – may or may not tell us much about the deeper patterns of interaction in those communities. An Ivorian visitor to England may find the changing of the guard at Buckingham Palace exotic and significant, yet barely notice that the English often form queues differently than in the Ivory Coast. The English orientation towards universalism may escape his attention while explicit and symbolic cultural elements are noticed. A wedding dress, the Magna Carta, and Waterloo may have symbolic significance for the English but they are, in the end, explicit phenomena. A few minutes of study are probably enough for foreigners to understand the historical facts related to the Magna Carta better than many English. A wealth of lived experience, however, is necessary to start to understand the place that *tea* occupies within the English perceptual world. The ability to interact naturally with the English over a cup of tea requires a greater depth of adaptation for non-English than an understanding of the Magna Carta.

This is not to say that objects of explicit symbolic importance do not hint at deep, underlying cultural differences. Learning about the five relationships emphasized by Confucius (husband and wife, parent and child, elders and youngsters, ruler and subject, friend and friend) may help someone see that hierarchical relationships are perceived differently in China than in England. The danger with these kinds of cultural explanations is that if one doesn't have extensive experience in China it is difficult to see what Confucian ideals mean to the lived experience of Chinese today. Sometimes, these ideas turn into half-explanations. One American, after studying world religions, concluded that the goal of Buddhism was to 'think about nothing', which to her seemed decidedly 'un-Godly'. This is not how Buddhists would describe Buddhism. Knowledge coupled with a lack of experience makes for simplistic explanations of behavior, for instance when American views on public morality are dismissed as 'puritanical' and conflict in Africa is described simply as 'tribalism'.

The reason that short-term stays in another cultural community are not deep is not that sojourners are not exposed to objects of symbolic importance, it is because they are not required to adapt to the hidden differences implied by those objects. When visiting a temple in Laos, a tourist may be told to remove his shoes and not to sit with his feet pointed at the altar. These adaptive changes (the new things this visitor is learning and doing) are related to explicit behaviors and don't require a deeper understanding of the symbolic significance of Buddhism in Laotian culture. Although if a visitor accepts the fundamental premise that Laotians have a different yet valid and functional worldview, it is more likely that a visitor will take these behavioral rules seriously. But just as learning how to pump one's own gas may initially be more important for getting along in the United

States than learning about Christianity, so is there often a gap between the objects of symbolic importance in a cultural community and the most pressing adaptive challenges.

The challenges of surface adaptation

It shouldn't be assumed that surface adaptation is easy. The reason that even the cheapest vacation packages usually include transportation from the airport to the hotel is that dealing with the uncertainty of finding transportation in a new country is extremely stressful for many people. When in a new environment, the inability to do things that we normally do without thinking – order food, use money, make a phone call, take a bus – creates stress and uncertainty. One powerful source of stress for many sojourners is the need to use a foreign language. It is not surprising, then, that many long-term sojourners don't learn the host language if they don't need to. The certainty and level of control permitted by expecting the host population to adapt to one's own language can be much more comfortable than the feeling of powerlessness and incompetence that can accompany poor foreign language skills.

In spite of these stresses, *surface adaptation* is relatively straightforward because *explicit adaptive demands* tend to be highly systematic. Learning to use chopsticks or figuring out how to use a bus system may not be easy, but the tasks are explicit and one can predictably ask for help, measure progress and integrate new information into one's daily life. But people have different levels of tolerance even for *surface adaptation*. Research by psychologists such as Matsumoto *et al.* (2001) shows us that flexibility, tolerance for ambiguity and the successful management of one's emotions are strong predictors of intercultural success. When a sojourner lacks these emotional capacities, they have less of the cognitive detachment necessary to relativize their experiences. When these sojourners must remain for an extended period of time abroad, they may isolate themselves and surround themselves with the accouterments from back home. This not only serves the purpose of reducing the stress that they feel, it also limits their need to adapt to more implicit cultural differences.

Deep Adaptation

Deep adaptive demands are diffuse. They do not revolve around a conceptual understanding of a discrete phenomenon but rather involve intuitive interpretation of attitudes, intentions and ways of thinking. Deep cultural difference often involves obvious but difficult-to-understand differences in how daily tasks or interactions are carried out. Kensuke, a

Japanese college student studying abroad, couldn't understand the concept of 'to party' at his University in the United States.

> And [when] I attended a party that was when I got kind of a shock. That was a party held by the rugby team, and I didn't understand [how] they could stand like that, with one keg, and people sit there and talked about something [with] each other without really having an order. ... They were just there and talked with just one keg of beer. I just couldn't believe it ... But the place was somehow managed and organized in that way.

Takeshi found his American college parties difficult to understand because in Takeshi's experience, 'parties' among college students in Japan are more highly organized, often at a restaurant or bar, involving advanced planning, reservations, greetings or explanations by the organizers, recaps of events of particular significance, a clear beginning and ending, and so on. The party that Takeshi attended in the United States, on the other hand, seemed chaotic. He could find no explicit order or code of expectations. People simply stood around talking.

The social, cultural and linguistic skills that are required for a sojourner to get along in these contexts are, for the most part, implicit and unconscious. If an American is asked how one goes about making friends and striking up a conversation at a party such as Takeshi attended, he or she may say 'be friendly' or 'be yourself'. But what that entails and how to learn to do it is largely beyond explanation. Functioning socially in a group of people from a host culture requires extremely advanced linguistic skills. Mayumi also talks about the difficulty of American 'parties' as a university student in the United States:

> It was hard, especially in the beginning. Mostly because [it was hard] to get along with the people the same age. I was able to understand my professors talk, but my friends used very colloquial forms and the content was very difficult. They would be talking about TV programs. The things they talked about were very different than the things I was used to talking about. ... You were often invited to parties or something, and you can't go alone. When I tried that I always felt really strange. If you go alone, you have to mingle without losing your friends. You don't have a base, and there is no organized arrangement, so it's hard and you have to take initiative.

Deeper adaptation requires significant changes in how we communicate and carry on relationships with the people around us, and ultimately, how we view ourselves and the world. As we have seen with Mayumi, her attempts to change herself to better fit the social style of Americans gave her a feeling of not being herself.

> In the beginning I was trying to act like Americans but I wasn't very comfortable ... I tried to participate in things that I wouldn't have done [in Japan], like sports, or things that I couldn't do even if I wanted to do it. ... I haven't yet figured out how this has all affected my identity. I try to accommodate to the other person, but sometimes that's at the expense of my true identity. If I continue to do that I reach a threshold, but when I got to the point that enough is enough, then I kind of retreated and tried to be more true to myself.

The reason that Mayumi feels the need to 'retreat' and be more true to herself is that *implicit adaptive demands* touch us at deep levels of the self. Strangely enough, adapting to behavior that is symbolically important – washing our hands before entering a shrine – is often felt as less threatening and difficult than adapting to differences in everyday interaction such as learning to be friendly in a new way. This is because explicit demands for adaptation are more predictable and so less threatening. More implicit demands create more uncertainty and therefore touch deeper elements of one's sense of personal competence.

Deep adaptation and language learning

Among those interviewed for this work there was a clear distinction between those sojourners who were, due to the circumstances of their stay abroad, required to speak a foreign language and extensively adapt to the host community, and those who had the choice of only adapting to the degree that they wanted to. The former included students studying abroad (in a foreign language) and long-term immigrants living in a community where their first language was not spoken. The latter included expatriates who were able to function largely independently of local norms because of their status and position in the host community. This means that although they were expected to follow obvious local etiquette, they were not required to have a high level of proficiency in the host language, or function socially following host community standards. They were largely seen as foreigners who needed special treatment to function.

Those who gained a high degree of competence in the host language were almost invariably those who needed it in order to function. Those who didn't learned less. Those who were more integrated were the ones that had no choice and made the best of it. Those who had the choice of whether to integrate or not, often had a shallower or more intellectualized intercultural experience. Compare, for example, the language learning and adaptation experiences of Mayumi, facing the need to learn Korean to survive and get along with her in-laws, with that of William, whose position as an English teacher in Japan allowed him more freedom to be different. William learns Japanese and uses it with his in-laws, as does Mayumi, but his pace of learning is much slower and his adaptive pressures are much less. When talking to William, one gets the impression that he is adapting to the degree that he is comfortable with – he is not being forced. Mayumi, on the other hand, gives the impression of someone who is adapting to survive (see Table 10.2).

The challenges that William refers to seem related to avoiding isolation: making friends, getting pulled out of his 'solitude', going an entire day without using English. Mayumi, on the other hand, feels pressure, gets stressed out trying to adapt, always has people around that she must keep in mind, feels that she should avoid talking about Japan, etc. Mayumi, it should be pointed out, learned Korean quickly and after a year and a half in Korea uses it as the primary means of communication with her husband. William, after living in Japan for four years, speaks with his girlfriend in English. The fact that he is ashamed of that seems to indicate that he recognizes that he is, at some level, choosing not to adapt and learn. This choice is a luxury that Mayumi didn't have and implies that her experience had more *implicit adaptive demands* than his.

Deep adaptation and cultural code switching

Overwhelmingly, the sojourners interviewed for this work who adapted successfully to deep cultural differences had a high degree of language ability and had integrated themselves into host cultural communities. They often described the empathy they gained in terms of a sort of cultural code switching – a shift into a different framework of communication or meaning. Paul, the multilingual son of a diplomat says:

[Y]ou are as many people as languages that you speak. When you speak a different language your thought patterns change and your gestures change. And when people tell jokes in that language you understand but you couldn't necessarily explain that to people in

Table 10.2

William	*Mayumi*
I have a few friends who can't speak English, so we had to speak in Japanese.	(Studying Korean) was different than studying English because I needed it in real life.
When I talk to my girlfriend's family, I guess hours can pass (only speaking Japanese). Her mother doesn't speak English. I can go a day speaking Japanese. I especially like to speak Japanese to people who don't speak any English. I'm tempted to insert English words for example if I know they speak English. It's hard for me to speak to my fellow teachers in Japanese.	(Koreans) expected me to behave like a Korean and assumed similarity. But there were subtle differences which were hard to accept, and I tried to be accommodating and then got frustrated and finally exploded at the end ... very close family relationships, and I had to call my mother-in-law every day. And I was nervous talking to her in Korean without knowing what to say. My husband was working late and a lot of things we had to do with the family.
In Hiroshima I went every Saturday to this all-volunteer classes and that's how I learned the basics of Japanese grammar and conversation. And actually that class pulled me out of my solitude because I met people and made friends there.	In Korea I felt I really shouldn't talk about Japan.
	My mother-in-law could come to my apartment unannounced. I left Korea a couple of times that I got stressed out.
It seems to me that the people who are bilingual are happier, they travel more, their conversations don't dig into a dark zone of complaints and frustrations.	I really love his parents. (But) I don't think I could live with them, because of the differences in customs.
My girlfriend and I usually speak English too, I'm kind of ashamed of that.	In a way I was lucky because I was forced to make friends in the US and I had family in Korea, so I always had people around.

another language. The reference points and assumptions are just so different.

When you are in an environment, like in Germany if you come to a pedestrian crossing you come to a red light and you don't cross, whereas in the US you would go ahead, or probably France too. Or eating, in the US you put one hand on your lap, but not in Europe. And this time when I came back to the US I found myself putting my hands in my pockets more. I find that I'm more on time when I'm in Germany.

And Yuko, the Japanese woman who grew up in India, Europe and the US, also speaks of how changing languages involves a deep shift in meaning.

When I get angry I prefer to speak English. I'm extremely polite in Japanese. I don't have the vocabulary to get angry in Japanese. The Japanese I know is polite, it's *aimai* [lit. vague]. When I talk in Hindi, there's 'tomorrow'. My way of thinking in each language changes, in Hindi it's slower, there's tomorrow, like something will happen, in Japanese it's *aimai* and in English it's more direct. ... In Japan Hindi doesn't come out. When I went back to India it comes right back.

I strongly believe that it's not possible to be culturally sensitive if you only speak one language. Otherwise you can't understand how people think. ... The reason you become a chameleon ... you want to fit in and you want to get along. So you try hard. A lot of third culture kids try to get along and not be too different.

Steven and Jack, who both spent a long time abroad without speaking a foreign language well, never spoke about feeling that they were different people depending on the language they spoke or that they switched between different behavioral modes. People in this situation may have a quite sophisticated understanding of cultural difference, at least at the conceptual level, and may also function very well in their particular environment. Their cultural understanding, however, does not seem to involve the kind of cultural code switching found among those who are more fully bicultural. The sojourners discussed in this work who became bilingual and adapted deeply concluded that speaking the host language is essential for the deeper levels of intercultural understanding. Presumably, this is because many of the deepest differences found can only be experienced when one takes part in host communities and functions more as an insider than an outsider.

Deep adaptation and identity shifts

As bicultural sojourners shift back and forth between different language and modes of behavior, they may create, in effect, multiple selves – for example a Spanish self and a Chinese self. Abdou, for example, reports that when he returns from France to visit Senegal, he puts on his 'Senegal glasses' to look at the world in the Senegalese way and becomes a different person than in France. These shifts may be disconcerting and create identity conflicts, a feeling of alienation, or culture shock when returning to one's home environment. Mayumi says:

I didn't feel like I was my true self. I hated it because I didn't seem like my usual self – I'm outgoing but I wasn't seen that way. I was seen as a quiet Asian girl. I thought the food would be difficult but it wasn't. ... I try to accommodate to the other person, but sometimes that's at the expense of my true identity. If I continue to do that I reach a threshold, but when I got to the point that enough is enough, then I kind of retreated and tried to be more true to myself.

Sojourners who feel a strong rapport for their host cultural environment may have somewhat less trouble with identity questions since they may feel little conflict between the expectations of their new environment and their existing sense of self. For other sojourners, shifting between different selves can raise the question of what one's 'true self' is. Resolving this dilemma may represent one of the ultimate challenges of intercultural learning which, as we will see in Chapter 12, is resolved fully by very few people.

Rapport and cultural identity

As Sparrow (2000) argues, for most sojourners successful cultural learning results primarily in a sense of belonging and engagement in a new community. This process generates cultural empathy: the ability to step into the worldview of the new community, sometimes without a great deal of conscious reflection. This may be especially true for sojourners who feel rapport with their new environment. It's not that unusual for a sojourner to feel more at home in their new environment than they were back at home. And if it feels good, the reaction seems to be, why question it? It seems that a fair number of 'accidental biculturals' – those exposed to two cultures in the process of growing up – don't feel a great need to reflect on their cultural identity or the fact that they may have integrated two worldviews into their identity.

This kind of less-reflective biculturalism seems to be quite different from that experienced by those who have dealt with progressively deeper adaptation challenges, first as an outsider and then as an insider in a new cultural environment. Having passed through these development stages seems to allow for a transcendent view of cultural difference. These sojourners seem to develop more *cognitive empathy*, the ability to look at cultural difference on the meta-level, with a deep and conscious acceptance of the validity of different worldviews. As we will explore more fully in Chapter 12, this can lead to the seemingly contradictory state in which a sojourner feels a sense of detachment at the same time that he participates fully in different communities. This experience has been described as the feeling of being on a fence, interacting with people on either side who can't see each other. One has a kind of meta-perception, recognizing one's own role as a cultural bridge. The understanding that one's perspective is functioning at a more inclusive level than the less culturally experienced people one deals with does not seem to inhibit forming positive relationships with people on both sides. The next chapter will look at learners who seemed to have an unusually easy (or occasionally difficult) time entering into a host community. As we will see, that doesn't mean that they have achieved the same kind of *cognitive empathy* as sojourners such as Mayumi.

Chapter 11

Resistance and Rapport – Why Not Everyone Reacts the Same

I was so burned out. Now that I'm back [in Switzerland] again I
don't feel any desire to go back to Japan.
Andre

Everyone is Different

One challenge of intercultural education is the difficulty of understanding why individuals react to new intercultural environments in such different ways. In this work, we have looked at length at how cultural difference influences the cultural learning process but very little at how individual difference does. This chapter will examine the cases of sojourners who seemed to have a strong personal reaction (either positive or negative) to their particular host cultural community. It will also look at some of the external factors that seemed to predict a great deal about the depth of intercultural learning and the success of particular sojourners. We will look at the kinds of relationships that successful sojourners develop and their experience with learning the host language. Finally, we will examine whether the cultural distance between the sojourner's home and the host community plays an important role in sojourners reactions to adaptive demands.

Resistance and Rapport

The sojourners interviewed for this book had a wide range of individual responses to their intercultural experiences. The differences between how different individuals react to similar adaptive challenges involve at least two considerations. First, different people deal with stress in different ways. Matsumoto *et al.* (2001), for example, has created a measure called the Intercultural Adjustment Potential Scale which attempts to measure the psychological coping strategies which help with intercultural adjustment. These include *emotion regulation, critical thinking,* and *openness/flexibility*. In this view, intercultural adaptation is fundamentally a stress reaction to a new environment and requires particular psychological adaptive strategies. Measuring these capabilities is purported to be able to predict with some degree of accuracy who will have a positive intercultural experience. These psychological factors may explain, to some degree at least, why some sojourners had more positive experiences than others.

Among the sojourners interviewed for this work, however, it seems that there was another highly personal element at play. Some individuals' personality seemed particularly suited – or not suited – to a particular new cultural environment. Jack, for example, was happy with life in Japan and was not stressed even though he spoke little Japanese, while another American, Adele, had spent years learning Japanese and investing herself in the culture but had extremely negative reactions to cultural difference. It does not seem enough to say that Adele simply had less openness and flexibility than Jack. It seemed that there was something about Japanese values which particularly bothered Adele – one would almost say that she seemed offended by Japanese cultural values. And while some individuals seemed to feel a particularly strong *resistance* to a particular cultural community, others seemed to feel the opposite, an attraction or *rapport* for a particular community.

Adele was mentioned as someone who certainly did not feel comfortable in Japan. It is informative to compare her with Andre, a Swiss man who studied Japanese, graduated with a master's degree from a Japanese university (taking his classes and writing his thesis in Japanese) and then worked in Japan before returning to Switzerland. He reports that he was fascinated by Japanese culture, and felt a tremendous mysterious attraction:

> I was so desperately trying to integrate into Japan ... it became kind of a religion for me. [I started to believe that] I am kind of by destiny bound to Japan. It's crazy ... I actually kind of admired Japan without even knowing it and projecting a lot into it. ...I tried to be more Japanese than the Japanese themselves. ...[While in Japan I felt] I love Japanese aesthetics. I love everything. I feel so good because people tell me 'Hey Andre, you're so good at Japanese. Wow you look great. I would like to know you.'

It seems that Andre's reaction to Japan cannot be explained simply as a result of his particular coping strategies. While his case is extreme, others also sometimes spoke of a naturalness they felt in a new culture. Neil, for example, says:

> Yes I am [happy living in Japan]. ...When I came back the second time from New York, I felt immediately, 'I'm back home'. I didn't have any

readjustment period. ...In fact, I had more of a problem with getting along with my American and British colleagues [than with Japanese].

I'm not hard-core competitive like Americans are. ...I've learned many things about how different I am from many Americans. I wasn't a misfit when I grew up, but I wasn't the one in the popular crowd. Maybe I fit the profile of someone who would fit life in Japan. ...I'm willing to do more to fit into this culture than would many Americans.

Another person who seems to feel *rapport* with a new cultural environment is Gail, a British woman who has moved to France and acquired French citizenship after more than 10 years there. While talking about why she came to France she says:

I think there was a kind of fascination. People say that the British and the French find it very hard to get on, and you know, they could easily be at one another's throats. I've never had any problem with that. There's obviously the joke about Waterloo and the 100 years war, and things like that that are annoying. I just think also that French people live for communication a lot more, and I need to communicate, and I think especially when you are growing up and becoming an adult you want to feel the communication is easier. And with the French communication is very easy. Cause they like to talk.

Some of what Gail says echoes the statements of Linda, the British woman who felt so much more comfortable in France than the US:

I'm still on a voyage of discovery. I know I want to be here but I'm still learning how I feel about everything. But I think it's exciting. ...I'm getting used to things. I'm trying to become or look or sound more French ... In Paris you can be poor or rich and you are accepted. People will talk to each other no matter what class you belong to. On the level I operate on it seems that people will talk to anyone, even a homeless person. That's something I really like. I hate class and snobbism.

The *rapport* that these sojourners describe seems quite diffuse and not entirely related to the particular circumstances of a sojourn. In Linda's case, she seems much more willing to change herself to adapt to France than she was when she lived in the United States. This is despite the fact that living in France demands much more change (at least in terms of language learning) than living in the United States. So while some people felt at ease – or _rapport_ – with their new environments, there were others who inexplicably felt ill at ease.

Another example of a lack of rapport – or _negative rapport_ – is Joanna, the French woman who disliked American attitudes about terrorism.

Joanna: After a while in the States, I was like 'Wow, where am I?' I didn't appreciate parts of American culture. For me it was a great experience, but just if I look back, I couldn't have stayed in this country. I was definitely not part of it. For one year it was great, but ... It was not groovy enough for me.

Interviewer: Your comment 'I couldn't have stayed in this country' is interesting for me.

Joanna: It didn't improve my opinion about Americans, especially the foreign policy of the country. I think I'm too politically conscious. It's too important to ignore that when you are in the country. Especially in the United States. They dominate the whole world. Their behavior influences the rest of the world. You cannot be indifferent.

Once again, what bothers Joanna is diffuse, it is not 'groovy' enough for her, and she apparently finds Americans overbearing. The parallel that can be found between both these strongly positive and negative reactions is that they are highly personal and seem to be generated not only by predictable elements of cultural difference, but by the particular personality of the sojourner. While this result may not be surprising, it does raise issues related to developing a model for intercultural learning.

Obviously, someone like Adele, who seems to feel a strong negative rapport with Japanese culture, will clearly face difficult adaptive challenges. But how about people who feel positive rapport with a particular culture? Does this mean that they are overall better cultural learners? Or is their identification with their host culture simply a product of a good match between personality and environment? If so, does that mean that while they may fit well into a new environment, they won't easily gain more generalized intercultural empathy? Bennett (M.J. Bennett, 1993) refers to this issue indirectly when speaking of _accidental biculturals_, people who happen to grow up in two cultures, but who still are ethnocentric. According to Bennett, the ability to switch back and forth between different cultural points of view does not automatically confer intercultural sensitivity. It is the ability to abstract meaning about the significance of cultural difference that marks true intercultural sensitivity.

If Bennett's view is true, it could mean that sojourners who feel a great affinity towards a host culture may fail to learn some of the broader lessons offered by intercultural experiences. Andre, for example, the Swiss man who was so enamored with Japan, ended up coming back to Switzerland and eventually rejecting the life he had created in Japan. In discussing Japanese culture, he seems unable to relativize his experience. Perhaps because his attraction to Japan was so personal, he does not find cultural difference very important:

> I think that within [the same culture] we can be as different as people are between Switzerland and Japan. And there were people like [his ex-girlfriend] who I got so very well along with because it was kind of souls that we had that went very well along with each other. Non-verbal communication, whatever it was. We were just understanding each other very well. And *no*, I do not think that the culture has such a really big influence.

Yet, even as he dismisses the importance of culture, he seems to have run into some powerful barriers of implicit difference:

> I was so burned out. Now that I'm here back again I do not feel any desire of going back to Japan ... I do read Japanese. I do speak and write Japanese. [I experienced] all of these prejudices [that Japanese have]. They weren't even meant in a negative way. As a foreigner, they were astonished and they showed their astonishment. And I got tired doing that. ... Although I wanted to prove [to] the world that I can become 100% Japanese and feel very much at home there, that I preferred [returning to Switzerland and] being myself and having the possibility to being myself and to live straight away in a place where it [is] easy for me to live ... In Japan it would have cost me so much more energy. And I would have been frustrated that I can't express what I really want. ... And here I just can use few words. And speak so very naturally and they do understand perfectly. I know they do understand me. It is very important to get that feedback. I did not get that feedback in Japan.

And so Andre seems not to have fully accepted the prospect that Japanese cultural values and communication styles represent a valid alternative worldview. He has not achieved the meta-view of cultural difference emphasized by Bennett. Interestingly, Andre uses precisely this word when describing his feelings about the cultural discoveries he is making now that he is back in Switzerland:

Giving birth to myself again in my own culture here, I do rediscover it and yes I'm back again. It's not learning about my culture in a distant way, on a meta-level, kind of looking down upon my culture and I learn something. I'm living it now. I am living my culture again and this feels good. ... Here, I'm back. I do not think about myself. I do not learn about my culture. I just live it and I feel right.

One final clue to Andre's state of intercultural sensitivity is related to comments he made when discussing France. He expressed distaste for the French in general, saying:

Their time has passed. It might be that something new is coming but, desperately they're trying to adhere to an old heritage, the Alliance Française, and they have tried to keep their language from changing, having everything in their own words, they do not talk about software, it's *logiciel*. So much force trying to, forcedly trying to, keep the culture and its own identity.

So once again, Andre does not seem to be viewing other cultural points of view as valid alternatives. This is in spite of his deep intercultural experiences, and an apparent facility for languages. In addition to Swiss German, High German, and Japanese, Andre speaks excellent English as well as Italian and French.

Other sojourners who expressed a positive *rapport* for their host cultural environment were not nearly as extreme as Andre in their cultural learning. It was difficult to tell whether they had the kind of detached meta-level cultural empathy emphasized by Bennett. It seems, however, that we cannot conclude that a personal affinity towards a particular cultural environment greatly contributes to *cognitive empathy*. It also highlights once again the importance of the hidden sides of our identity. The overall tone of Andre's interview, for example, paints the picture of someone who felt alienated by certain elements in his home cultural environment and felt an attraction to another environment that seemed to offer an escape. This dynamic can function at the unconscious level and had his language education or study abroad preparation included more of an emphasis on the hidden nature of intercultural learning, he might have had more opportunities to reflect on his motivations and reactions when going to Japan. This might have spared him some of his later difficulties.

Relationships and Language Learning

Among the sojourners interviewed for this work, there were two factors that predicted, to some degree at least, increased *cognitive empathy*: language learning and the types of relationships with members of the host community. These two factors are often associated with intercultural success, but the sojourners interviewed in the book painted a rather complex picture of the relationship between language learning, relationships and increased cognitive empathy.

Perhaps surprisingly, learning a foreign language didn't seem to necessarily bring with it a high degree of cultural sensitivity. Andre, who spoke at least four languages at a high degree of proficiency, seemed not to have gained much cultural relativism in the process. One participant, Mayumi, referred to speaking a foreign language *too well*. In discussing how she is perceived by the English speakers she knows, she says:

> The reason I give the impressions of being nice is that I love learning languages, and so my linguistic skills were advanced. But my perception is that I don't have the social skills to match my linguistic skills.

Based simply on these two cases, it would almost seem that a high language learning aptitude can be a disadvantage in terms of cultural learning. Could Andre and Mayumi's experiences refer more easily to the acquisition of the external forms of language than the underlying value system and codes of interaction? Andre seems to have felt extremely frustrated by communication difficulties in spite of highly advanced linguistic skills. When discussing how frustrating it was not to be able to express his emotions in Japanese, he says:

> Here [in Switzerland] I can get angry also. I can have real relationships and it doesn't cost me a lot of energy. It's so easy for me to pick up the phone at 11:30 to ask (my friend) why doesn't she come over for wine; and we talk until 2 o'clock in the morning. And I have so many friends here. And with them it's so easy for me ... In Japan it would have cost me so much more energy. And I would have been frustrated that I can't express what I really want. Here I can do that in my own mother tongue which is Swiss-German dialect, and I feel very, very free here.

> And here I just can use few words. And speak so very naturally and they do understand perfectly. I know they do understand me. It is very important to get that feedback. I did not get that feedback in

Japan. Only with very, very few people. And even if I wanted to get it I felt I could not express myself to the extent that I wanted to. I couldn't express myself as perfectly as I wanted to.

One gets the impression that Andre feels that Japanese never express their emotions. This, of course, is not true. Japanese may express their emotions in a reserved way but it is part of a code that other Japanese understand. One illustration is the story of the Japanese man who came home from work and was served tea by his wife soon after arriving. Upon tasting it he discovered that it was only lukewarm. This alerted him to the fact that his wife was upset with them and he understood that it was because he had promised to be home much earlier. Andre clearly wants more verbal feedback than this man received. Perhaps mastering the verbal forms of the language did not improve Andre's communicative competence as much as he had hoped.

Both Mayumi and Andre make specific references to being 'good' at learning languages and make reference to the difference between linguistic skills and cultural skills. Much more common, however, were participants who talked about language learning in terms of how it gave them access to another social world. For these participants, learning a foreign language helped create the kind of meaningful relationships that characterize successful intercultural learning for Sparrow (2000). Some examples include, William:

In Hiroshima I went every Saturday to these all-volunteer classes and that's how I learned the basics of Japanese grammar and conversation. And actually that class pulled me out of my solitude because I met people and made friends there.

There was a woman at my university who didn't speak any Japanese and I used her as an anti-role model. I could see how she was seen in the school. She seemed unhappy. She was seen as lazy, and detached and not interested in getting involved. I decided early on that I didn't want to be like her.

It seems to me that the people who are bilingual are happier, they travel more, their conversations don't slip into a dark zone of complaints and frustrations ... My girlfriend and I usually speak English too, I'm kind of ashamed of that.

Also Neil.

Once you demonstrate that you have some ability to speak the language, people treat you more as an ordinary person. Maybe you won't get the special treatment, but at the same time you feel more part of the group instead of always being outside.... [W]hen someone came from [the phone company] and I could talk to them. I could interact with people. That has been a pleasant result of learning more Japanese.

Or Mayumi, a Japanese student who studied in the United States for a year:

With Americans, if I don't speak English well, I may think that I understand Americans but in fact not really understand them at all. It's necessary to involve myself with them. I thought that I spoke pretty good English before I went, but unless you really get into the culture, it's not possible to know.
My parents came over to me and told me that I had become Americanized. When I talk with my roommates, I show more emotion. Like they say 'Hi! How are you doing!?' and I started to adapt to that way of expressing myself. I felt that I have to adapt to their way of communicating. When I'm happy, I have to show I'm happy, and when I'm sad I do that.

In fact, most participants did talk about language learning in this way. Those that did not, tended to be those who had little language ability relative to the time they had spent abroad. We have seen Jack, who, having spent more than 10 years living in Japan, says the following:

My Japanese language ability is pretty low. I can have a basic conversation, talk about what they did or what they are going to do, making plans, I can express my feelings on some topics, I'm limited in vocabulary and grammar. ... I've only learned what I needed to learn to survive and get by ... what I need in my job, being an English teacher. I don't have a chance to use Japanese. I've made some attempts at times, joining language schools. I guess there are other things I've been interested in. I can experience the culture doing other things. I can experience the culture with people through English.
I passed the *nihongo kentei* third level [Japanese proficiency exam – equivalent to lower intermediate] years ago, if I had to take it again I'd probably fail. If I listen to the news I don't understand a thing. Dramas are much, much easier. I don't use it. I went to the post office today.

They said 'sign' and I said *'hai'* [yes/okay]. I really don't have the opportunities. I would have to create opportunities. For example I could go to the store, even though I don't need tuna fish I could ask for the tuna fish. I could call a department store on the phone and ask for something.

It is hard to guess what precisely Jack means by 'experience the culture with people through English' but he does not seem to be looking at his intercultural experiences in terms of relationships. Even more remarkable is his statement that he does not have the chance to use Japanese. His example of creating an opportunity to use Japanese by asking for something he does not really need in the supermarket seems to be a reflection of how little he sees Japanese as a tool for interaction and relationships. The shallowness of his linguistic ability reflects his isolation – the extent to which he keeps himself at the explicit levels of cultural learning. This makes his reported satisfaction and enjoyment of his life in Japan that much more remarkable.

Another participant who has spent six years in Korea and six years in Japan without much foreign language learning is Steven:

I tried to study on my own and also went to a language school for three months while in Korea. Students often tried to help. That's about my language experience. I developed a survival/functional ability, not conversational. Ask for directions and buy stuff in the store. I could tell them I'm a teacher, and what subject I teach, but not in depth. Couldn't discuss any abstract topics, basically functional stuff.

Like Jack, Steven is focused on the explicit elements of cultural learning:

But [cultural adaptation] wasn't that big of a problem because once you get your lifestyle settled you don't need to be shopping every weekend.

For me, learning a culture starts with their history. To me the history will give lots of clues to current behaviors customs and values, and trying to learn how the local people think and behave.

[Cultural understanding] helped me understand why things worked the way they did. For example if I wanted to see someone, and I was told that I couldn't, it helped me understand that it was because of their status. It even helps with body language. Once I was in a restaurant sitting with my back to the door and suddenly everyone stood up and bowed. What gave me the clue was that it was a very deep bow. That let me know that the person who entered the room was very important.

There's a lot of people who say that if you are a foreigner there's always a limit [to what you can understand culturally]. It's a question of degree. I'm sure that being fluent in the foreign language would help. But there are also other ways of getting that information, like how I did.

So Steven sees himself as having gained a high degree of cultural insight without speaking a foreign language, though it's not clear that this·is true.

Cultural Distance

It is generally assumed that greater cultural distance makes for more challenging intercultural experiences. Paige (1993), for example, lists the degree of difference between a sojourner's own culture and the host culture as a factor which contributes to the psychological intensity of an intercultural experience. And indeed, this may explain to some degree David's inability to make an empathetic leap with his Asian student pilots. The experiences of other participants, however, indicated that it would be misleading to say that increasing cultural distance automatically means that an intercultural experience is more demanding and/or deeper. The demands of the specific context of the sojourner's living situation seemed even more important in trying to understand an individual's cultural learning than broadly-defined cultural distance. This is one of the reasons that this work has focused on *adaptive demands* faced by sojourners, including the depth of those demands. Knowledge of a particular type or degree of cultural difference is not enough, by itself, to explain the intercultural learning process for a given individual.

The depth of adaptive demands seems to affect the cultural learning process more than the degree of cultural difference between two communities. Mayumi first lived in the United States as a university student and later married a Korean man and moved to Korea. Mayumi gives an articulate account of the adaptation process in these two situations. In theory, the cultural distance between Korea and Japan is much less than that between Japan and the United States. Korean and Japanese societies share many deep-rooted cultural characteristics such as an emphasis on explicit hierarchy and a preference for high-context communication. Many common cultural value orientations in Korea such as a Confucian emphasis on respect towards elders, the importance of effort and study or an acceptance of hierarchy are easily recognizable for Japanese. Japanese and Korean belong to the same language family (Altaic) and the two languages share similar grammatical structures, systems of deferential language and a high number of cognates. Mayumi refers to the ease with which she learned Korean:

It was easy to learn Korean. It took me less time [than English]. I studied first in the States, and I had Korean friends. I took a semester and learned to write the basic alphabet. Then I visited for five days to Korea, and I thought it would be cool to learn. Then I met my husband and I went to live in Korea and I studied there for about six months of classes.

Mayumi actually refers to the ease of expressing her personality in Korean relative to English. When talking about ways in which her personality changes depending on the language she speaks, she says:

I think there is some parts that I change because of language. The differences are more obvious between English and Japanese. I can present my personality more easily in Korean because of that.

Yet despite this cultural and linguistic similarity, and the fact that she is married to a Korean, she describes adaptation to life in Korea as being extremely difficult:

I had a very mixed feeling. I became strongly attracted to Korea, but at the same time it wasn't easy because I was Japanese. One thing that was great about Korea was that I didn't stand out as foreigner. No one realized I was Japanese so I was able to mingle more smoothly. At the same time, they expected me to behave like a Korean, and assumed similarity. But there were subtle differences which were hard to accept, and I tried to be accommodating and then got frustrated and finally exploded at the end. Very close family relationships, and I had to call my mother-in-law every day, and I was nervous talking to her in Korean without knowing what to say. My husband was working late and we had a lot of things we had to do with the family.

It is important to note that blending in physically meant that Mayumi was expected to act like Koreans. In this sense, her physical similarity and relatively small culture distance made the demands *more* intense. If Mayumi had been an American, perhaps Korean's would have expected less from her and her adaptive demands would have been, at least in some ways, easier to deal with. In the case of the adaptive demands

Mayumi faced in the United States, she refers primarily to challenges she dealt with successfully:

> I was [happy] for the most part. It was hard, especially in the beginning. Mostly because to get along with the people the same age, I was able to understand my professors talk, but my friends used very colloquial forms and the content was very difficult. They would be talking about TV programs. The things they talked about were every different than the things I was used to talking about. I didn't feel like I was my true self. I hated it because I didn't seem like my usual self – I'm outgoing but I wasn't seen that way. I was seen as a quiet Asian girl. I thought the food would be difficult but it wasn't. Also, there were few Japanese at the undergraduate level so there wasn't much support. It was tough in the beginning, mostly for social reasons, not academic.

In spite of these understandable difficulties, Mayumi integrated into university life in the US, made friends, and describes herself as having been happy with life there. She had a circle of American friends and an American boyfriend. Her stories about life in the US were primarily about having overcome the difficulties of adaptation, while in Korea it seems certain issues could not be resolved. In addition to her statement above about having mixed feelings about her Korean experience and having 'exploded at the end', she talks about difference that seemed to have left lasting frustration:

> My mother-in-law could come to my apartment unannounced. I left Korea a couple of times that I got stressed out. When I wasn't there my mother-in-law would go and clean up for me, making me feel like a failure when I returned. She even bleached the teapot. Of course she felt she was being kind, and I didn't take it as an offense, and I felt a bit angry at my husband for letting her do it. Don't get me wrong, I really love his parents. I don't think I could live with them, because of the differences in customs. I have lots of complaints against their son but not them.

As we have seen, Mayumi felt many frustrations with her life in Korea. An obvious lesson in Mayumi's accounts is that the degree of cultural distance does not automatically translate to increased intercultural learning demands. The pressures Mayumi faced seemed more related to the depth of the relationships and roles she played – a student in the US and a wife and daughter-in-law in Korea. It is easy to imagine that the social pressures she faced with her Korean in-laws were in many ways greater than those faced as a student at an American university.

Another participant who faced cultural adaptation challenges in more than one culture was Linda, the British woman who first lived in the United States with her family as a trailing spouse, and then after divorcing went to live in France. In a way that parallels Mayumi to a certain degree, Linda has highly negative things to say about her experience in the United States compared to her life in France. This is in spite of the obvious challenges in France of learning a new language and dealing with cultural frameworks that are, in theory at least, more different from those found in Britain.

Linda talks about her experiences in a very personal way without the kind of detachment that Mayumi displays when expressing her frustrations in Korea. We have seen her statements about life in the United States compared with those of life in France. Of the United States, Linda says:

Linda: Everyone said Americans are so open, it will be great, but when we were going into our first house the neighbors wouldn't talk to us because we were renters not owners ... They had such a snobbish attitude. It was unbelievable. I detest things like that. ... They just didn't like outsiders, especially the English.

Interviewer: How could you tell?

Linda: By the fact that no one would speak to me. Even when we moved in, the one neighbor came with a bottle of wine, but after that I didn't meet anyone for nine months. Later, I decided to have a party together with that neighbor, and we invited everyone in the whole neighborhood, and they came, and they said: 'Oh, I'm sorry, I should have come.' Some of it was my fault ... There was a group of people that had coffee and I was supposed to go and do that with them, a kind of coffee klatch, but I hate that kind of thing. I hate having to forcibly go and meet people. It was partly my state of mind because I didn't really want to be there. Things got better after that, but I was still doing things I didn't want to do just to survive.

Linda's description of her life in France, on the other hand, is much more positive:

I'm still on a voyage of discovery. I know I want to be here but I'm still learning how I feel about everything. But I think it's exciting. ...I'm still changing and adapting. I'm happier because my marital circumstances have changed. I'm getting used to things. I'm trying to become or look or sound more French. ...I just couldn't take the whole money thing where we lived [in the US]. In Paris you can be poor or rich and you are accepted. People will talk to each other no matter what class you belong to. On the level I operate on it seems that people will talk to anyone, even a homeless person. That's something I really like. I hate class and snobbism.

As with Mayumi, it is hard to say why specifically Linda had more trouble getting used to life in the US than in France. It seems apparent, however, that a sojourner's individual circumstances (student versus daughter-in-law, trailing spouse versus sojourner by choice) can be larger factors in an individual's cultural learning than abstractions about presumed cultural distance. In addition, a learner's personality may simply be more suited to a particular set of cultural frameworks. People have complicated reactions to new cultural environments, some of which may be contradictory. The demands of a particular learning context are clearly important, including the relative depth of the experience, and the kind of demands being placed on the learner. Many of these factors relate to whether individual sojourners develop deeper relationships with members of their host community and how well they end up learning the language. In the next chapter we will look at the most successful sojourners and see what they have to teach us about ideal outcomes for intercultural learning.

Chapter 12
Beyond Adaptation

I sometimes feel like I am a bridge, between cultures or groups, with a foundation on both sides, but also a foundation in the middle which doesn't belong to either side.
Paul

It is interesting to compare the definitions of successful intercultural learning with the experiences of the best adjusted sojourners interviewed for this work. In particular, we can see how their sense of personal identity evolves as their membership in different cultural communities changes. Throughout much of this work, cultural communities have been discussed in terms of shared frameworks of meanings, not one's personal sense of identity. It is clear, however, that deep intercultural learning does have an impact on a sojourner's sense of cultural identity. In the case of Paul (above), there is a sense that he doesn't feel completely connected to any particular cultural community. Does this indicate that he has gone 'beyond' culture? Or does he simply feel detached?

Defining Intercultural Success

As we have seen in Chapter 5, Sparrow (2000: 173) has argued that a fully engaged membership in a host community is a primary indicator of successful intercultural learning. She argues for a need to go beyond a focus on 'enhanced cognitive awareness, to a view of identity development which is interactive, highly dependent on context, and ultimately rooted in gender, race, ethnicity and religion'. She argues that it is difficult or impossible to ever go 'beyond' one's cultural frameworks in the way described by Bennett. According to Bennett, at advanced stages of cultural learning, one no longer has a primary affiliation with a single culture, but rather is engaged in a constructive marginality. Sparrow finds this view, which originated with Adler's description of the 'multicultural man' (Adler, 1977), to be overly intellectualized and to reflect a particularly male, Cartesian view of development which emphasizes finding an ultimate objective point of view from which to observe reality. For Sparrow, intercultural learning is closely wedded to a feeling of connectedness to particular cultural communities, not the kind of detachment described by Bennett and Adler.

213

Whereas Sparrow refers to successful learners as feeling strong connections to particular communities, M.J. Bennett (1993) talks about successful sojourners feeling they don't totally belongs to *any* cultural community. Among those interviewed for this work, there were three participants who seemed to match Bennett and Adler's (1977) description of the 'multicultural' person. That is to say, even more so than Mayumi, they seemed to have learned to function comfortably in multiple cultural frameworks, to be fully engaged in their social environments and not feel limited or inseparably attached by a primary cultural affiliation. This is not to say that they did not feel a primary affiliation, but they each talked about their identity in terms of multiple frameworks as much as in terms of membership in a particular community.

Two of these three sojourners grew up in many different cultures due to the circumstances of their family and childhood. Paul is an American citizen, son of a diplomat, who was born in Nepal, raised in Morocco, Europe and the United States. He has German grandparents and grew up speaking English, French and German. Paul describes his identity in terms of a multiplicity of perspectives. For example:

Paul: I sometimes feel like I am a bridge, between cultures or groups, with a foundation on both sides, but also a foundation in the middle which doesn't belong to either side.

Interviewer: How would you describe your cultural identity? How American do you feel?

Paul: On one level I've always seen myself as a world citizen, and then I'd have to drop down one level and say German American. My mother's German, but my father also has a strong German cultural identity. His parents spoke German and he learned German and his grandparents came over from there and we have maintained ties to family there that go back 100 years.

So even when Paul 'drops down' a level of abstraction, he does not define himself as an American, but as a 'German-American'. But he feels like a bridge between cultures, not only between Germany and the United States, but in a more general way related to adapting to different cultural circumstances.

When I moved to India from Morocco my mother spoke to me in French and I refused to speak in French. I told her 'but they don't speak that here' and I refused to speak. I had lots of Indian friends, and lots of Moroccan friends ... people from countries all over. ... You are as many people as languages that you speak. When you speak a different language your thought patterns change and your gestures change.

I don't always feel like I fit in. You overlap to a certain degree, but there's always a place that doesn't overlap, and so your identity is always separate in some way.

Paul illustrates his shifting identity by talking about how his code shifts in different languages. He is clearly referring to highly implicit parts of cultural identity when referring to changing 'thought patterns' and gestures. Notice that while Mayumi and other participants described their adaptation process in terms of joining or being accepted by other cultural communities, Paul defines himself by a degree of *separateness*, saying that there's 'always a place that doesn't overlap' and describing himself as a bridge with a more solid foundation in the middle than on either side.

So Paul describes himself as being American, with strong German roots, yet always detached in some way. His stories of growing up are stories of ongoing adaptation – cultural learning as a primary focus of identity:

In Morocco I actually spoke better French than English. That had to do with the maid Fatima, and I went to a French nursery school. In that sense I didn't have a developed sense of being an American. According to my mom she once took me to the bazaar and I spit in the face of a man that my mom was haggling with.

When I was about five or six my family got home leave and we took an extended period over Christmas and we went to Germany, but I didn't want to go, so my grandmother promised me a cowboy outfit. And it was the first time I saw snow and it was the wildest thing. I showed a snowball to each of my relatives and said 'It's cold'. We first went to Nuremberg, and stayed with my aunt and uncle and I felt really out of place, out of my comfort zone, culture context. I had never seen so many Caucasians, and only Caucasians. Having grown up in Morocco and India I wasn't used to so many white people. I felt really uncomfortable. First time I saw television.

When I moved to India from Morocco my mother spoke to me in French and I refused to speak in French. I told her 'but they don't speak that here' and I refused to speak. I had lots of Indian friends, and lots of Moroccan friends ... people from countries all over.

I had culture shock coming back to the States in high school. We lived there from '73 to '77, then went to France and came back to home leave in '79, then permanently in '81. Each time I came back, in the US things change faster than in other places. I used to measure change by the kind of cash register in MacDonald's. That was what I looked at. And they are still changing.

In high school I had to start Grade 12 in the US, and high school was like four times bigger than the Canadian school in France and everyone had been in the school for many years, and it was one of the few times of my life that I didn't make many friends. I just didn't feel like I had anything in common with people. Other guys were talking about cars, and I didn't have any interest.

In his description of going back to high school in the US, Paul refers specifically to trouble making friends, yet overall it seems that he was capable of integrating into a wide range of cultural communities and code switching between different languages. He certainly does not express the kind of frustration of someone like Adele, who hates Japanese culture so much, or even Mayumi, who struggled to adapt to life in Korea. Adaptation, it seems, is a primary and integral part of his cultural identity.

This view of having cultural adaptation at the center of one's identity closely mirrors M.J. Bennett's (1993) description of the end product of cultural learning in the DMIS. As quoted earlier:

> marginality describes exactly the subjective experience of people who are struggling with the total integration of ethnorelativism. They are outside all cultural frames of reference by virtue of the ability to consciously raise any assumption to a meta-level (level of self-reference). In other words, there is no natural cultural identity for a marginal person. There are no unquestioned assumptions, no intrinsically absolute right behaviours, nor any necessary reference group. (p. 63)

This description seems to match Paul's discussion of his cultural identity. He has a meta-level ability to see all behavior existing in equally viable, yet varying cultural contexts:

> When you go somewhere, the way that people do things is simply the way people do things and so you adapt to that. Of course it doesn't mean that you don't judge, or that you like it, but you adapt. It also has to do with the environment that you are used to. When things are different it might create some internal tensions, but you adapt. ...You just get used to the way people expect you to do things.

Paul does not imply that he is equally comfortable everywhere or that he does not have personal preferences about how to do things. But he recognizes that his personal preferences are simply that, and he is capable of understanding different expectations about behavior at the meta-level of varying interpretive frameworks maintained in different cultural communities.

The 'Chameleon'

Another participant whose description of her intercultural experiences closely mirrored Paul's, and who matches very well Bennett's description of the most-advanced state of cultural learning, was Yuko. Yuko is a Japanese citizen who was raised first in India (16 years) speaking Japanese with her family and Hindi and English in school and with friends. She later lived in the United States and finally went to live for an extended period for the first time in Japan. Yuko's first language learned was Hindi, but she now feels most comfortable in English and then Japanese. She learned written Japanese by visiting Japan on holidays and by being taught by her parents. Like Paul, Yuko defines her cultural identity not in terms of connection to a primary cultural community, but rather to the process of cultural learning itself.

> I was a very fast learner. I went to an international school. Me and my brothers and sisters are chameleons.
> The important thing is knowing what the rules are. When I first came to Japan it took me three years to learn how to slurp.
> With me and my sister borders don't matter, and it's no longer about language. My brother, who has lived in Japan less than I have, and he has the least Japanese tutoring only speaks Japanese, so nobody would realize that he spoke English. A lot of people are surprised that he can speak English. His English is really good. I have an American friend who has never spoken to my brother in English. She would speak to me in English and to my brother in Japanese. He [the brother] has that big chameleon thing. He says 'Yuko you're not a very good chameleon'. When my sister speaks she throws in different words from different languages because she feels they express things better.

Yuko's use of the word 'chameleon' is striking, as is her statement that 'borders don't matter'. Yuko is very aware of the fact that different cultural contexts involve different expectations about what is normal, and like Paul, while she finds cultural expectations that she does not like, she recognizes that they represent a viable reality and that one can use those varying cultural frameworks to express an individual identity. In Yuko's case, the process of adapting to life in Japan as a university student and company employee is remarkable. Because she grew up outside of Japan, though Yuko spoke Japanese, she didn't have a deep understanding of Japanese cultural norms and values. She made a conscious effort, however, to learn and adapt. Her account of learning to be a 'submissive woman' after having been raised in the cosmopolitan environment of international schools, and places such as Europe and the United States, is fascinating:

> I worked very hard at adapting and blending in. So, I was able to get even very traditional friends. One way I decided to improve my Japanese was to get a part time job at Itoyokado [a Japanese department store – a traditional working environment]. Also I wanted to work for a Japanese company. Going to an international school you represent your culture and country, but having never lived here you get a stereotypical view of Japan so I wanted to experience a Japanese company so I worked there. The reality is very different from the stereotypes: The *sempai-kohai* [lit. superior–subordinate] concept, the whole hierarchy. I don't think anyone can understand it.
>
> Well, I went through the whole range, I tried everything once. Serving tea, opening the elevator doors for me, the whole *aisatsu*, [lit. greeting – also refers to ceremonial speeches/introductions] it's hard to put my finger on it. Now I live my way, but when I came here I tried really hard to blend in, the way of socializing, you know when you have an opinion, the way you express it people might think you are pushy. When you do *settai* [socializing with customers for the purpose of relationship building], I was just a *kazari* [lit. decoration, meaning she was meant to be seen but not heard], I was not part of the *settai*. They needed a young female to pour so they brought me along instead of being there to contribute to the business. I spent so many evenings pouring beer and translating.
>
> It's a give and take. Being Japanese in one situation asks for it. Since my name is Japanese I'm a Japanese and they expect a very submissive person. The salespeople think they can get their way with me because I am young. But I can yell when I want to, or speak up when I want to, when the situation calls for it. But at the same time it doesn't mean that I don't know what the manners are. I just choose. For example I don't send *ochuugen* or *seibo* [seasonal gifts] and I send Christmas cards instead of *nengajo* [New Year's greeting card].

One striking thing about Yuko's account is her reference to 'trying everything once'. The examples she gives, such as serving tea and being a 'decoration' that pours drinks for customers, refer to parts of Japanese culture that are the most traditional and could be considered hardest for foreigners – particularly those with a background emphasizing individualism and gender equality – to get used to. She seems proud of having been able to get 'traditional friends' and chose a job at a very traditional department store (one in which staff is trained in proper bowing etiquette and honorific language and in which staff greets customers at store opening in uniforms with deep bows). This is quite a different world from her previous experiences, feeling most comfortable in English, going to international schools, studying in the United States and hanging out with friends from all over the world. Yet for Yuko, like for Paul, this conscious process of cultural adaptation seems to be an important part of her cultural identity.

Notice that Yuko does not seem to be trying to 'find her roots' in Japan. She wants to understand the cultural 'system'. Once having learned the system, however, she makes choices about how to express herself as an individual – yelling at salespeople and sending Christmas cards rather than New Year's greeting cards. She is proud of her success integrating and forming relationships with Japanese, yet maintains an identity separate from this:

> In my first apartment, when I invited my Japanese friends over they saw me just like a typical young Japanese girl. But when I moved I decided to change it ... My aunt was very surprised when she visited my [new] apartment because when I talk to her I'm really Japanese, but when she came to my apartment she saw a very different side of me.

So, like Paul, Yuko seems the archetype of the 'constructive cultural marginal' described by Bennett. Given that she is so flexible, and clearly is a member of multiple cultural communities, one wonders if she has a primary affiliation – as Sparrow's description of successful interculturalists suggests. But when asked if there were people from a particular culture that she felt most comfortable with, she says: 'Third culture kids. For example my best friends are people that grew up in more than one culture and speak several languages.' It seems that Yuko is a cultural marginal to the core.

While Paul and Yuko do not invalidate Sparrow's point that feeling connected to and gaining membership in particular cultural communities is an important marker of intercultural learning, they do lend weight to Bennett's idea that in some ways at least, it *is* possible to go beyond a single cultural affiliation and achieve a kind of constructed cultural identity. So it could be argued that constructive cultural marginality represents a kind of end product of very deep cultural learning. However, both Yuko and Paul were raised in circumstances that are extremely rare, speaking multiple languages and being exposed to many different cultural frameworks. One could almost say that multiculturalism *is* their culture. This is echoed in Yuko's statement that the people she feels most comfortable with are 'third-culture kids' – people who have been raised in multicultural environments like she has.

This does not mean that this 'third culture' is just another cultural framework like any other. They are certainly more adapted intercultural learners than people growing up in more limited intercultural contexts. But the fact remains that they were, in effect, *forced* to adapt by virtue of their international background. We can't assume, however, that being raised in a multicultural environment automatically confers this 'beyond culture' state. In the case of one participant – Liz – though she was raised in a bicultural environment, as a child she 'chose' a primary cultural affiliation. Ultimately, the participants in this study support both Bennett's idea that a form of deep intercultural relativism can represent an end product of intercultural learning, as well as Sparrow's idea that forming relationships with members of a host cultural community is an important element of intercultural adaptation.

Identity Questions and Deep Cultural Learning

Cultural learners who confront the need to code-switch between different cultural worlds often confront questions about their personal identity. Those who didn't speak a foreign language did not seem to do this sort of code switching. Jack and Steven, who both had long experiences abroad, did not mention identity issues in their discussion of cultural learning. Adele never spoke of her language learning in terms of code switching and it seem that her identity as an American was even reinforced – she was glad that she was born in the United States. Andre, the talented linguist from Switzerland, seemed uncomfortable with the deeper value and identity changes implied by adapting to a very different communication style. Like Adele, his Swiss identity was reinforced by his intercultural experiences, and it seemed that he never became comfortable doing cultural code switching.

Learners who had deep experiences in several different cultures, including Abdou, Yuko, Paul and Mayumi, all talked about changes in their sense of cultural identity. While the first three talk about their intercultural selves primarily from the perspective of having resolved identity issues, Mayumi gives the impression of still grappling with them:

I didn't feel like I was my true self. I hated it because I didn't seem like my usual self – I'm outgoing but I wasn't seen that way. I was seen as a quiet Asian girl. I thought the food would be difficult but it wasn't.

I try to accommodate to the other person, but sometimes that's at the expense of my true identity. If I continue to do that I reach a threshold, but when I got to the point that enough is enough, then I kind of retreated and tried to be more true to myself.

I think there is some parts that I change because of language. The differences are more obvious between English and Japanese. I can present my personality more easily in Korean because of that. Sometimes I really feel a difference in behavior or how to talk to people in different languages and I don't know which approach to take. In that sense I ... do change. I guess there are changes that I make but that I don't notice them.

I haven't really figured out who I am yet, or I haven't accepted my self yet.

Unlike Paul, Abdou and Yuko, who seem to be highly comfortable shifting between different cultural realities, Mayumi seems to feel that there are limits to how much she can change and still be her 'true self'. She apparently hasn't fully resolved the potential conflict between having a stable sense of self and shifting between different social and cultural frameworks. Given her apparent deep acceptance of the validity of other cultural worldviews, however, she may well be at the threshold of the kind of 'integrated marginal' state constructed by the other three.

Confronting cultural difference at very deep levels can easily be threatening. Joanna's distaste for Americans who do not see 'reality' and Adele's conclusion that she was happy to be born in the United States seem indicative of this. Some sojourners seemed to deal with this issue by isolating themselves. Jack and Steven seem to be in this category. Some others, such as William and Neil, seemed to have felt a good personal fit between their personalities and their host cultural surroundings. As noted, only a few sojourners seemed to have resolved the deeper issues of identity and shifting cultural frameworks.

One participant who spoke specifically of cultural identity issues was Liz. She lived in Japan with her family as a very young child then lived there again from the age of 11. At the time, she seems to have been well on her way to forming an identity within Japanese cultural frameworks:

> [I] stayed in international school for two years and most of the other students were Japanese and after class everyone spoke Japanese. I was looking for friends and so had to speak Japanese. ... In junior high school I tried to be Japanese. I wanted to be the perfect little Japanese girl – I had the backpack and all the gear. I actually liked the uniform. I loved riding the train. ... It was very natural. I was reading a lot. My friendships were in Japanese. Every morning I used to ride the same train in the same car and there was this businessman who rode it too. We would always sit together and he would help me with my homework.

At this point, however, something happened:

> I was 13 years old. I think I had a little identity crisis. I wanted to hang out with Americans for a while. I hung out with the swim team over the summer and I wanted to be with them. I think it was the first conscious decision to be American.
>
> Being around Americans I felt a sense of relaxation ... not trying to fit in. I was too tall, I was too bulky. I didn't speak the language. With the Americans I fit in and I liked it. I had several really close Japanese friends and that was really hard. That was the downside. My very best friend I still keep in touch with. I felt like I was letting her down.

This decision seems to have been a critical juncture for Liz. She eventually went back to the US and developed her identity as an American. She maintained a strong interest in Japan, however, and did not lose the Japanese that she had learned. She studied Japanese in college and later got a job in Tokyo working for an American organization. She married an American.

In spite of her continued involvement with Japan and the subsequent improvement of her Japanese – she reads Japanese newspapers as part of her job – Liz seems to never have regained the feeling of being an insider in Japan. She talks almost as though Japan has failed her. She does, however, identify with Japan. She speaks about this primarily in the context of her work with Japanese businesses:

I don't want Korea to pass Japan. I identify with a lot of Japanese. I talk with my husband and we say aren't we glad we have an option. [Because, as Americans, they have the choice of leaving the country.] I don't like it when I'm this cynical. I go to Korea and I come back with this big high because Korea has figured some things out. They've made some big changes.

It's hard to respect Japanese leaders when things are, from an American's perspective, so backwards. To be honest, my business in the last three months couldn't be better. I'm a pretty competitive person too. I love the program on NHK [Japanese television station] about the creative Japanese inventors of the past. I just wish there were a little more pride in oneself here. Patriotism is taboo, loyalty to companies is going out the window. Creativity is just starting to be valued, so where do you get the esteem? And most of my Japanese friends, we start talking about the economy and we all get depressed. I get out of Tokyo every weekend and I try not to think about it. I do ask myself if I should start cutting my losses and start learning Chinese.

In personal situations I've been known to use bad Japanese to be the stupid *gaijin* [foreigner]. Recently I got free admission to a museum by saying *'nihongo tabemasen'* [I don't eat Japanese (language)]. And it worked!

Given the depth of Liz's involvement with Japan, it is perhaps surprising that she is willing to pretend to be an ignorant foreigner simply for the sake of gaining admission to a museum. This seems to reflect, however, a fundamental feeling that her identity is not attached to any potential she might have for being an insider in Japan. It is as though her decision at 13 has carried through into her adult life. The strength of her 'non-Japanese' self is evidenced by her statement that she sometimes feels she should 'cut her losses' and start learning Chinese.

Binary intercultural experiences and triangulation

Liz seems to root her identity clearly in a particular culture – American. She has this in common with all the participants in this study, with the exception of the three 'integrated marginals': Yuko, Paul and Abdou. In addition, like most others who were interviewed for this work, she has primarily a binary experience of cultural difference. She faced a choice of American and Japanese identity. For most sojourners, cultural learning primarily involves experiencing a single new environment. Once again, the primary exceptions to this were Yuko, Paul and Abdou, all of whom

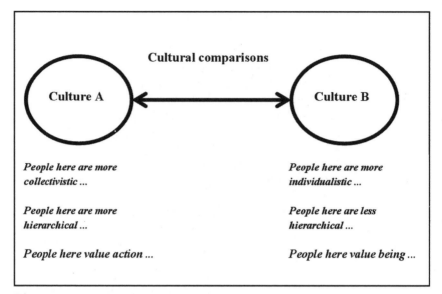

People here are more
collectivistic ...

People here are more
individualistic ...

People here are more
hierarchical ...

People here are less
hierarchical ...

People here value action ...

People here value being ...

Diagram 12.1

had deep intercultural experiences in multiple cultural settings. Their experiences hint at a qualitative difference between having deep intercultural experiences in two cultures and multiple cultures. When someone experiences two cultural frameworks, only a binary comparison is possible (Diagram 12.1):

Someone who has three or more deep experiences, on the other hand, can do a kind of *triangulation*, in which they recognize not only that it is possible to look at the world in a different way, but also a greater sense of the range of possible differences. For example, someone who has experienced the relatively collectivist cultural frameworks in India as well as the relatively individualistic frameworks of England, who then has a deep intercultural experience in Japan, will be exposed to a much more nuanced view of collectivist and individualist thought. The sense of community among Hindus and the sense of community among Japanese colleagues may both be collectivist relative to a traditionally British view of the individual, but having this third point of comparison makes it much easier to extrapolate as to the potential for other combinations of cultural characteristics (Diagram 12.2).

A sojourner who can *triangulate* in this way could therefore more easily escape an *either/or* view of cultural difference. No longer would belonging to a particular set of cultural frameworks imply an absolute choice. It would instead represent a set of choices within the context of an infinite

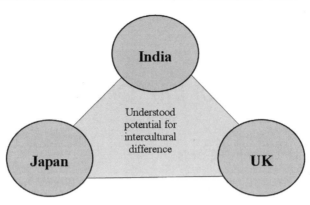

Diagram 12.2

variety of potential cultural difference. When integrated marginals like Yuko or Paul speak about their identities – as chameleons, for example, or bridges which have their strongest support in the middle – they seem to be functioning in this triangulated fashion. This does not seem to be related simply to speaking more languages – since Andre, for example, spoke multiple languages – but rather to being deeply accepting of cultural difference, and having deep experiences in multiple cultures. The one other multilingual participant who had deep experiences in more than one culture – Philippe, who told the horror stories about German trash collection – seems to be fundamentally less accepting of cultural difference. Mayumi, who is highly functional in Japanese, Korean and English, and who seems quite accepting of cultural difference, may be struggling with the identity issues which arise from having had this kind of triangulated experience.

Chapter 13

Implications for the 'Global Village'

Intercultural Learning Goals

This work has emphasized a description of intercultural learning which finds both positive and negative outcomes of intercultural experiences to be normal. For educators, of course, negative outcomes are less desirable and it is important to consider how this description of intercultural learning can inform intercultural education. The successes of intercultural learners can act as signposts in intercultural education and successful sojourners can be learning models. We have seen highly successful interculturalists, such as Paul and Yuko, and thus need to consider if they should serve as the model for intercultural learners. As we have seen, however, the kind of deep cognitive empathy and 'beyond culture' state they reported are so rare that it may not be appropriate to consider their experiences as the target of intercultural learning. For most sojourners, success may more reasonably be defined not by an abstract meta-consciousness of cultural difference, but rather by the ability to understand and accept difference at a deep level and use this acceptance as a base to build relationships and develop communication skills in new cultural communities. It remains, then, to find ways to apply this insight.

A vocabulary for intercultural experiences

It is striking that among the typical goals of intercultural learning there is little emphasis on the possibility of negative outcomes – there doesn't even seem to be neutral terminology to express this phenomenon. Yet, this work has shown that intercultural contact can reinforce or create negative attitudes and intolerance. This is a serious problem because such negative attitudes are embedded in the lived experience of sojourners and not easily altered. Terms such as *culture shock* or *culture stress* articulate the psychological stresses of intercultural adaptation, but do not go so far as characterizing the long-term possible negative consequences of intercultural learning. For terms like 'cultural awareness' there seems almost no negative counterpart, other than 'not being aware'. Words such as *intolerance, racism,* and *prejudice* describe accurately negative attitudes towards cultural difference, but they are pejorative. Few learners would say 'I felt intolerant' to describe an intercultural reaction.

In this sense also, the terminology presented here may be of use. *Resistance* as a term describes a reaction to an experience and not an absolute measure of intercultural sensitivity. Thus, it's easier for learners to apply it to themselves. In this work, we have seen the difficulty of accepting more implicit levels of intercultural difference. For Philippe, Germans were simply unreasonable in their trash sorting, and for David, Asian students had no 'survival instincts'. The challenge for learners like this is to identify what precisely they are resisting. This implies going beyond the superficial level of explicit behavior – separating the trash – and examining the reasons for one's particular reaction. In this sense, the term *resistance* may provide a neutral label for the experience. This neutrality is important if learners are going to reflect openly on the deeper layers of their personal and cultural identities.

The intercultural learning process described in this work emphasizes the importance of *acceptance* of cultural difference as a way of gaining *cognitive empathy*. For educators, helping intercultural learners to recognize the importance of *acceptance* as a factor in enhancing their intercultural experience would seem an appropriate pedagogical goal. In addition, learners need to recognize that *resistance*, *acceptance* and *adaptation* function not only at explicit levels but deeper ones as well. It is not enough to know that *acceptance* is important, it must also be realized that discovering the cultural differences that need to be dealt with is not that easy. Fortunately, as a goal of intercultural education, *acceptance* is relatively easy to describe, give examples of, explain the importance of, etc. In addition, since most people accept a certain degree of intercultural difference, the task of an intercultural educator becomes not so much changing a learner's attitudes or awareness, but rather helping learners explore acceptance and resistance more fully.

Applying the vocabulary of intercultural experiences

The concepts *resistance*, *acceptance* and *adaptation* can be integrated into existing intercultural training techniques. For example, one common intercultural training technique makes use of 'critical incidents', or narratives, describing an instance of cross-cultural conflict or misunderstanding and involves asking learners to make cross-cultural judgments. If, in addition, learners are asked to imagine themselves in these situations and discuss their reaction in terms of *resistance*, *acceptance* and *adaptation*, they can use these incidents in a more personal way. Thus, the use of critical incidents becomes not only a way to highlight the particular points of intercultural conflict, but a kind of virtual intercultural experience with an emphasis on the *reaction* to cultural difference and not simply on having the 'correct' interpretation of a given intercultural situation. This shifts emphasis towards a more process-oriented or developmental view of intercultural learning. Intercultural education that focuses on cross-cultural comparison can also benefit from these concepts. Rather than simply describing cultural difference as something to be quantified, as in 'When in the Middle East you should be prepared to eat with your fingers', emphasis can be placed on how one might react (or has reacted to) differences. In other words, it is not the specific cultural differences that are the defining characteristic of intercultural learning, it is one's reaction to differences found.

For culture-specific intercultural education, such as predeparture training for study-abroad students or expatriates, *resistance, acceptance* and *adaptation* lend themselves to a case-study approach. The stories of those who have 'gone before' can be an entry point for learners to examine their potential reactions to their new environment. To use an example from the study of Australian students learning to deal with French universities, predeparture training could focus on having prospective students analyze the stories of other students from previous years. Learners could analyze stories as well as specific statements such as 'the French are incredibly bureaucratic' in terms of whether this represents *resistance* or not. This may help learners to be more aware of their reactions to cultural difference and encourage the suspension of judgment and increased empathy.

Another common culture-general training activity is games such as Bafa Bafa (D.G. Carroll, 1997) or Barnga (Thiagarajan & Steinwachs, 1990) in which learners have a controlled intercultural experience in the form of card games or role play. Generally, this involves a debriefing after the game in which participants discuss their reactions to their experience. The terms *resistance, acceptance* and *adaptation* seem very well suited to this kind of debriefing. Not only do they give participants a vocabulary to talk about their subjective reactions, they are connected to larger goals of empathy and suspension of judgment. These are just a few examples of the ways that these terms may be able to be applied to a variety of intercultural education contexts. Their potential usefulness hinges on their ability to join theory and practice, to serve as a bridge between the intercultural experiences and the conceptual goals of intercultural learning.

Explicit/Implicit Culture – Surface/Deep Intercultural Experiences

Just as intercultural experiences are diffuse, the elements of an intercultural experience that cause problems or create resistance or misunderstanding can be difficult to describe or characterize. An expatriate manager who plans to work in a foreign country may want to know what 'problems' he is going to have working with, say, Malaysians. But attempting to answer a question like that presents a challenge to intercultural educators because cultural differences that are easy to explain are often the easiest to deal with. Rules of etiquette or a list of cultural taboos – e.g. pointing the feet at someone in Thailand or asking about salary in the United States – are relatively straightforward to learn but provide little guidance outside of very particular situations.

As we have seen, the deeper challenges of intercultural learning involve reacting to cultural phenomena which have deeper symbolic meaning – such as when Philippe reacts to the requirement to separate garbage in Germany – or more simply the stress of learning new life routines in a new environment. In both these cases, the salient feature is the implicit nature of much intercultural difference and the fact that our responses to a new environment take place largely at the unconscious level. This fundamental insight seems not to have become a major component of intercultural education. As we have seen, however, explicit versus implicit intercultural phenomena, and their experiential parallel of surface and deep cultural learning, are at the core of this model of intercultural learning. Finding a way to make productive use of these organizing principles seems a primary challenge in intercultural education.

One result of this work which may be a step in that direction is the visual representation of intercultural learning which has been used to make the profiles of the participants of this study (see Diagram 13.1). It should be possible to include this kind of diagram or visual representation in materials that describe cultural difference and intercultural experiences. Diagram 13.1 lends itself both to a case-study approach to intercultural learning, in which the experiences of other intercultural learners are discussed and interpreted, as well as activities in which learners talk about their own experiences and use this diagram to clarify their own reactions to an intercultural experience.

Integral to this characterization of intercultural learning is the distinction between _surface_ cultural learning and _deep_ cultural learning. As discussed previously, this refers not so much to how much emotion we feel in an intercultural context, but whether the cultural phenomenon that provoke

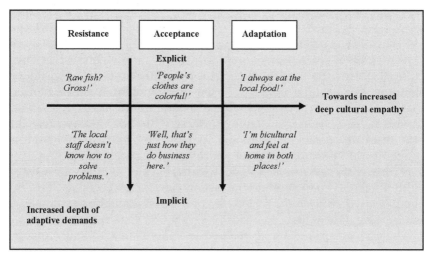

Diagram 13.1

the reaction are relatively explicit or implicit. In practical terms, this distinction seems important for distinguishing between the experiences of travelers who do not have an opportunity to experience the hidden side of a new cultural environment and expatriates who go further into a new cultural community. The expatriates in this study seemed to seek a comfortable depth of intercultural learning; isolating or integrating themselves depending on their reaction to their environment. An awareness of the importance of the choices that lead to increased isolation or integration would seem to fit well with intercultural education.

The terms *explicit/implicit* and *surface/deep* can be useful pedagogically because they provide a conceptual lens through which to examine intercultural experiences and cultural phenomena. The challenge for learners is not understanding the concepts per se, but coming up with examples from their own intercultural experiences, or explaining the implicit elements of their own cultural background. The gap between the conceptual understanding of these terms and the challenge of applying them was seen in a class with British students. They understood easily that the norms dictating when it is generally appropriate to call someone by their first name or shake hands are largely implicit, yet they had much more trouble determining what those norms were. The attempt to isolate and articulate these implicit elements of one's intercultural experience or one's usual cultural environment can lead toward the goal of cultural awareness pursued by many educators.

This is not to say that these terms are new. As we have seen, the implicit versus explicit nature of cultural phenomena is a foundation of intercultural communication theory. What is new, however, is that these terms have been connected to a more complete model of intercultural learning. In addition, the corollary of explicit and implicit cultural phenomena – *surface* and *deep* intercultural learning – is not commonly used in intercultural education. It should be possible to design learning activities around evaluation of the depth of an intercultural experience. One example is to ask learners to compare the traveler who visits 50 countries in a year and the one who stays in the same place but goes more deeply into the host community. Profiles of expatriates who are relatively more or less integrated into their host cultural communities could be used in case studies and learners could be asked to describe their own cultural experiences in these terms.

The distinction between explicit versus implicit cultural phenomena and *deep* versus *surface* intercultural learning seems particularly important for expatriates in today's increasingly interconnected world. In the past, sojourners had less choice about the degree of depth of their intercultural experiences. Today, it is much easier for expatriates to insulate themselves within a cocoon of familiarity and long-distance relationships. Increasingly, deeper intercultural experiences may be a conscious choice – a reflection of a better understanding of what one has to gain by going deeper into a host community – rather than simply a reflection of a need for psychological survival. Perhaps sojourners can also more consciously retreat to more familiar environmental cues when they feel high degrees of stress and increased *resistance*. This approach to intercultural learning may help modern day sojourners take more advantage of all the learning possibilities inherent in our new global age.

Relationships, Language Learning and Intercultural Learning

This work has highlighted the importance of using relationships with people from the host cultural community both as a measure and goal of intercultural learning. Closely related to this is the importance of language learning, since learning the language of a host community allows for relationships with hosts with no foreign language ability and allows sojourners to step more fully into the perceptual world of their hosts. Relationship formation, then, could be described as the meeting point between language education and intercultural education. This insight may provide new ways for language teaching methodology and materials to encourage intercultural learning.

One area that this emphasis on relationship formation could be applied is in the teaching of English to speakers of other languages. Unlike foreign language learning in which the language spoken has a relatively clearly corresponding 'target culture', English is often learned as an international language. This means that for a Korean learning English, it is not possible to learn specific norms related to speaking English, since the learner does not know what cultural background the people they may speak with will come from. It could equally be Philippine, Nigerian or Australian. In this context, language educators who want to focus on issues of intercultural understanding or cultural difference must do so in a culture-general way. Since typical goals of culture-general education are often highly abstract, language learners face the additional challenge of dealing with these topics in a foreign language.

Shaules has developed the idea of language learning as a 'cultural performance' and has emphasized relationship formation is a key goal in language education (Shaules, 2003, 2004b). This has also led to the development of an English skills textbook with intercultural themes (Shaules *et al.*, 2004). In terms of curriculum planning, the focus on relationships served as a criterion for course planning. Courses that emphasized speaking were focused on giving learners practice presenting personal opinions about social topics. This led to a final exam in which students were required to give in-class presentations in English. The goal of the course was to lead students towards the linguistic ability to offer their opinions and express their personality in intercultural relationships. In the case of the teaching materials developed, intercultural concepts were presented in the form of personal narratives of people from around the world who commented on cultural issues from their own cultural environment. Students used value-clarification questionnaires as a basis for discussions about the issues raised by the narratives. It was hoped that this pseudo exchange of opinions could foster empathy and act as preparation for future intercultural relationships. For a more detailed description of the thinking behind these initiatives, see Shaules (2004b).

Principles for Intercultural Education

A number of organizing principles have emerged in this book which may be able to act as a guide in intercultural education settings. These can be represented in the form of statements about cultural learning that should be kept in mind for intercultural education. They represent a distillation of the most important elements of the cultural learning experience as examined in this work.

Cultural learning is developmental

This principle reminds us that cultural learning is an ongoing process with no absolute end state or final goal. This means that learners' attention is most productively focused not on absolute ideals or rigid categories of cultural difference, but rather on the process of discovering and reacting to cultural difference.

Successful cultural learning implies recognition of cultural difference

Acceptance of other worldviews is challenging because it is easy to react to implicit cultural difference without recognizing that the source is cultural. Intercultural education initiatives should, therefore, give learners the opportunity to do critical reflection on the hidden nature of intercultural experiences, values, norms and hidden cultural assumptions.

Successful cultural learning implies acceptance of cultural difference

Acceptance of the validity of other worldviews at a deep level leads towards increased empathy, improved relationships with cultural hosts, easier adaptation to new cultural environments, an ability to suspend judgment, biculturalism and the ability to gain *cognitive empathy*. The importance of *acceptance* makes it a useful organizing principle for intercultural learning initiatives.

Resistance to difference is natural.

It is important not to 'moralize' intercultural learning by implying that one state of intercultural learning is superior to another. Everyone *resists*, *accepts* and *adapts* to difference to varying degrees in different settings. It is the awareness of this process that constitutes the salient feature of intercultural learning.

Cultural learning involves relationship formation

The human need to create meaning and form relationships with others is the driving force behind intercultural learning. This is true as we try to make sense of a new environment and as we relate to cultural hosts. Relationship formation is also a measure of success in intercultural learning and can be used as an organizing principle in language education. Language education should involve learning about other cultures and expressing one's own personal and cultural identity in a new language.

Language is a reflection of worldview

Because language is a primary vehicle for people of a particular community to encode the meanings of their worldview, it can act as an entry point into that worldview. This implies that words, expressions and proverbs that reflect important implicit cultural values should be given particular emphasis in language learning. Language teachers should emphasize not only grammatical accuracy and proficiency in pronunciation, but also use of language in social contexts.

Process not product

There is a tendency in language education to focus on an idealized final product, whether linguistic (perfect grammar and pronunciation) or cultural (having perfect knowledge of host etiquette). In fact, deep cultural learning requires such long and involved interactions in a host community that this kind of perfect understanding is difficult or impossible. Language teaching methods should emphasize and model the process of learning new cultural lessons, not the desired end state of being a kind of cultural expert. This can be done by using materials which aren't afraid to show the mishaps, misunderstandings, resistance and stress that go along with cultural learning. It should also include the understanding that the easiest to learn facts about a cultural community (e.g. the year of the French revolution) are often the least useful in coming to grips with deep learning challenges.

Conclusion

As pointed out at the beginning of this work, our more interconnected world has given rise to the notion that we are now living in a 'global village' where cultural difference may be less problematic than in the past. This work has highlighted the possibility that this may not be as true as we might like to think. While it is true that many interculturalists adapt successfully and there is an increase in inclusive multicultural communities, it is also true that cultural convergence on the explicit level can be misleading. Jack has experienced life in Japan for more than 10 years, yet his perceptual world seems not to have changed much at the deeper levels of self. While the interconnectedness of our global village is very obvious, many deeper differences remain hidden. We must also remember that the sojourners introduced in this work are among the most privileged interculturalists in the world. Not only do they come from advantaged socio-economic circumstances but for the most part they chose their intercultural experience. A study of sojourners who had returned early from postings abroad because of intercultural stresses may have painted a somewhat different picture of intercultural learning, though it is assumed that the model presented here would largely be valid.

There are millions of people in the world who have enforced intercultural experiences, for example economic and political refugees. This work has not dealt with what may be the most difficult challenge of intercultural learning – the embedded resistance to difference that can come with prolonged enforced exposure. The deep embedded resistance that was found in sojourners like David – who concluded that Asians have no 'survival instinct' – is perhaps the most troubling aspect of the sojourners we have met. This same dynamic can be seen in reports of ethnic conflict throughout the world. Discouragingly, it seems that prejudice is more easily passed on from generation to generation than empathy and tolerance. This may mean that distrust of a particular ethnic group or people with particular physical characteristics become a deep part of one's implicit values and worldview. Given the challenge for advantaged interculturalists to accept change at deeper levels of the self, it is not surprising that intercultural conflict is so persistent.

This work has argued that deep intercultural sensitivity is rare, even among privileged sojourners. Negative judgment and resistance remains even among well adjusted long-term sojourners. And if this is true for those living in the midst of intercultural difference, it may be even more so for majority members of a multicultural community. Sojourners in this work faced powerful demands for change in their everyday lives. But this is less true for someone whose experience with difference does not come from travel, but from contact with people from a cultural or ethnic minority at home. For better or worse, it seems that many people achieve a level of cognitive empathy necessary for them to function comfortably, but not much more. This may reflect the realities of our evolutionary biology which dictates not that we strive to fulfill our greatest potential, but simply that we fit into our environment in a way which lets us perpetuate ourselves. The experiences of highly developed interculturalists point towards an ongoing developmental struggle with our tendency to rest within the limits of our perceptual routines.

Ideally, this work hopes to inform the educational choices of future intercultural educators. The ultimate challenge of understanding cultural learning is not only to examine the learning process, but to find ways to pass on the understanding that intercultural experiences bring. With this in mind, during an unrecorded conversation with Yuko – perhaps the most highly-developed interculturalist interviewed – the author asked whether she thought that her cultural understanding could be passed on to other generations. Her reply was that it could not, since it is a product of a highly unstable, albeit constructive, upbringing. She said that even with highly intercultural parents, a child will naturally take on the worldview of the community that he or she grows up in, and have, just like everyone else, a primary cultural affiliation. This acts as the starting point for intercultural exploration. Yuko feels that increased intercultural contact has led only to shallow intercultural understanding. If she is correct – and the experiences of the sojourners we've met do not contradict her – then, as has been the case throughout human history, it remains up to each generation to discover the deeper truths of human learning. Hopefully, however, today's interculturalists can leave clues about the capacity for human development for the increasing number of people who will face these challenges in the future.

A Glossary of the Intercultural Experience

This glossary explains key terms related to the Deep Culture Model

Adaptive demands

Adaptive demands are defined as the gap between one's internal competencies and the demands of one's environment, or *cultural difference*. This gap may involve a lack of concrete competencies such as geographic knowledge, or language ability, or more implicit competencies such as an intuitive understanding of value orientations or behavioral expectations. When faced with adaptive demands one may *resist* the cultural differences encountered, *accept* them or *adapt* to them. We may have mixed reactions in which we accept one element of an experience while resisting another.

'Animal trainer' adaptation

The 'animal trainer' style of intercultural adaptation refers to one who learns how to manage relations to get what one wants without ever accepting the fundamental validity of the worldview of the people one is dealing with. In deeply prejudiced environments such as apartheid South Africa or the slavery-era in the south of the United States this may be the default setting among those in a position of dominance.

Acceptance

Acceptance is defined as perceiving as valid alternative interpretations of the cultural phenomena that one experiences. This doesn't necessarily imply changing oneself in order to better align one's internal patterns with those of a new environment. *Acceptance* indicates the recognition of the validity of other worldviews. *Acceptance* implies a construal of cultural difference as valid and encourages *cognitive empathy*.

Adaptation

Adaptation is defined as allowing for change in oneself as a response to adaptive demands from a different cultural environment. Adaptation doesn't guarantee that one sees the demands being adapted to as valid. One can adapt (change oneself) and resist (see as invalid the source of the demand) at the same time. Adaptation at deep levels of the self often involves changes in one's sense of identity. Adapting behavior is much easier than adapting deeper elements of the self.

Cognitive empathy

Cognitive empathy is considered the desired outcome of intercultural learning. It is defined as an increased ability to consciously differentiate cultural phenomena. *Differentiation* refers to the ways in which one creates meaning from the perceptual phenomena in one's environment. One's worldview becomes more differentiated by increasing the perceptual categories used to make sense of one's experiences. This allows for the ability to construct varying yet valid interpretations for a given phenomenon. A high degree of cognitive empathy means that one can consciously shift between competing frameworks of meaning. One can understand competing cultural logics and choose one's own behavior accordingly.

A high degree of cognitive empathy implies that one no longer sees one's own worldview as primary – a state of ethnorelativism. Having less cognitive empathy implies being more ethnocentric. An increase in cognitive empathy accompanies a decrease in making absolute cultural judgments. One can learn about the degree of cognitive empathy an individual has by examining the way he or she talks about cultural difference. Denigration of cultural difference implies less cognitive empathy, while acceptance of cultural difference implies more cognitive empathy. Thus, the statement 'The people there are all snobs. You can tell by the way they dress.' implies less cognitive empathy than the statement 'You should see how people dress up there! It's really something!' The process of gaining cognitive empathy has nearly defined end-point.

Culture and cultural communities

Culture refers to the shared products and meanings which act as the interactive frameworks in a given community. A community may be as small as a family or as large as a nation or region. *Products* refer to the objective output and visible elements of a community. They may include physical objects such as food, music, churches and architecture, but also reified conceptual structures such as cosmologies or language. Behavior which has a shared cultural interpretation – for example a handshake as a greeting – is a cultural product. Products are said to be 'objective' because they have an existence which can be demonstrated in a way which can be observed by all.

Meanings refer to the shared sense of how *products* are interpreted. This includes the conceptual frameworks used to interpret behavior. Behavior is interpreted contextually but that doesn't mean that behavior is interpreted arbitrarily. Individual variation in a cultural community is seen as an emphasis on one particular interpretation over another. Thus, while one person may see a sports car as a sign of success, another may see it as a waste of natural resources. These competing interpretations do not imply that the individuals do not share the same cultural frameworks, but that they emphasize certain meanings over others.

Culture is not static and cannot be isolated and described definitively because it is the result of the ongoing process of interaction between those who make up a cultural community. Since any individual participates in any number of cultural communities, that person's sense of social and cultural identity will be multiple and contextual. Cultural identity is related to but not identical to participation in cultural communities. One may identify with a community that one doesn't understand or participate in and one may participate in a community but not wish to identify with it.

One often doesn't notice one's participation or membership in a cultural community until interacting with people that don't share one's cultural frameworks. Someone from London may not feel British until going to France. It is easy to confuse the difference between identifying with a cultural community, i.e. 'I feel British', and the competencies required to interact with members of a cultural community. The one does not guarantee the other. Intercultural learners must deal with a lack of cultural competencies. This process can call into question one's cultural identity.

Culture is seen as existing at different depths as illustrated in the diagram on the next page. At the surface are explicit products and behaviors. Beneath that are the *values* and *norms* that underlie those meanings given to those products and behaviors. Beneath that are *deep assumptions* which form the basis for what a cultural community accepts as true and reasonable.

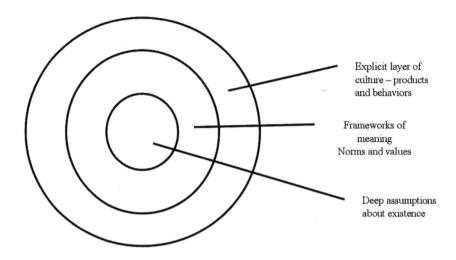

Explicit layer of culture – products and behaviors

Frameworks of meaning Norms and values

Deep assumptions about existence

Cultural code switching

In the same way that those who are multilingual may switch back and forth between different languages, sojourners may switch back and forth between different modes of behaving, communicating and thinking based on who they are interacting with. Cultural code switching involves a bicultural or pluralistic ethnorelativism. Those who do cultural code switching may feel that they have different selves, or may switch back and forth without feeling that they change themselves in fundamental ways.

Cultural difference

In a general sense, cultural difference simply refers to ways in which products of meanings of a cultural community differ in systematic ways from those of another. For intercultural learners, *cultural difference* implies that a sojourner's knowledge of his or her environment is inadequate in systematic ways. That is to say, sojourners must deal with not only new facts, but also new systems of meaning. They must learn not only 'things' but also 'how things work'. Cultural difference is often (but not always) experienced as incompetence, since there is a gap between their internal competencies and the demands of their environment. As sojourners (hopefully) learn new systems of meaning, their new environment becomes more predictable and they develop a higher functional fitness in relationship to their environment. A tourist who learns the money of a country or how to use the subway system in a new city are obvious examples of cultural learning at the most explicit level necessitated by cultural difference. Once these systems are understood and internalized a traveler can function more freely and can express more fully their individual predilections and intentions. Concrete demands of intercultural learning such as these are perhaps not easy, but they are at least easily defined. Learning the subway system can be done consciously and in a relatively predictable way. The more subtle and difficult elements of intercultural learning, however, exist at the hidden level of values, norms, implicit beliefs and assumptions. Cultural difference at this *deep culture* level is the most fundamental challenge of intercultural learning.

Cultural frameworks

The shared meanings in a cultural community act as frameworks for interaction. Language is the most obvious example. Sharing a cultural framework doesn't imply identical behavior or an identical sense of identity, just as sharing the same language doesn't make people say the same things. Sharing frameworks do, however, give people a set of tools that allow for meaningful interaction. One's individual personality is expressed within the framework of expectations that are shared. Someone who speaks up more than is considered typical may be seen as 'outgoing', while someone who speaks up less may be seen as 'reserved'. The shared expectation of how much is 'typical' represents the shared framework of meaning within which 'outgoing' and 'reserved' people express their individuality. Any shared meaning provides an opportunity for interaction. Thus we may have meaningful interaction with those who don't speak our language because some other shared meaning allows us to interpret the other's behavior. There are a few meanings which are universal, or nearly so, such as obvious expressions of anger, joy and aggression. Commerce provides an important shared framework of interaction among many different cultural communities.

Any individual shares multiple and overlapping frameworks of meanings as he or she participates in many communities. Young people share frameworks that they don't with their elders. Those from the same region, the same religious faith, with the same hobbies, and so on, also share frameworks of meaning. Membership in a community implies that one shares enough frameworks of meaning to develop relationships and participate in that community. Interaction within groups of people requires a great number of shared frameworks of meaning, both explicit and implicit. This involves explicit frameworks such as laws and contracts and implicit frameworks such as how to interact with strangers, how and when to show deference, when to make eye contact, what is seen as polite in a give situation, and so on. Language learners who can communicate one on one, but who still could not with a group of native speakers, experience this difference. It takes years to share enough frameworks of meanings to participate fully as an insider in a different society. Interacting as a 'visitor foreign resident' (not fully subject to the expectations of host community members) is often much easier.

Deep (hidden) assumptions

Deep assumptions form the hidden framework that norms and values are based on. They include things such as assumptions about hierarchy and equality, degree of gender separation, the importance of independence, and so on. The norm 'bow when the teacher enters the room' may be explained by the value 'respect is important'. These may be based on the deep assumption that hierarchical relationships are normal and should involve deference and caretaking. The norm 'don't have sexual relations before getting married' may be explained by the value that 'chastity is good'. One deep assumption behind this value may be that sex outside of marriage is impure. A deep assumption behind having infants sleep separately from their mother may be that independence is important. A deep assumption behind having infants sleep with their mother may be that children need nurturing.

Deep assumptions are rarely questioned and often form the framework within which problems are resolved. If one assumes that 'freedom' involves having the choice to do as one pleases, one will seek freedom by trying to provide for more choices. If one assumes that 'freedom' involves the security of not having to face the antisocial behavior of others, one will seek freedom by imposing limits to extreme behavior. In this way, deep assumptions form the starting point for debate and can lead to opposite results. 'Freedom' as choice assumes the individual is primary. 'Freedom' as security from antisocial behavior assumes relationships between people as primary.

Demanding, deep and meaningful experiences

A demanding intercultural experience is one that requires a high degree of change and adjustment on the part of a visitor. A *meaningful* experience has personal significance for a sojourner. A *deep* intercultural experience is one that involves adaptive demands at the deeper levels of implicit culture. Just because an experience is meaningful does not mean that it is deep. A short trip abroad may be meaningful enough to change one's life. This doesn't mean, however, that the cultural differences experienced were implicit. It takes extended interaction in a new environment to have a deep intercultural experience. Deep cultural learning involves a trial and error process which leads to an intuitive understanding of how things work or are perceived. Hitchhiking through Africa and sleeping in small villages could be a demanding experience that requires great flexibility. The adaptive challenges are, however, mostly related to explicit elements of culture. Spending two years in the Peace Corp in a rural village in Africa is most likely deep, demanding and meaningful. Most sojourners find experiences that are more demanding to be more meaningful.

Ethnocentrism, racism and prejudice

Ethnocentrism is the normal (though not necessarily desirable) tendency to judge one's experience from one's own cultural viewpoint. Ethnocentrism involves using pre-existing categories to judge phenomena while ethnorelativism involves the creation and integration of new perceptual categories. Ethnocentrism is a built-in part of human perceptual reality, meaning that it is difficult or impossible to ever avoid completely.

Racism is a belief that race determines human traits and capacities and that racial difference involves the superiority of one race over another. Racism is learned.

Prejudice refers more generally to the irrational belief in the superiority of one thing over another and may or may not be inculcated. It implies an inclination to see something as better even when it is not. Prejudice may be a result of an inculcated attitude of superiority or of an ethnocentric reaction to an intercultural experience, or both.

Enforced adaptation

Enforced adaptation involves adaptive change undertaken in the face of *resistance*. At some level the sojourner does not perceive of *demands for change* as being legitimate. It may involve being obliged to adapt by external forces, such as when an economic immigrant is obliged to adapt behavior to local norms to get work. Sometimes sojourners may impose enforced adaptation on themselves. They may desire status or other benefits that come from association with the host culture. Expatriates who resist a cultural community but stay in order to make money or gain status often experience enforced adaptation. Marginalized minority communities also often experience enforced adaptation. Enforced adaptation is psychologically unhealthy and leads to denigration of the host cultural community and sometimes even denigration of oneself.

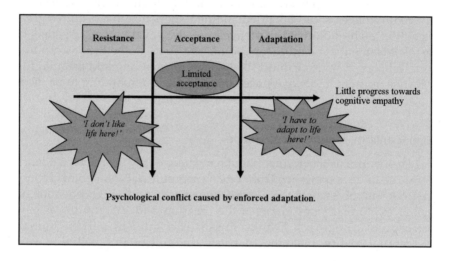

Enforced resistance

A desire to change may not be accepted by members of a host community. This *enforced resistance* can mean that even when a sojourner tries to *adapt*, he or she is excluded. It is difficult to maintain acceptance towards cultural difference if one's attempts to adapt are not recognized or valued. Enforced resistance can be psychologically damaging to those who face it.

Deep Culture Model

The Deep Culture Model describes how sojourners react to the *adaptive demands* of being in a new cultural environment. One's response to adaptive demands constitutes the intercultural learning process. Intercultural learning involves *resistance, acceptance* and/or *adaptation* to cultural difference. The adaptive demands faced may be explicit, related to obvious visible cultural difference, or deep, related to implicit elements of cultural difference. In this way, intercultural experiences can be 'surface experiences' or 'deep experiences'. The difference between 'surface' and 'deep' is not how meaningful the experience is for the sojourner, but the degree to which the sojourner faces hidden adaptive demands. Sojourners who learn a foreign language and involve themselves deeply in their host community often face deep adaptive demands. Sojourners may have contradictory or multiple reactions, *resisting* certain things and *adapting* to others or *resisting* at the deep level even while *adapting* at the surface level. One's reaction to intercultural demands can be measured to some degree by the way people talk about their intercultural experiences and can be illustrated as below:

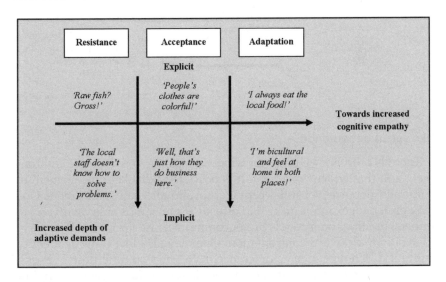

The horizontal line represents the fact that intercultural learning is developmental and can lead to increased cognitive empathy. The vertical lines represent the varying depths of an intercultural experience. Tourists, for example, may experience only explicit cultural difference and react to it in ways illustrated by the three quotes above the horizontal line, each representing *resistance, acceptance,* and *adaptation* respectively. Longer-term sojourners may (but not necessarily) experience more implicit cultural difference and may react with *resistance, acceptance,* and/or *adaptation* as represented by the quotations below the horizontal line.

Intercultural learning

Intercultural learning consists of the ongoing process of responding to the adaptive demands of a new cultural environment. Facing adaptive demands that touch on the deeper sides of one's own cultural programming bring about a deep intercultural experience. Cultural learning is seen as developmental because one has the possibility of going from the state of ethnocentricity, which is incapable of shifting perceptual frameworks in a systematic way, to ethnorelativism, in which one understands competing yet valid frameworks of meaning.

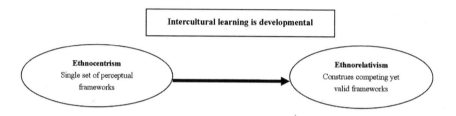

Like versus acceptance

There is a difference between what we *like* in a new cultural environment and that which we accept. It is possible to dislike some element of cultural difference, yet still accept it as a valid alternative for others. One may prefer, for example, to be told directly if someone is angry with us, yet understand that some people prefer communicating through a third party to avoid an awkward confrontation. One may also like some element of cultural difference, such as deference from one's cultural hosts, yet still find it not legitimate. In this case, the deference may seem 'phony' or somehow illegitimate.

Long-term tourist

Some sojourners continue to react to their intercultural experiences only with *surface acceptance* even though their sojourn may go on for years. This implies that in addition to this *surface acceptance* that they are also engaged in a *deep resistance* of cultural difference. This can be described as a long-term tourist phenomenon. Generally, only sojourners who are in a position to isolate themselves from deeper adaptive demands (such as those who live in sheltered expatriate communities) can maintain this state.

Mixed states

A reaction in which certain elements of an intercultural experience are accepted or adapted to, and others are resisted, can be referred to as *mixed states*. This can also refer to *accepting* certain cultural differences but *resisting* others. In the diagram below, this sojourner accepts explicit difference, seen in an acceptance of obvious difference such as food and clothing, even while resisting cultural difference which makes this sojourner feel that people are 'half-assed' and that people don't plan ahead.

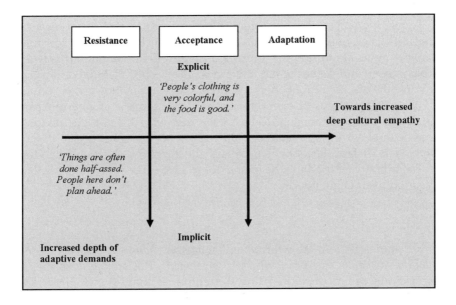

Norms

Norms tell us what acceptable behavior is. They may be explicit, as in laws, contracts and regulations, or informal as in customs about how to shake hands or eat food. Informal behavioral norms, such as when to make eye contact, usually function out of awareness. Norms function as a form of social regulation with negative consequences for those who don't follow them.

Rapport

Some sojourners feel a particular attraction or *rapport* for a particular community. They may feel more at home in their new environment than their old. It may be a result of their personality or the fact that the lifestyle of values of that community provide the sojourner with something that they want. Sometimes sojourners feel a *rapport* for a community that they don't fully understand and project their desires onto this community. This can lead to disappointment as they become more involved with the community if it doesn't live up to their expectations. Those who *adapt* to a community based on rapport may denigrate their original home community, leading to reversal.

Relativization

To *relativize* an experience refers to looking at the contextual reasons that influence one's experience of it. This often leads to a perceptual *decentering* as standards for judging a given phenomenon shifts away from oneself and moves to larger frames of reference. Relativization can involve the discovery that one's reactions to a phenomenon are a product of one's expectations or experiences and don't come from any intrinsic quality of the phenomenon itself. A sojourner who doesn't like the food that he or she tries may relativize the experience concluding that it may be a lack of familiarity which causes the reaction. A sojourner who doesn't relativize food that he or she doesn't like may simply decide that the food itself is not good.

Resistance

Resistance is defined as an *unwillingness to change in response to the adaptive demands of a new cultural environment*. Resistance describes a (conscious or unconscious) unwillingness or inability to allow for internal change in response to the patterns or expectations of a new environment. *Resistance* is considered to involve denigration or being dismissive of difference as a way to uphold the primacy of one's internal cultural patterns. *Dislike* is a negative reaction to difference that does not involve a negative value judgment. *Resistance* can be the source of ethnocentric judgments, such as 'the bread here isn't nearly as good as that back home' or 'you can't trust people there'. While dislike more often involves descriptive statements such as 'the food had a lot of spice in it'. The most typical strategy to deal with feelings of *resistance* seemed to be avoidance – isolating oneself from adaptive demands. Avoidance doesn't mean that sojourners don't spend time with people from the host community, it means they avoid putting themselves in situations in which they need to adapt themselves to the host community. The inability to accept adaptive demands as legitimate is a sign of resistance.

Sometimes, *surface resistance* results from the 'inefficiency of the unfamiliar'. Deep resistance is characterized by an *absolute judgment*, in which a group of people is found lacking based on a principle that the sojourner assumes to be universal, yet which is based on ethnocentric assumptions.

Reversal

Reversal refers to when a sojourner takes on the values and behavior of a new environment but denigrates their home environment. Reversal is a form of adaptation founded fundamentally in a resistance to the validity of cultural difference.

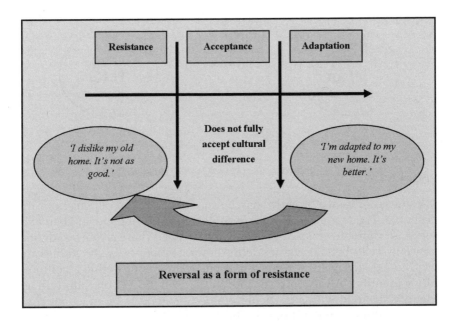

Triangulation

Triangulation refers to going beyond a binary A versus B view of cultural difference. Having three or more deep intercultural learning experiences may have a greater sense of the range of possible cultural differences. For example, someone who has experienced the relatively collectivist cultural frameworks in India as well as the relatively individualistic frameworks of England, who then has a deep intercultural experience in Japan, will be exposed to a much more nuanced view of collectivist and individualist thought. Having this third point of comparison makes it much easier to extrapolate potential combinations of cultural characteristics

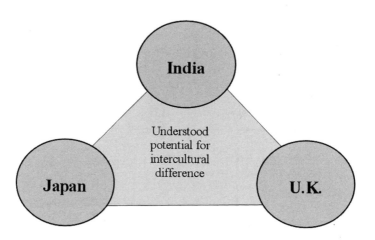

Values

Values represent a broadly shared sense of what kind of behaviors are desirable. They reflect a cultural group's definition of good and bad and serve as criteria to choose between alternatives. Whereas 'norms' define how one *should* behave, values define how one *wants to behave*. Values are used to explain or justify one's particular choices or define a community's identity. In this way, an individual or cultural community may identify strongly with a particular value (it's good to be independent). We use values to make choices in behavior. When given a gift we don't really like should we follow the value 'be honest' and say so or 'be kind' and lie about it? Naturally, we try to find ways to solve this contradiction.

Some values exist as statements of absolute good such as 'be kind to others' or 'love they neighbor'. Some values, however, exist in relation to an opposing value orientation. Individualism exists in opposition to collectivism. These opposing value orientations exist because of fundamental dilemmas in social organization and human relations. In any group, for example, the desires and priorities of any given individual will sometimes conflict with the consensus of the group. Cultural communities may give priority to one or the other of these two orientations. Thus, some cultural communities may emphasize individualism (emphasizing the need for individuals to develop themselves independently of the group) while others emphasize collectivism (emphasizing the need for the group to nurture the individual).

Background of the Sojourners

(names have been changed)

Name	Country of origin	Intercultural experience and language ability
Jack	US	Has lived 14 years in Japan, speaks only basic Japanese. Mostly foreign friends. Seems happy as a sheltered expatriate.
Paul	US/Germany,	Father is American diplomat. Born in Nepal and raised in many countries. Speaks English, German and French.
Rieko	Japan	College student who attended a one year study abroad in US. English/Japanese.
Adele	US	Lived in the Middle East during a stay in the Peace Corps. Later spent seven years in Japan. Scholar of Japanese literature. Fairly high level of Japanese ability but very frustrated with life in Japan. Can't wait to go back to US.
Joanna	France	Raised in France but studied for one year in Dublin. One year working as French teacher in US. Frustrated with her experience in the US. French/English.
Mayumi	Japan	Raised in Japan but attended university in US. Later lived in Korea with Korean husband. Japanese, English, Korean.
William	US	Expatriate American living in Japan. Works as an English teacher. Japanese spouse. Intermediate Japanese.
Liz	US, lived as child in Japan	As a child, family lived in Japan. Spent junior and senior high school in Japan. Later went to live in US and returned to Japan to work as an expatriate. Bilingual. English/Japanese.

Name	Country of origin	Intercultural experience and language ability
Linda	UK	Raised in the UK. Lived in US as trailing spouse. Unhappy there. Moved to France. English plus intermediate French.
Steven	US	Twelve years living in Korea and Japan. Language teacher. Speaks little Korean or Japanese.
Neil	US	Expatriate in Japan, Japanese spouse, semi-bilingual.
Yuko	Japanese parents, raised in India	Grew up abroad with Japanese parents. Lived extensively in India, Europe, US and later in Japan. Trilingual. Hindi, English and Japanese.
Abdou	Senegal	Raised in Dakar. University studies in Austria, lives and works in France as German teacher. Wolof, English, French, German.
Donald	UK	Raised in UK. Lived extensively in Japan and Switzerland. English, Japanese, German.
Gunter	Germany	Raised in Germany. Attended graduate school in US. Spent three years as an expatriate manager in Japan
Gail	UK	Ten years in France. Raised in UK but has now received French nationality. Loves life in France.
Andre	Switzerland, Italian father	Raised in Switzerland. Studied and worked in Japan. Talented language learner. Swiss German, High German, Japanese, English, French, Italian.
David	France	Lived and worked in US for several years. Returned to France and works with people from many countries as a commercial pilot instructor. Bilingual. French and English.
Philippe	France	Parents are French. Lived in US as child then moved back to France with family. Did research in Germany. French, English, German.

Name	Country of origin	Intercultural experience and language ability
Eun Suk	Korea	Raised in Korea. Many years experience living and working in Japan. Korean, Japanese, English.
Kensuke	Japan	Raised in Japan. Studied at university in the US. Japanese, English.
Masako	Japan	Raised in Japan. Studied at university in the US. Japanese, English.

References

Abbink, J. (1984) The changing identity of Ethiopian immigrants (Falashas) in Israel. *Anthropological Quarterly* 57(4), 139–153.

Adler, P.S. (1975) The transitional experience: An alternative view of culture shock. *Journal of Humanistic Psychology* 15(4), 13.

Adler, P.S. (1977) Beyond cultural identity: Reflections upon cultural and multicultural man. In R. Brislin (ed.) *Culture Learning: Concepts, Application and Research.* Honolulu: University Press of Hawaii.

Agar, M. (2002) Transcultural self, multicultural world: Dialectic or disaster. Paper presented at the Transcultured Self: Experiencing Languages and Intercultural Communication. Johannes Kepler University, Linz, Austria.

Alptekin, C. (2002) Towards intercultural communicative competence in ELT. *ELT Journal* 56(1), 57–64.

Amersfoort, H. (1984) *Immigration and the Formation of Minority Groups: The Dutch Experience 1945–1975.* (L. Lyng, trans.). New York: Cambridge University Press.

Ansari, A. (1988) *Iranian Immigrants in the United States: A Case Study of Dual Marginality.* Millwood, NY: Associated Faculty.

Au, T.K. (1983) Chinese and English counterfactuals: The Sapir–Whorf hypothesis revisited. *Cognition*, 15, 155–187.

Babiker, I.E., Cox, J.L. and Miller, P. (1980) The measurement of cultural distance and its relationship to medical consultations, symptomatology and examination of performance of overseas students at Edinburgh University. *Social Psychiatry* 15, 109–116.

Barnard, A. (2000) *History and Theory in Anthropology.* Cambridge: Cambridge University Press.

Barnard, A. and Spencer, J. (eds) (1996) *Encyclopedia of Social and Cultural Anthropology.* London: Routledge.

Barnlund, D. (1989) *Communication in a Global Village, Public and Private Self.* Yarmouth, ME: Intercultural Press.

Benedict, R. (1934) *Patterns of Culture.* Boston: Houghton Mifflin Company.

Benedict, R. (1943) *Race and Racism.* London: Scientific Book Club.

Bennett, J. (1993) Cultural marginality: Identity issues in intercultural training. In R.M. Paige (ed.) *Education for the Intercultural Experience* (pp. 109–135). Yarmouth, ME: Intercultural Press.

Bennett, J. (1998) Transition shock: Putting culture shock in perspective. In M. Bennett (ed.) *Basic Concepts of Intercultural Communication.* Yarmouth, ME: Intercultural Press.

Bennett, M.J. (1986) A developmental approach to training for intercultural sensitivity. *International Journal of Intercultural Relations* 10, 179–200.

Bennett, M.J. (1993) Towards ethnorelativism: A developmental model of intercultural sensitivity. In R.M. Paige (ed.) *Education for the Intercultural Experience* (pp. 21–71). Yarmouth, ME: Intercultural Press.

Bennett, M.J. (ed.) (1998) *Basic Concepts of Intercultural Communication*. Yarmouth, ME: Intercultural Press.

Bennett, M.J. (2004) Becoming interculturally competent. In J. Wurzel (ed.) *Towards Multiculturalism: A Reader in Multicultural Education* (2nd edn, pp. 62–77). Newton, MA: Intercultural Resources Corporation.

Berry, J.W., Kim, U. and Mok, D. (1987) Comparative studies of acculturative stress. *International Migration Review* 21, 491–511.

Black, J.S. and Stephens, G.K. (1989) The influence of the spouse on American expatriate adjustment and intent to stay in Pacific Rim overseas assignments. *Journal of Management* 15, 529–544.

Bloom, A.H. (1981) *The Linguistic Shaping of Thought: A Study in the Impact of Language on Thinking in China and the West*. Hillsdale, NJ: Erlbaum.

Boas, F. (1928) *Anthropology and Modern Life*. New York: Dover Publications, Inc.

Bourdieu, P. (1991) *Language & Symbolic Power*. Cambridge: Harvard University Press.

Bourdieu, P. (1998) *Practical Reason*. Stanford: Stanford University Press.

Bourdieu, P. and Wacquant, L.J.D. (1992) *An Invitation to Reflexive Sociology*. Chicago: The University of Chicago Press.

Brill, A.A. (ed.) (1995) *The Basic Writings of Sigmund Freud*. New York: The Modern Library.

Brislin, R. (1981) *Cross-cultural Encounters*. New York, NY: Pergamon.

Brooks, D. (February 19, 2006) Questions of culture. *New York Times*.

Brown, D.E. (1991) *Human Universals*. New York: McGraw-Hill.

Browning, C., Masako, K., and Haruko, S. (1999) Comparative cultures course: education in ten countries. *The Language Teacher* 23(1), 27–31.

Brussow, H.L. and Kohls, L.R. (eds) (1995) *Training Know-how for Cross-cultural and Diversity Trainers*. Adult Learning Systems.

Byram, M. (1987) *Cultural Studies in Foreign Language Learning*. Clevedon: Multilingual Matters.

Byram, M. (1997) *Teaching and Assessing Communicative Intercultural Competence*. Clevedon: Multilingual Matters.

Byram, M. and Feng, A. (2004) Culture and language learning: Teaching research and scholarship. *Language Teaching* 37, 149–168.

Byram, M., Nichols, A. and Stevens, D. (eds) (2001) *Developing Intercultural Competence in Practice*. Clevedon: Multilingual Matters.

Candlin, C.N. (ed.) (1991) *Language Awareness in the Classroom*. London: Longman.

Carroll, D.G. (1997) BaFa BaFa: Does it work with university EFL learners? [Internet]. *The Internet TESL Journal*, March 1997. Retrieved April 15th, 2004. On WWW at http://iteslj.org/Techniques/Carroll-BaFa.html

Carroll, J.B. (ed.) (1956) *Language, Thought, and Reality: Selected Writing of Benjamin Lee Whorf*. Cambridge: The MIT Press.

Carroll, J.B. and Casagrande, J. B. (1958) The function of language classifications in behavior. In E.L. Hartley (ed.) *Readings in Social Psychology* (pp. 18–31). New York: Holt.

Castaneda, C. (1972) *A Journey to Ixtlan: The Lessons of Don Juan*. New York: Simon and Schuster.

Cates, K.A. (1997) New trends in global issues and English teaching. *The Language Teacher* 21(5), 39–41.

Cates, K.A. (1999) Teaching English for world citizenship: Key content areas. *The Language Teacher* 23(2), 11–14.

Chalmers, D.J. (1996) *The Conscious Mind – In Search of a Fundamental Theory.* New York: Oxford University Press.

Clarke, M.A. (1976) Second language acquisition as a clash of consciousness. *Language Learning* 26(2), 377–389.

Coleman, D. (1987) UK statistics on immigration: Development and limitations. *International Migration Review* 21, 1138–1169.

Cornes, A. (2004) *Culture from the Inside Out.* Yarmouth, ME: Intercultural Press.

Cushner, K. and Brislin, R. (1996) *International Interactions* (2nd edn). Thousand Oaks, CA: Sage Publications.

Damen, L. (1987) *Culture Learning: The Fifth Dimension in the Language Classroom.* Massachusetts: Addison-Wesley Publishing Company.

David, S.J. (1996) Developing sociolinguistic competence through learner-centered dialogues. *The Language Teacher* 20(3), 13–15.

Davies, I.R.L., Sowden, P.T., Jerrett, D.T., Jerrett, T. and Corbett, G.G. (1998) A cross-cultural study of English and Setswana speakers on a colour triads task: A test of the Sapir–Whorf hypothesis. *British Journal of Psychology* 89(1), 1–15.

de Nooy, J. and Hanna, B. (2003) Cultural information gathering by Australian students in France. *Language and Intercultural Communication* 3(1).

Dinges, N. (1983) Intercultural competence. In D. Landis and R. Brislin (eds) *Handbook of Intercultural Training* (Vol. 1, 176–202). New York: Pergamon Press.

Dinges, N.G. and Baldwin, K.D. (1996) Intercultural competence – A research perspective. In D. Landis and R.S. Bhagat (eds) *Handbook of Intercultural Training* (2nd edn, 106–123). Thousand Oaks, CA: Sage Publications.

Dinges, N.G. and Lieberman, D.A. (1989) Intercultural communication competence: Coping with stressful work situations. *International Journal of Intercultural Relations* 13, 371–385.

Doi, T. (1995) *Anatomy of Dependence*: Kodansha International.

Durkheim, E. (1938) *The Rules of Sociological Method.* New York: The Free Press.

Friedman, J. (1994) *Cultural Identity and Global Process.* London: Sage Publications.

Futuyma, D.J. Evolution, science & society: Evolutionary biology and the national research agenda. The A. P. Sloan Foundation/The National Science Foundation. Retrieved February 9th, 2006, from the WWW at http://evonet.sdsc.edu/evoscisociety/what_is_evo_biology.htm

Gaston, J. (1984) *Cultural Awareness Teaching Techniques.* Brattleboro: Pro Lingua Associates.

Goffman, E. (1967) *Interaction Ritual.* Garden City, NY: Anchor Books.

Goldstein, D.L. and Smith, D.H. (1999) The analysis of the effects of experiential training on sojourners' cross-cultural adaptability. *International Journal of Intercultural Relations* 28(1), 157–173.

Gordon, M. (1973) Assimilation in America: Theory and reality. In P. Rose (ed.) *The Study of Society* (pp. 350–365). New York: Random House.

Hall, E.T. (1959) *The Silent Language.* New York: Anchor Books.

Hall, E.T. (1976) *Beyond Culture.* New York: Anchor Books/Doubleday.

Hall, E.T. (1984) *The Dance of Life: The Other Dimension of Time.* New York: Anchor Books.

Hall, E.T. and Hall, M.R. (1987) *Hidden Differences: Doing Business with the Japanese.* New York: Anchor Books/Doubleday.

Hall, S. and Du Gay, P. (1996) *Questions of Cultural Identity.* London: Sage Publications.

Hammer, M.R., Bennett, M.J. and Wiseman, R. (2003) The Intercultural Development Inventory: A measure of intercultural sensitivity. In M.Paige (guest ed.) *International Journal of Intercultural Relations.*

Hammer, M.R., Gudykunst, W.B. and Wiseman, R.L. (1978) Dimensions of intercultural effectiveness: An exploratory study. *International Journal of Intercultural Relations* 2, 382–393.

Hampden-Turner, C. and Trompenaars, F. (2000) *Building Cross-cultural Competence.* New Haven, London: Yale University Press.

Hannigan, T.P. (1990) Traits, attitudes, and skills that are related to intercultural effectiveness and their implications for cross-cultural training: A review of the literature. *International Journal of Intercultural Relations* 14(1), 89–111.

Hanvey, R. (1979) Cross-cultural awareness. In E.C. Smith and L.F. Luce (eds) *Toward Internationalism: Readings in Cross-cultural Communication* (pp. 46–56). Rowley, MA: Newbury House.

Harrison, D. (1999) Communicating classrooms: English language teaching and world citizenship. *The Language Teacher* 23(2), 29–31.

Hess, J.D. (1994) *The Whole World Guide to Culture Learning.* Yarmouth, ME: Intercultural Press.

Higgings, M. and Tanaka, B.M. (1999) Empowering ESL students for world citizenship. *The Language Teacher* 23(2), 15–19.

Hofstede, G. (1980) *Culture's Consequences: International Differences in Work-Related Values.* Beverly Hills, CA: Sage Publications.

Hofstede, G. (1983) Dimensions of national culture in fifty countries and three regions. In J.B. Deregowski, S. Dziurawiec and R.C. Annis (eds) *Expiscations in Cross-cultural Psychology.* Lisse, Netherlands: Swetz and Zeitlinger.

Hofstede, G. (1986) Cultural differences in teaching and learning. *International Journal of Intercultural Relations* 10(3), 301–320.

Hofstede, G. and Hofstede G.J. (1997) *Cultures and Organizations: Software of the Mind.* New York: McGraw-Hill.

Hofstede, G. and Bond, M.H. (1984) Hofstede's culture dimensions: An independent validation using Rokeach's Value Survey. *Journal of Cross-Cultural Psychology* 15(4), 417–433.

Hu, A. (1999) Interkulturelles Lernen: Eine Auseinandersetzung mit der Kritik an einem umstrittenen Konzept. *Zeitschrift für Fremdsprachenforschung* 10(2), 277–303.

Hu, H.C. (1944) The Chinese concept of 'Face'. *American Anthropologist* 46, 45–64.

Imahori, T.T. and Lanigan, M.L. (1989) Relational model of intercultural communication competence. *International Journal of Intercultural Relations* 13(3), 269–286.

Ingulsrud, J.E., Kaib, K., Kadowakic, S., Kurobanec, S. and Shiobarad, M. (2002) The assessment of cross-cultural experience: Measuring awareness through critical text analysis. *International Journal of Intercultural Relations* 26(5), 473–491.

Jack, G. and Phipps, A. (2005) *Tourism and Intercultural Exchange.* Clevedon: Channel View Publications.

Jaffe, A. (ed.) (1979) *C.G. Jung: Word and Image.* Princeton: Princeton University Press.

James, C. and Garrett, P. (eds) (1992) *Language Awareness in the Classroom.* London: Longman.

Jandt, F.E. (1995) *Intercultural Communication Student Workbook*. Thousand Oaks: Sage Publications.

Kamal, A.A. and Maruyama, G. (1990) Cross-cultural contact and attitudes of Qatari students in the United States. *International Journal of Intercultural Relations* 14, 123–134.

Kay, P. and Kempton, W. (1984) What is the Sapir–Whorf hypothesis? *American Anthropologist* 86, 65–89.

Kemp, J.B. (1995) Culture clash and teacher awareness. *The Language Teacher* 19(8), 8–11.

Kim, Y., Triandis, H.C., Kagitcibasi, C., Choi, S.-C. and Yoon, G. (1994) *Individualism and Collectivism: Theory, Method and Applications*. Thousand Oaks, CA: Sage.

Kim, Y.Y. (2001) *Becoming Intercultural: An Integrative Theory of Communication and Cross-cultural Adaptation*. Thousand Oaks, CA: Sage.

Kluckhohn, F. and Strodbeck, F. (1961) *Variations in Value Orientations*. New York: Harper & Row.

Kramsch, C. (1998) *Language and Culture*. New York: Oxford University Press.

Kramsch, C. (2005) Intercultural literacy vs. communicative competence. Paper presented at the International Forum: Kotoba, Bunka, Shakai no Gengo Kyouiku, Waseda University, Tokyo, Japan.

Kraus, S.J. (1995) Attitudes and the prediction of behavior: A meta-analysis of the empirical literature. *Personality and Social Psychology Bulletin* 21, 58–75.

Labov, W., Ash, S. and Boberg, C. (eds) (2005) *Atlas of North American English: Phonetics, Phonology and Sound Change*. Berlin: Mouton de Gruyter.

Landis, D. and Bhagat, R.S. (eds) (1996) *Handbook of Intercultural Training* (2nd edn). Thousand Oaks: Sage Publications.

LaPiere, R.T. (1934) Attitudes vs. actions. *Social Forces* 13, 230–237.

Lévi-Strauss, C. (1958) *Anthropologie structurale*. Paris: Plon.

Lewin, K. (1936) Some social-psychological differences between the US and Germany. In K. Lewin (ed.) *Principles of Topological Psychology*. McGraw-Hill.

Lewthwaite, M. (1996) A study of international students' perspectives on cross-cultural adaptation. *International Journal for the Advancement of Counselling* 19(2), 167–185.

Marrett, C.B. and Leggon, C. (eds) (1982) *Research in Race and Ethnic Relations* (Vol. 3). Greenwich, CT: JAI.

Matsumoto, D. and Juang, L. (2004) *Culture and Psychology*. Belmont: Wadsworth.

Matsumoto, D., LeRoux, J., Ratzlaffa, C., Tatania, H., Uchida, H., Kima, C. and Araki, S. (2001) Development and validation of a measure of intercultural adjustment potential in Japanese sojourners: The Intercultural Adjustment Potential Scale (ICAPS). *International Journal of Intercultural Relations* 25(5), 488–510.

McGuigan, J. (1999) *Modernity and Postmodern Culture*. Buckingham and Philadelphia: Open University Press.

McLuhan, M. (1964) *Understanding Media*. New York: Mentor.

McLuhan, M. and Fiore, Q. (1968) *War and Peace in the Global Village*. New York: Bantam.

Mead, M. (1961) *Coming of Age in Samoa*. New York: Perennial Classics.

Mead, M. (1995) *Blackberry Winter: My Earlier Years*. New York: Kodansha International.

Mehrabian, A. (1968) Communication without words. *Psychology Today* 2(4), 53–55.

Merriam-Webster Online Dictionary. Retrieved March 27th, 2006.On WWW at http://www.m-w.com

Moran, P. (2001) _Teaching Culture: Perspectives in Practice._ Boston: Heinle & Heinle.
Morris, M.W. and Peng, K. (1994) Culture and cause: American and Chinese attributions for social and physical events. _Journal of Personality and Social Psychology,_ 67, 949–971.
Morse, G. (January 2006) Decisions and desire. _Harvard Business Review_ 42–51.
Muller, B.-D. (2003) Linguistic awareness of cultures: Principles of a training module. In P. Kistler and S. Konivuori (eds) _From International Exchanges to Intercultural Communication: Combining Theory and Practice_ (pp. 50–90). Jyvaskyla: University of Jyvaskyla.
Nagata, A.L. (2005) Promoting self-reflexivity in intercultural education. _Journal of Intercultural Communication_ 8, 139–167.
Nisbett, R.E. (2003) _The Geography of Thought: How Asians and Westerners Think Differently ... and Why._ New York: Free Press.
Noels, K., Pon, G. and Clement, R. (1996) Language, identity, and adjustment: The role of linguistic self-confidence in the acculturation process. _Journal of Language and Social Psychology_ 15, 246–264.
Oberg, K. (1960) Culture shock: Adjustment to new cultural environments. _Practical Anthropology_ 7(177).
Olson, C.L. and Kroeger, K.R. (2001) Global competency and intercultural sensitivity. _Journal of Studies in International Education_ 5(2), 16–137.
Paige, R.M. (ed.) (1993) _Education for the Intercultural Experience._ Yarmouth, ME: Intercultural Press.
Paige, R.M. (1993) On the nature of intercultural experiences and intercultural education. In R.M. Page (ed.) _Education for the Intercultural Experience_ (pp. 1–20). Yarmouth, ME: Intercultural Press.
Paige, R.M., Jacobs-Cassuto, M., Yershova, Y. and DeJaeghere, J. (1999) Assessing intercultural sensitivity: A validation study of the Hammer and Bennett (1998) intercultural development inventory. Paper presented at the International Academy of Intercultural Research Conference, Kent State University, Kent, OH.
Parry, M. (2002) Transcultured selves under scrutiny: Whither languages? Paper presented at the Transcultured Self: Experiencing Languages and Intercultural Communication, Johannes Kepler Universitat, Linz, Austria.
Pinker, S. (1995) _The Language Instinct: How the Mind Creates Language._ New York: HarperCollins.
Redfield, R., Linton, R. and Herskovits, M. (1936) Outline for the study of acculturation. _American Anthropologist_ 38, 149–152.
Ruben, B.D. (1972) General systems theory: An approach to human communication. In R. Budd and B.D. Ruben (eds) _Approaches to Human Communication_ (pp. 120–144). Rochelle Park, NJ: Hayden.
Santa, J.L. and Baker, L. (1975) Linguistic influences on visual memory. _Memory and Cognition_ 3(4), 445–450.
Sapir, E. (1921) _Language an Introduction to the Study of Speech._ San Diego: Harcourt Brace & Company.
Sapir, E. (1958[1929]) The status of linguistics as a science. In D.G. Mandelbaum (ed.) _Culture, Language and Personality._ Berkeley, CA: University of California Press.
Schuetz, A. (1963) The stranger: An essay in social psychology. In A.J. Vidich (ed.) _Identity and Anxiety: Survival of the Person in Mass Society._ Glencoe, IL: Free Press.

Scollon, R. and Scollon, S.W. (2001) *Intercultural Communication: A Discourse Approach.* Oxford: Blackwell.

Scott, J. (ed.) (2003) *Travel Industry World Yearbook – The Big Picture.* Spencertown, NY: Travel Industry Publishing Company Inc.

Scully, G. (2000) Does the distributions of income affect life expectancy? *National Center for Policy Analysis.* Retrieved February 27, 2006. On WWW at: www.ncpa.org/ba/ba328/ba328.html

Seelye, H.N. (1984) *Teaching Culture – Strategies for Intercultural Communication.* Lincolnwood: National Textbook Company.

Seelye, H.N. (ed.) (1996) *Experiential Activities for Intercultural Learning.* Yarmouth, ME: Intercultural Press.

Sharp, J. (March 12th, 1997) Communities of practice: A review of the literature. Retrieved April 15th, 2004. On WWW at: http://www.tfriend.com/cop-lit.htm

Shaules, J. (November 2003) Student identity: From personal to global. *Oxford News for Japan*, 4–5.

Shaules, J. (2004a) Explicit and implicit cultural difference in cultural learning among long-term expatriates. Unpublished Doctoral Thesis, University of Southampton, Southampton.

Shaules, J. (2004b) Going mainstream: The role of intercultural education in Japan. *The Journal of Intercultural Communication*, SIETAR Japan 7.

Shaules, J. (2006) Assessing intercultural learning strategies with Personal Intercultural Change Orientation (PICO) profiles. *Rikkyo Journal of Intercultural Communication* 4, 61–80.

Shaules, J. and Inoue, A. (2000) Relativism and universalism – opposing views of education for internationalization. *The Language Teacher* 24(5), 13–17.

Shaules, J., Tsujioka, H. and Iida, M. (2004) *Identity.* Oxford: Oxford University Press.

Sherbert, G., Gerin, A. and Petty, S. (eds) (2006) *Canadian Cultural Poesis: Essays on Canadian Culture.* Waterloo: Wilfrid Laurier University Press.

Simmel, G. (1950) The stranger (K.H. Wolff, trans.). In K.H.Wolff (ed) *The Sociology of George Simmel.* Glencoe, IL: Free Press.

Singer, M.R. (1968) *Perception & Identity in Intercultural Communication.* Yarmouth, ME: Intercultural Press.

Smith, R. (1999) Intercultural network theory: A cross-paradigmatic approach to acculturation. *International Journal of Intercultural Relations* 23(4), 629–658.

Sparrow, L.M. (2000) Beyond multicultural man: Complexities of identity. *International Journal of Intercultural Relations* 24(2), 173–201.

Spiro, M. (1955) The acculturation of American ethnic groups. *American Anthropologist* 57, 1240–1252.

Stevick, E. (1980) *Teaching Languages: A Way and Ways.* Rowly, MA: Newbury House Publishers.

Stone, F.E. and Ward, C. (1990) Loneliness and psychological adjustment of sojourners: New perspectives on culture shock. In D.M. Keats, D. Munro and L. Mann (eds) *Heterogeneity In Cross-Cultural Psychology* (pp. 537–547). Lisse, Netherlands: Swets & Zeitlinger.

Stoorti, C. (1994) *Cross-Cultural Dialogues.* Yarmouth, ME: Intercultural Press.

Taylor, E. (1871) *Primitive Culture.* London: John Murray.

Terreni, L. and McCallum, J. (2003) Considering culture. Ministry of Education, New Zealand. Retrieved March 27, 2006. On WWW at www.ecd.govt.nz.running/ profdev.html: Consideringculture1.pdf

Thiagarajan, S. and Steinwachs, B. (1990) _Barnga: A Simulation Game on Cultural Clashes._ Yarmouth, ME: Intercultural Press.

Ting-Toomey, S. (ed.) (1994) _The Challenge of Facework: Cross-cultural and Interpersonal Issues._ Albany: State University of New York Press.

Ting-Toomey, S. and Oetzel, J.G. (2001) _Managing Intercultural Conflict Effectively._ Thousand Oaks, CA: Sage Publications.

Tomalin, B. and Stempleski, S. (1993) _Cultural Awareness._ New York: Oxford University Press.

Tomlinson, B. (2000) Materials for cultural awareness. _The Language Teacher_ 24(2).

Triandis, H.C. (1972) _The Analysis of Subjective Culture._ New York: Wiley.

Triandis, H.C. (1995) _Individualism and Collectivism._ Boulder, CO: Westview.

Triandis, H.C., Lisansky, J., Marin, G.B.H. and Betancourt, H. (1984) Simpatia as a cultural script of hispanics. _Journal of Personality and Social Psychology_ 47(6), 1363–1375.

Trompenaars, F. and Hampden-Turner, C. (1998) _Riding the Waves of Culture._ New York, NY: McGraw Hill.

Trompenaars, F. and Hampden-Turner, C. (2004) _Managing People Across Cultures._ Chichester: Capstone Publishing.

Valdes, J.M. (ed) (1986) _Culture Bound._ Cambridge: Cambridge University Press.

Valdes, J.M. (1994) _Cross-cultural Dialogues._ Yarmouth, ME: Intercultural Press.

Ward, C., Bochner, S. and Furnham, A. (2001) _The Psychology of Culture Shock_ (2nd edn). Philadelphia, PA: Routledge.

Ward, C. and Kennedy, A. (1993) Where's the 'culture' in cross-cultural transitions? _Journal of Cross-cultural Psychology_ 24, 221–249.

Ward, C., Okura, Y., Kennedy, A. and Kojima, T. (1998) The U-Curve on trial: A longitudinal study of psychological and sociocultural adjustment during cross-cultural transition. _International Journal of Intercultural Relations_ 22(3), 277–291.

Weaver, G. (1993) Understanding and coping with cross-cultural adjustment stress. In R.M. Paige (ed.) _Education for the Intercultural Experience._ Yarmouth, ME: Intercultural Press.

Weaver, G. and Uncapher, P. (1981) The Nigerian experience: Overseas living and value change. Paper presented at the Seventh Annual SIETAR Conference, Vancouver, BC, Canada.

Weber, M. (1968) _Economy and Society: An Outline of Interpretive Sociology_ (E. Fischoff, trans.). New York: Bedminster Press.

Wicker, A.W. (1969) Attitudes vs. actions: The relationship of verbal and overt behaviour responses to attitude objects. _Journal of Social Issues_ 25, 41–78.

Williams, R. (1958) _Culture and Society 1780–1950._ London: Flamingo.

Wilpert, C. (1984) International migration and ethnic minorities: New fields for post-war sociology in the Federal Republic of Germany. _Current Sociology_ 32, 305–325.

Yamamoto, S. (1998) Applying the developmental model of intercultural sensitivity in the Japanese context. _Journal of Intercultural Communication_ 2, 77–100.

Yoneoka, J. (2000) What is a Kokusaijin? A 10-year study. _The Language Teacher_ 24(9), 7–13.